DEMOCRACY IN THE CONNECTICUT FRONTIER TOWN OF KENT

Number 601
Columbia Studies in the Social Sciences
Edited by the Faculty of Political Science
of Columbia University

Democracy in the Connecticut Frontier Town of Kent

CHARLES S. GRANT

Columbia University Press
New York 1961

The Columbia Studies in the Social Sciences (formerly the Studies in History, Economics, and Public Law) is a series edited by the Faculty of Political Science of Columbia University and published by Columbia University Press for the purpose of making available scholarly studies produced within the Faculty.

Published in Great Britain, India, and Pakistan
by the Oxford University Press
London, Bombay, and Karachi

Library of Congress Catalog Card Number: 61-7713
Manufactured in the United States of America

Gratefully dedicated to my father
Harry L. Grant

Preface

Midway through the eighteenth century Connecticut pioneers completed their colony's filling-up process with the settlement of the northwest corner, the so-called Western Lands. Kent was one of the eight new auction townships into which this frontier[1] region was divided, the town being sold at "public vendue" in 1738 and settled in 1739.

This study is an examination of economic opportunity and democracy in the town of Kent. Students of American history tend to have fixed notions about opportunity and democracy on the New England frontier during the colonial period. Most high school students and some college students in the more general survey courses emerge from their studies in step with the traditional idea that our pioneering forefathers were liberty-seeking individualists and that the overall spirit throughout the New England colonies was democratic. Students in more advanced college courses receive a contrary impression. From the pages of Frederick Jackson Turner, James Truslow Adams, Roy H. Akagi, Carl W. Bridenbaugh, and Leonard W. Labaree they learn of many undemocratic tendencies. The present study of Kent will produce a mixed verdict for that one community but will in the main support the traditional theory of democratic tendencies and take exception to some generalizations of twentieth-century scholarship.

In organizing the evidence from Kent land, church, and court records, vital statistics, and petition literature it has seemed advisable to let the data throw light on three basic questions raised by leading students of New England history. The first question pertains to economic opportunity; that is, the extent to which the common settler was or was not hampered by such restrictions as an inequitable land policy, oppressive debt-collection procedures, or general limitations on free enterprise. The question on the extent and nature of economic opportunity or economic conflict was posed in an important article written in 1914 by Turner. Inquiring about the New England frontier, he wrote:

> How far was this first frontier a field for the investment of eastern capital and for the political control by it? Were there evidences of antagonism between the frontier and the settled, property-holding classes of the coast? Did "Populistic" tendencies appear in this frontier and were there grievances which explained these tendencies?

Although much scholarly writing has produced affirmative answers to Turner's questions, Kent evidence suggests extensive opportunity and a minimum of conflict or oppression.

The second question concerns the extent of political democracy. Albert E. McKinley, in *The Suffrage Franchise in the Thirteen English Colonies in America*, published in 1905, paved the way for a number of scholarly comments emphasizing the limited nature of a colonial's political rights. McKinley's argument covered mainly the colony level (to what extent could a common citizen raise his voice in colony affairs?) but also extended to the local level (how much did the common man participate in his town government?). The present study, however, finds that at Kent political rights were generally widespread.

Both the first and second questions are involved mainly with external relationships where outsiders oppose town inhabitants. These questions refer to the attempt of a group of eastern capitalists to impose economic control and political control on the group of local settlers. The third question, on the nature and extent of social democracy, is, on the other hand, a problem of internal relationships. It asks the extent to which class lines erected barriers within the town and "kept the lowly in their places." Bridenbaugh, Labaree, and Akagi have observed the influence of the gentry and the ability of the "New England squires to see to it that the town thought as they thought and acted as they would have it act." In this area of class barriers and thought control, Kent again reveals differences from the standard version.

Thus the interpretation of evidence found in Connecticut's Western Lands is mainly revisionist. Where time and effort have gone into the study of a town and where unexpected currents have been discovered, there arises the temptation to project such findings beyond the town and to attribute to them broad significance which they do not possess. A prudent course is for the author to abide by rules of evidence, to acknowledge that he has furnished data for only a small sector of the colonial frontier, and to assure authors whose works are cited that where exceptions to their versions occur, they occur (for all the author knows) because Kent was an exceptional community. But—and this is a large *but*—there may be some obligation to the reader. If Kent is assumed to be exceptional, then the reader is asked to spend his time examining statistics and arguments about what is no more than a bizarre colonial backwater. To the reader, then, the author would like to convey his own supposition that Kent was not necessarily exceptional.

A major factor to be considered is that of pioneer mobility. A student of frontier New England during the eighteenth century can scarcely fail to note the seeming ease and frequency with which settlers came and went. Granting this mobility, one finds difficulty in postulating great differences between towns of similar size. It would seem absurd, for example, to envision 300 Kent inhabitants enjoying bonanza conditions while to the north 300 fellow citizens chose to languish under proprietor tyranny in, say, Westminster, Massachusetts. Probably each town maintained an equilibrium between the hopeful arrivals and the disappointed departers. The existence of a "free market" as to where a pioneer might establish himself would discourage great differences between towns.

The differences between conditions in Kent as revealed by this study and the situation elsewhere as indicated in accounts by Turner, Adams, Akagi, and others might be attributed in part to different research techniques. These writers produced studies in breadth and used research methods to facilitate such wide coverage. This Kent history sacrifices breadth for depth. For example, a study in breadth might rely on inhabitants' petitions to the colony legislature (often full of descriptive detail) or on travelers' impressions. A study in depth might record for each inhabitant his property (tax lists), his speculative activity (land records), and his status as a leader (rolls of freemen, lists of officeholders). Conceivably this breadth-versus-depth issue could be all important. Conceivably one could find one story at one level and a different story at a deeper level. For Kent, at any rate, the type of evidence used by historians writing in breadth does indeed substantiate their versions; and the reversals occur only when one probes deeper. Do studies in other towns parallel the Kent differences between breadth and depth? Unfortunately the issue has seldom been joined and there are few data on which to draw. The scholars interested in economic, political, and social history who have worked in breadth from central archives have not been challenged. The numerous local historians who could challenge them have pursued different objectives and have raised their own questions about genealogy, folklore, and the locations of early homesites, roads, and bridges.[2]

The writer is indebted to so many friends for advice, cooperation, and assistance during the years when this work was in preparation that in expressing gratitude he hardly knows where to start or stop. Much as he would like to offer individual thanks, it seems better to submit this blanket statement of appreciation to the patient town clerks, the helpful librarians, and the interested and ever-watchful historians.

A few individuals must be mentioned. Any project will have its ups and downs and during the downs of this one Mr. Frank Spencer of Sharon, Connecticut, did much to spur the writer on. His outstanding collection of eighteenth-century travel accounts provided an invaluable source, but the real boost came from the encouraging conversations by the fireside of his study. The two most inspiring proofreaders, tabulators, and document copiers ever encountered are the author's mother, Margaret S. Grant, and wife, Katharine G. Grant. Wives of historians know all too well what happens to them when a book is put together. Finally, to the author's father, Harry L. Grant, goes deep gratitude. His understanding, assistance, and encouragement have made the work possible.

CHARLES S. GRANT

Middlebury College
Middlebury, Vermont
December, 1960

Contents

Tables

PART I

The Settlement of Kent

The town of Kent lies in the westernmost part of Connecticut midway between Long Island Sound and the Massachusetts line. Immediately to the west lies New York State. The Housatonic River, flowing south from Massachusetts, tumbles through Kent in a series of rapids and departs with a roar at Bull's Falls on the southern border. A visitor to Kent feels hemmed in by the steep mountain walls, which, like the river and Route Seven, run north and south. But these are not mountains. To ascend Mauwee Peak or scale St. John's Cliffs is merely to reach the normal level of western Connecticut. Take a flat board to represent the surrounding Connecticut terrain; then chisel out a deep groove and you have an example of what the Housatonic and glacial action have formed at Kent.

Kent was one of seven townships comprising Connecticut's so-called Western Lands in the northwest corner of the colony. These lands, about 450 square miles in extent, were first opened to settlement in 1738. In that and in subsequent years Kent, Cornwall, Sharon, Salisbury, Canaan, and Norfolk were sold, organized, and settled.[1]

Part I of this study has two purposes. The first is to examine the preliminaries to settlement: Connecticut's filling-up process, the pressure of population, the Indian problem, and the steps taken by the General Assembly to organize the sale of the seven auction townships in the Western Lands. Chapter 1 is intended to set the stage, to place Kent in proper historical perspective. The second purpose is to move from preliminaries to problems of the original settlement in 1738 and 1739. Treatment of these problems in

Chapter 2 stresses the success of the proprietary system of land distribution and the ability of the General Assembly to maintain effective control. Operation of the proprietary system at the founding of Kent reinforces the standard version of such eighteenth-century settlements in one area but proves exceptional in several. Where some versions picture an underprivileged class migrating to the west and then resisting exploitation by an eastern capitalistic class, the Kent evidence shows the migration of the capitalistic class itself and the absence of class conflict.

1

PRELIMINARIES TO SETTLEMENT

"A hideous, howling wilderness" was the first known description of the region occupied by Kent and her six sister towns in the northwest corner of Connecticut. The Reverend Benjamin Wadsworth, guarded by thirty troopers, passed by present-day Kent on August 26, 1694. His *Journal* recorded his discomfiture at the "long, tedious hills" and his uncertainty on geography. Crossing the Housatonic River, he hesitantly but correctly observed: "This river is the same which some say runs through Stratford." Wadsworth also noted: "We rode through very good land: some intervale by the side of the river." [1] Wadsworth's "good land" and not the "howling wilderness" provided a key to the future. During the next forty-four years the tide of Connecticut settlement pressed in, Indian threats diminished, and colonial legislators and surveyors laid the legal foundation for settlement. Early in 1738 Stephen Pain's axe and hammer might be heard as the first Kent cabin was erected and the settlement got underway.

Connecticut's Filling-Up Process

The founding of Kent in 1738 was a final step in the gradual expansion of Connecticut settlements. This expansion was carried by two main currents, both of which affected the settlement of Kent.[2] First was the impulse from the Connecticut River line. Much of Connecticut was settled by migrations to both the east and the west from the three original "river towns," Windsor (1633), Wethersfield (1634), and Hartford (1635). Other river towns, Middletown (1640) and Saybrook (1639), also furthered expansion by throwing off new towns to the east and west. The second main current was from the coastal towns spread along Long Island Sound. New Haven (1638), Milford (1639), and Fairfield (1639) were centers from which population pressed northward. Of the forty families who settled Kent in 1738, sixteen (or 40 percent) were of the "first current," having moved on an east-west axis from the Connecticut River. The majority of Kent families (twenty-four or 60 percent) had moved north via the "second current" from the southern coastal towns.

TABLE 1

TOWNS OF ORIGIN OF ORIGINAL KENT SETTLERS [a]

Numbers from towns in east-west settlement pattern: east of Connecticut River	*Numbers from towns in east-west settlement pattern: west of Connecticut River*	*Numbers from towns settled by movements north from Long Island Sound*
5 Colchester	1 Farmington	9 Danbury
1 Coventry		3 Fairfield
1 Lebanon		3 New London
2 Mansfield		2 New Milford
1 Plainfield		3 Norwalk
3 Tolland		1 Stonington
1 Willington		1 Stratford
1 Windham		2 Woodbury
15	1 (total)	24

[a] Tabulated from Kent, Proprietors. The deeds recording original land purchases in Kent indicate towns of origin for each buyer.

Table 1 reveals a curious feature about settlement along the east-west axis. Although towns were moving west from Hartford and the Connecticut River in orderly sequence (Farmington 1640, Simsbury 1670, Waterbury 1673, and Litchfield 1719), Kent was not a final step in this sequence. Only one Kent family, the Brownsons of Farmington, came from settlements west of the river. Instead, Kent's founders in the east-west stream had first moved east of Hartford to Windham and Mansfield (1686), Plainfield (1689), Lebanon (1697), Colchester (1699), and Tolland (1715).[3] Having reached Connecticut's eastern boundary, these families reversed direction and leaped westward to Kent and the extreme western frontier of the colony.

On the other hand, the movement of population from the south into the interior reached Kent in more orderly sequence. English settlers reaching New Haven in 1639 moved on to found Milford at the mouth of the Housatonic. This town in turn sent inhabitants up the river to New Milford in 1670; [4] and from here it was only a twelve-mile jump north for the New Milford Canfields and Hamiltons who settled Kent. Similarly Kent inhabitants worked their way north by the Stratford (1639)–Woodbury (1673) line, [5] the New Haven–Wallingford (1673) line; [6] and the Norwalk (1649)–Danbury (1687) line. [7]

Pressure of population appears to have been the outstanding force propelling Connecticut citizens into the colony's uninhabited regions. Connecticut's population was augmented by a steady stream of English immigrants, [8] but natural increase from an "astonishing" birth rate seems mainly responsible for the population growth. At Kent few settlers were recent immigrants and a majority were fourth-generation descendants of "first comers" at Hartford, New Haven, or other Connecticut river and coastal towns. [9]

John Beebe, an original Kent settler, was the great-grandson of an English "husbandman" who migrated to New London, Connecticut, in 1660. When John was settling in Kent, at least one hundred other Beebes of the third and fourth generations were settling other Connecticut towns. Beebe descendants of the original New London patriarchs were numerous in Norwich, Colchester, Danbury, and Stratford. Beebes helped found Canaan and Salisbury in 1738, both just to the north of Kent. [10] Daniel Comstock, another founder, was one of 126 descendants of Christopher Comstock of Fairfield. [11] Abraham Fuller of Kent was descendant number 101 of Joseph Fuller of Haddam. [12] Barnums, Carters, Geers, Hatches, Hubbels, Judds, Newcombs, Millses, and many other Kent families boasted seventy-five to one hundred and fifty cousins in Connecticut, all descendants of some patriarch who had reached Connecticut in the mid-seventeenth century.

If pressure of population was the basic force impelling Beebes, Comstocks, Fullers, and countless other families toward the colony's unsettled lands, then the Indian problem and the slow mechanism of government planning and supervision were the brakes retarding such impulses. These Indian and organizational problems were gradually solved in the eighteenth century, and in 1738 the currents of settlement reached Kent on Connecticut's western boundary.

The Indian Problem

As the settlers pressed west from the Connecticut River and north from Long Island Sound, the Indians presented them with two problems, neither especially serious. First, there was the danger from Indians on the warpath. The farther frontiersmen advanced to the north and west away from the thickly settled and easily defended seaboard sector, the more vulnerable they became to Indian raids. Second, there was the legal problem of extinguishing Indian titles to the desired land. These problems need not be considered serious because no Indian massacre blighted Connecticut in the eighteenth century and Indian sachems appeared pathetically eager to deed away their lands.

The original Indians of Connecticut, Pequots and Mohegans, were weak tribes quite easily crushed in the Pequot War in 1637.[13] Some survivors of the "Swamp Fight" at Fairfield are said to have drifted north and joined other Indians already at Weantanuck (New Milford). Around 1730 about one hundred fighting men are said to have moved up the Housatonic from Weantanuck to Kent.[14] Pockets of dispirited Mohegans and Pequots in the New Milford–Kent region posed little or no threat. Indeed, the coming of white men may have been a temporary boon to them for they had been paying tribute to Mohawks (in New York) and looked to Connecticut's early settlers for aid against their Indian foes.[15] During King Philip's War these Pequots and Mohegans west of the Connecticut River did not join the league against the English. In 1684 they joined in a general treaty with the English and the Five Nations directed against the French and Indians from Canada.[16]

It was the Canadian tribes allied with the French that sent chills up and down Connecticut spines and tended to delay any rush for lands in the northwest corner of the colony. These invaders from the far north had access to western Connecticut as late as 1747 via a sort of wilderness corridor that projected south from Lake Champlain. This corridor, flanked by the Hudson River and Albany County settlements on the west (Hoosick, Scatacook, Turconick) and by a line of forts in Massachusetts on the east, followed the spine of the Berkshire and Taconic Mountains through western Massachusetts and Connecticut.[17]

After 1694 the Connecticut line of settlements slowly tended to pinch the wilderness corridor from the south and east while similar penetrations came from New York to the west. During Queen Anne's War, 1702–13, the Connecticut towns of Woodbury and Danbury were on the colony's northwest frontier. Each built forts, provided two scouts per village, and were ordered to range the woods for approaching enemy "as far north as Ousatonnock" (present-day Stockbridge, Massachusetts).[18] Alarms were sounded in 1704 after the Deerfield massacre and in 1707 when invasion was rumored and it was feared the Indians at Weantanuck (New Milford) would go over to the enemy. In 1710 Canadian raiders actually penetrated down the corridor to Waterbury, Connecticut in a raid which killed one settler and captured three others.[19]

In 1707 New Milford was settled and in 1719 Litchfield joined it as another more westerly outpost. Both claimed Indian adventures, with Litchfield suffering her last raid in 1724. At this time settlers were ordered to remain for defense, with anyone who departed to forfeit his land.[20]

Fourteen years of quiet after the Litchfield raid of 1724 encouraged numerous settlers to move on to Kent and fill the last of Connecticut's Western Lands. However, the founders of Kent still peered anxiously up the corridor. They were alarmed at their situation when King George's War, 1740–48, brought in the usual flood of rumors. On May 10, 1744, the Kent militia captain, Abel Wright, petitioned the General Assembly for a sufficient stock of ammunition at public charge and noted "that the town of Kent is one of the frontier towns and since there is so much noise of war with the French we but look upon ourselves as much exposed." [21] Inasmuch as this petition brought no answer, on June 20, 1774, the selectmen of Kent appealed to Colonel Joseph Minor of nearby Woodbury. Minor was commanding officer of the regiment of which the Kent trainband was a part. This message was more urgent: "Our town is now under difficult circumstances reporting the Indians that are round about us and the difficulty that now attends us respecting the want of powder." [22]

The most detailed analysis of the vulnerability of the western towns was presented in a petition to Roger Wolcott, deputy governor and head of the Committee on War during King George's War. This petition from the inhabitants of Kent, Canaan, Goshen, Cornwall, Salisbury, and Sharon bears no date but was undoubtedly written in the spring of 1747.[23] It insisted that forts must be furnished or the towns would be abandoned. The argument ran as follows:

Crown point is only 120 miles from Albany and there is nothing but a final garrison at Saratoga between Albany and Crown Point to intercept the enemy in descent on the English northwest frontier. The settlements above us in York government east of the Hudson River being drawn in, viz. Sanhocky, Scatacook, and Hoosac which leaves a vacancy of at least thirty miles in thick woods between the line of forts in Massachusetts and the settlements in Albany County. So now there is nothing to prevent the enemy coming down to Stockbridge and on to the ruin of the new settlements, especially since soldiers posted the winter at Stockbridge are now recalled which leaves us the more exposed.[24]

Becoming more eloquent about their peril, the petitioners from Kent and the other western towns then elaborated on some rumors.

We have a report which has never been contradicted on what the enemy declared during retreat from Saratoga while in their liquor. That they had by their spies taken a view of the whole country on each side of the Housatonic River to the lower end of Sharon and found they were able to lay all waste in one night time with very little hazard to themselves; and that this design they intended to put in execution early this spring. This was confirmed by a letter found after the destruction of Saratoga written by a French priest.[25]

This petition is the last evidence of an Indian threat to Kent. The apprehension expressed in it is probably exaggerated. The forts were not built, the towns were not abandoned, and the dreaded raids were not forthcoming.

The second problem, acquisition of Indian titles to lands in the northwest portion of the colony, was cleared up during the first half of the eighteenth century. The largest individual transaction appears to have occurred in 1716 when one Benjamin Fairweather approached one Chief Waramaug and bought the Indian title to a vast tract including most of the present towns of Kent, Cornwall, and Goshen. The price paid by Fairweather was £19.[26] Records of "Fairweather's Purchase" are missing from the *Public Records* and the Connecticut Archives. Probably Fairweather sought confirmation of his title from the General Assembly. Instead of receiving his entire purchase, he apparently obtained only the much smaller parcel in southern Kent referred to as "Fairweather's Grant."

The process whereby private individuals bought Indian lands and then sought confirmation from the government was extremely lucrative for seventeenth-century opportunists,[27] but by 1720 the General Assembly had grown wary. In October, 1722, the Court passed an act assessing triple damages on any person purchasing an Indian title and attempting to sell it to third parties.[28] The act does not appear to have been rigidly enforced but it did make bonanza profits a thing of the past.

By 1738 the Indian "brakes" on settlement in the Western Lands had been virtually eliminated. Canadian Indians might still raid down the wilderness corridor, but fears of such unlikely forays seem to have been no deterrent to settlement. Indian titles to the land had been extinguished by individuals like Benjamin Fairweather, giving the government clear title. The sole remaining task was governmental organization of the Western Lands and arrangement for their sale to actual settlers.

Organization and Sale of the Western Lands

Settlement in Connecticut was in the final analysis dependent on the approval of the government. From the first settlements of the 1630s and 1640s to those of the mid-eighteenth century the Court, or General Assembly, was interested in an orderly advance. Would-be settlers had to apply to the government for permission "to plant settlements" and for confirmation of titles to the desired land. The Court was pleased to have wilderness land improved and granted applications when assured that procedures would be orderly.[29]

By the second decade of the eighteenth century Connecticut lands had been generally settled except for those in the northwest corner. As pressure on the lands mounted, the General Assembly attempted to forestall any disorderly land rush. In the May session of 1719 the Court put up a no-trespassing sign. "The whole of said tract of land shall lie for further disposal of this Assembly. . . . All surveyors are forbidden to lay out land without the leave of this Assembly." [30]

From April, 1724, to May, 1726, the General Assembly wrangled with Hartford and Windsor, both of which objected to the no-trespassing sign on the grounds that the lands were theirs.[31] The issue was compromised in 1726 by running a line north and south along the western boundary of Litchfield extending north to Massachusetts and south to the New Milford town line. Ungranted lands east of this new line went to Hartford and Windsor and are of no further concern here.[32] Lands to the west went to the General Assembly and continued to be called Western Lands.

Commencing in 1726 the General Assembly instituted surveys, heard reports, proposed various settlement plans,[33] and finally produced a definitive act in the October session of 1737. This

TABLE 2

THE AUCTION TOWNSHIPS OF THE WESTERN LANDS [a]

Town	Site of Auction	Date of Auction	Minimum Price (in pounds)
Goshen	New Haven	December, 1737	60
Cornwall	Fairfield	January, 1738	50
Canaan	New London	January, 1738	60
Kent	Windham	March, 1738	50
Norfolk	Hartford	April, 1738	50
Salisbury	Hartford	May, 1738	30
Sharon	New Haven	October, 1738	30

[a] Deming, "Litchfield Settlements," pp. 8–11. The early settlement of Salisbury occurred because of uncertainty over Connecticut's western boundary, with resulting habitation by Dutch and New Yorkers. Norfolk's late settlement may be attributed to her remote and mountainous location.

legislation, to which Kent and her sister towns of the Western Lands owe their existence, was entitled "An Act Ordering and Directing the Sale and Settlement of All the Townships in the Western Lands." [34] The act did not name the towns but dealt with five townships east of the Housatonic which subsequently became Kent, Cornwall, Goshen, Norfolk, and Canaan and with two townships west of the river which became Sharon and Salisbury. The land of each town was to be divided and sold at auction, or "vendue," in fifty-three rights, or shares; that is, fifty shares would be sold outright with the remaining three furnishing income for the first settled minister, the church, and the schools. The auctions were to take place in different towns and minimum acceptable prices were specified for each.

The auctions were generally successful. All shares were sold at prices between £150 and £200 and settlement got underway at all towns except Norfolk within the year. [35]

With increasing population and shortage of land driving the tide of settlement north and west, with Indian obstacles removed, and finally with organizational details completed by the government, Connecticut's filling-up process was completed and Kent and her six sisters joined the roll of Connecticut towns.

2

SETTLEMENT: THE SPECULATIVE
SETTLER PROPRIETORS

The sale of Kent at the Windham auction in 1738 and its settlement in 1739 provide an illustration of the operation of the Connecticut land system in the mid-eighteenth century. Students of
the New England land system have developed a version of its
functioning that might be called standard, and the purpose of the
present chapter is to show what occurred at Kent in comparison
with or contrast to that standard account.[1]

Kent evidence supports the authors of the standard version on
one important point, the prevalence of land speculation. It fails to
provide support, however, on seven points. The first divergence
from the usual presentation is one of fundamental importance.
Actually, the original settlers at Kent were not "common men"
opposed to a class of absentee proprietors. Rather, the first Kent
inhabitants were virtually all proprietors themselves. Second, at
Kent one finds a partial continuation, not a breakdown, of what
Turner called the "Seventeenth century socio-religious concept of
settlement."[2] Third, the oft-described iniquities of the proprietary
method of land distribution were absent at Kent. The failure of
proprietor absenteeism to continue at Kent and the lack of proprietor delinquency furnish the fourth and fifth differences. The
sixth exception to the standard account concerns the issue of political control at the time of settlement. Kent was not governed by
an oligarchy of absentees but instead was governed democratically
by residents. Here an understanding of the role of town incorporation is helpful. Lastly, Kent evidence suggests a different final
appraisal of the eighteenth century colony government and the

land system in Connecticut. If we may judge by what happened in the Western Lands, the Connecticut General Assembly did not "lose control" of the land system and did not "break down."

Proprietors and Land Speculation at Kent

The New England land system was based on grants by colony governments to so-called town proprietors. This system was designed to provide for orderly, mass migrations into unsettled regions. Historians are generally agreed that the system worked well in the seventeenth century when land was sought for use, not for speculation, but that it worked badly in the eighteenth century when a speculative mania developed.

Proprietors were the original grantees or purchasers of a tract of land, usually a township, which they held in common ownership.[3] Most proprietary grants in New England after 1640 were responses to petitions to the General Courts. The government, when satisfied that the petitioners were proper men to conduct the planting of a new settlement, would make the applicants grantees of a township. Thus fifteen to fifty proprietors would acquire exclusive title to the land of a new town. Originally, the group of proprietors and the group of settlers tended to be one and the same.[4]

During the seventeenth century the proprietors usually paid nothing for their lands except the cost of extinguishing Indian titles. (At Suffield this cost only 4 pence per acre).[5] In return for the land they did serve their respective colonies by assuming responsibility for the success of the new community. Proprietors formed the nucleus of a compact, migrating group, and they provided, minister, meetinghouse, roads, saw and gristmills, defenses, and other facilities for the new town.[6] However, during the eighteenth century proprietary shares tended to be acquired by cash purchase rather than by grants. Rapid turnover of such shares indicated speculative activity.[7] Absenteeism by the proprietors increased as many held large tracts in towns to which they had no intention of moving.[8] Even more spectacular were instances where whole towns became the property of only one or of a handful of

grantees. For example, the entire auction township of Murrays-
field was sold to the noted Connecticut patriot and speculator,
William Williams.[9] According to some historians, the spirit of
speculation reached its height in the 1738 sale of Kent and her six
sister auction townships.[10]

The auction sale of Kent at Windham and some events associated with the early settlement of the town sustain the idea that
speculation in land was widespread. Fifty shares in Kent land
were sold to the assembled bidders at Windham. Of the forty-one
men who became proprietors by the purchase of one or more of
these shares, the majority never came to Kent and never used their
land except as a trading commodity. To be precise, twenty-five
original purchasers fell in this absentee category, while only sixteen moved to the new town.[11] As a matter of fact, the label speculator can be applied as appropriately to the sixteen resident proprietors as to the twenty-five absentees. Whereas the resident
proprietors could clear and use only fifty to one hundred acres to
support their families in their subsistence way of life, they each
acquired better than 1000 acres via their proprietary shares. Frequently they were not satisfied with a holding ten times beyond
their needs. Settler Ebenezer Barnum bought four shares (4000
acres), settler Abel Wright bought three, while resident-proprie-
tors John Mills, Jonathan Morgan, and Thomas Beeman bought
two apiece. As will be shown below, virtually all Kent settlers,
proprietor and nonproprietor alike, speculated actively once they
had arrived in Kent. One cannot discover a single purchaser at
the Windham auction who was seeking merely a farm on which
to practice his husbandry.

A second type of evidence, minutes of Kent proprietors' meetings, also produces an impression of land hunger for speculative
rather than for farming purposes. The seventeenth-century proprietors had divided land among themselves according to farming
need. In Suffield, Massachusetts, for example, proprietors had allocated to themselves eighty acres apiece and had left the major part
of their town land as "undivided common." [12] At Kent the proprietors divided the "common" as rapidly as the mechanism of
surveying and division permitted.[13] On March 8, 1738, the day

following the Windham auction, the Kent proprietors held their first meeting. The first order of business was the appointment of a surveying committee: "To lay out such part of the lands . . . as they shall judge best for the interest of said proprietors . . . none of the lots to be less than fifty acres." [14] Kent contained about 50,000 acres. It took the proprietors only two years to divide about 32,000 acres of the best land among themselves. It seems significant that every proprietors' meeting except two during the two years following the sale at Windham was concerned with the distribution of land.

Settlement by Proprietors

Having noted the prevalence of speculation, we part company from the usual critical accounts of eighteenth-century settlements. A number of areas where Kent evidence produces a conflicting version will be noted. First, however, the major cause for differences with previous writers will be suggested. It seems hardly an overstatement to indicate that ones entire view of colonial society in the new towns of the eighteenth century should hinge on the question of who settled them. Many writers have described the erection of new communities by "common men," "humble pioneers," or perhaps just "frontier settlers." They have implied or stated that the majority of settlers were nonproprietors and thus were subject to exploitation by the proprietary body. These exploiters have been depicted as privileged speculators, mostly callous absentees residing in comfortable eastern towns and thus ripe targets for settler resentment.[15]

The settlement of Kent in 1738 was not carried out by any such group of exploited, humble men. By the end of 1739 (when the first tax list of names was prepared) Kent contained about forty-five adult males, mostly heads of families. Of these, thirty-two were proprietors and only thirteen were nonproprietors.[16]

However, Kent evidenced reveals no resentment on the part of the thirteen nonproprietors. Table 3 suggests that they were not a class apart from the proprietors but intermarried with them and shared in the town government.

TABLE 3

NONPROPRIETORS AT THE SETTLEMENT OF KENT

Nonproprietor	Relationship to Proprietor	Status or Town Office
Alexander Carey	none	left, 1739
Elisha Hamilton	son of Benjamin Hamilton	left, 1739
Silvenus Hatch	son of Timothy Hatch	became proprietor, 1742
Melatiah Lothrop	son-in-law of Timothy Hatch	town clerk in 1740s
Thomas Judd	brother of Philip Judd	left, 1740
Samuel Latham	son-in-law of Abel Wright	
Ebenezer Lyman	none	became proprietor, 1739
Stephen Pain	none	highway surveyor
Caleb Morgan	son of Jonathan Morgan	lister (tax)
William Porter	son of John Porter	hayward
Abraham Raymond	none	became proprietor, 1742
Gideon Root	none	became proprietor, 1743
Samuel Wright	son of Abel Wright	hayward

The Socioreligious Pattern of Settlement

Authors who compare speculative, eighteenth-century settlements adversely with the earlier movements of compact, covenanted groups (a Milford congregation moves up the Housatonic River to found New Milford) stress the loss of the socioreligious pattern of settlement. An element of stability was said to be lost when an eighteenth-century speculator might settle in a new auction town without knowing "who his neighbors would be and when they would arrive." [17] The spirit and character of settlement did undoubtedly change, but evidence at Kent suggests the contrast may have been overdone. Kent fails to sustain the idea that migrating groups were "scattered and accidental" or that "they were without spirit either of cooperation or of mutual interest." [18]

Of the forty families that settled Kent in 1738, twenty-six, or 65 percent, came in groups of three or more. Eighteen families came from Fairfield County and half of these were former neighbors in the town of Danbury. Only eight families, 20 percent, appear to have come to Kent alone.

The five families from Colchester (Pratts, Beebes, Lewises, Ransoms, and Fullers), for example, showed a close, social cohesiveness. The patriarch of the group, Sergeant Joseph Pratt, had been born in 1671 in Hartford, had once been a deputy from Milford, and later had become an original proprietor at Colchester. Records of 1724 show that John Beebe, also one of the Colchester-to-Kent migrants, had gone on an expedition to Hampshire County, Massachusetts, equipped with a gun "belonging to Sergeant Joseph Pratt and a hatchett belonging to Azariah Pratt" [19] (another prospective Kent settler). Pratts and Beebes intermarried. Meanwhile Samuel Lewis' daughter married John Ransom. Their son, John Ransom, Junior, later married Rhoda Pratt at Kent. The Fullers had not intermarried with these families in Colchester but did so after the party reached Kent.

Pratts, Beebes, Lewises, Ransoms, and Fullers moved together from Colchester to Kent in 1738. All made money in land speculations, and Joseph Fuller's transactions might qualify him as a typical speculative proprietor. But more outstanding than their economic record was their contribution to the growth and stability of Kent. Samuel Lewis, town clerk for three years, alone left early, for North Carolina. Joseph Pratt served Kent as deputy to the General Assembly, as selectman, and as tithingman. His son, Joseph, Junior, held numerous town offices. Azariah Pratt was a selectman, tithingman, and almost perpetual town treasurer during the early years. He was also sealer of leather and sealer of weights and measures each year. Azariah averaged three offices per year, and the only town positions he never held were pound-keeper, lister, and constable. His son Azariah, Junior was similarly active. John Beebe was the Kent constable each year from 1739 to 1745. He held six other offices before moving on to Amenia, New York, in 1763. Deacon Joseph Fuller headed one of Kent's first families in point of service to the town. He was a selectman for three years and also town treasurer. Squire Ransom served for many years as constable, selectman, justice of the peace, and town deputy.[20]

The Colchester group also formed a nucleus of strength in the church. Of the ten original incorporators of the Kent church, three were of this Colchester group, (Samuel Lewis, Azariah

Pratt, and Joseph Fuller). Joseph Fuller was one of two deacons for many years, and Azariah Pratt, Joseph Pratt, and John Beebe served as tithingmen.[21]

Most of the original proprietors of Kent probably had no intention of moving to their new lands. Those settler proprietors who did found the town were active land speculators and did not migrate as one church congregation or as a single group of neighbors. However, Kent was formed from several fragments, each of which broke off from a different home base and then moved into and settled Kent as a miniature, old style, socioreligious group. Once in Kent, the fragments tended to coalesce into a single social unit not unlike those of earlier times. This is not to suggest that Kent was identical with, say, Wallingford, Connecticut, which had broken off from New Haven in 1667. Kent did feature far more land speculation and a somewhat faster population turnover. The Kent story does suggest that in the auction towns there was not a complete break with the past. A nucleus of substantial, dependable proprietors shouldered the responsibilities of settlement in both the Kent of 1739 and the Wallingford of 1667. The quest for land profits did not destroy the older way.

Equitable Land Distribution at Kent

When writers praise the New England land system as it operated in the 1600s and criticize the speculative mania, inequity, and class struggles of the 1700s, they sometimes overlook a crucial point. It was in the 1600s that the system tended to be restrictive and arbitrary according to standards of free enterprise. For example, if one wished to settle in, say, Dedham, Massachusetts in 1640 but lacked the good fortune to have been one of the nineteen original proprietors to whom the entire town was granted, then one would have to ingratiate oneself with the nineteen and secure the best bargain possible on their terms. There was indeed land mongering in the eighteenth century but one suspects that prices, sales, and population movements were governed far more by free market conditions. Perhaps something can be said for a social arrangement where, if one wanted admission to a community, one bought his way in at the going price rather than se-curing admission by courting the favor of the town fathers.

At Kent it can be shown that the proprietary system prevailed and that all the land was disposed of originally in the lots and pitches of the various divisions. These were conveyed to proprietors, who in turn sold them to nonproprietors or to each other. It may be assumed that these nonproprietors were reconciled to the or-derly process of land distribution. An act of the General Assembly of 1723 had resolved earlier confusion by assigning all "common land" to proprietors and defining proprietor status and proce-dures.[22] Except for one minor slip the Kent Proprietors had pro-ceeded in strict conformity with the law.[23] More important, the nonproprietors were undoubtedly aware that the proprietors had attained their status by bidding high enough at a competitive auc-tion open to any Connecticut inhabitant. Proprietors of Kent did not owe their position to favoritism or haphazard chance. Each had paid a price for a share reflecting the risks, duties, privileges, and potentialities of proprietorship.

A nonproprietor could hardly complain of inability to buy a share. Although the lowest acceptable bid at the auction was £165 old tenor, no cash was required. Payment was not due for three years, and this date was later extended.[24] A nonproprietor need not have deplored a missed opportunity in failing to reach Windham. There appears to have been an open market for pro-prietary shares at all times. Indeed, a majority of the thirty-two settler proprietors had bought their shares second hand. Four of the nonproprietors were to buy shares during the forties. Over one hundred Kent residents became proprietors at some time dur-ing the speculative ferment that accompanied the settlement of the town.

The thirty-two original resident proprietors at Kent had gambled on the success of the town and a consequent increase in land values. Their gamble was successful and rewarded them many times. The nonproprietors, who lacked the inclination, time, or energy for share-purchasing and risk-taking, stood by and watched the orderly procedures of the proprietors' surveying committees and the division of the lots and pitches by lottery-style drawings.

They were free to buy into the proprietary body at any time (and many did) or to continue to stand by. Under such an arrangement, no controversy over land distribution developed at Kent.

If this settlement pattern at Kent, a pattern wherein the town was erected by a proprietor group speculating with their left hands and clearing the land with their right hands, was true of other new towns of the eighteenth century, then the class-struggle version might require some correction. A final answer awaits further research. It may be appropriate, however, to observe that there are two main research avenues for this question. The first, (and this has been employed generally in the past), is to read the settlers' own versions in their grievance petitions to the General Assembly. In these petitions, usually for tax relief or for moritoriums on debt payments, the settlers indeed sound like an oppressed and exploited class. Kent settlers too submitted such petitions; but on close inspection, these proved to be exaggerated and distorted to the point where they were more misleading than revealing. The other research avenue is to visit the town in question, settle down in the vault of the Town Clerk's office, and tabulate the names of all inhabitants. Who were proprietors or non-proprietors (land records)? What were the relationships and roles of the two groups (vital statistics, minutes of town meetings, and elections of town officers)? Conceivably this second avenue has received too little attention in the past.[25]

Absenteeism

It was noted earlier that the original proprietors, or first owners of all Kent land, were the forty-one men who purchased proprietary shares at the Windham auction in March, 1738. It was further indicated that only sixteen of these men came to Kent and that twenty-five were thus absentees. This sort of ratio is not unusual. Historians have used similar ratios elsewhere to deplore the evils of absenteeism whereby land owners avoided the danger, work, and problems of settlement.[26] However, the impression created by this initial, absentee-resident proportion is quickly altered if one studies the immediate sequel. The absentee proprietors soon sold their shares to residents.[27] Some of the men who attended the Windham auction may not have been certain as to whether they would move to Kent or not. However, they apparently bought for speculative purposes, and they presumably knew that the best way to realize speculative profits was to move to Kent. As will be shown, Kent became the trading mecca. Ninety percent of the numerous Kent land transactions involved Kent residents, and the biggest profiteers were those who moved to Kent. Once an absentee like Abel Barnum, Thomas Hatch, or Jonathan Dunham decided he would not move to Kent, he perhaps lost his desire to remain a proprietor; for as an absentee, he would be at a disadvantage trading with those more familiar with the lay of the local land. When such men learned of settlers going to Kent, they often sold them their shares. One of the twenty-five temporary absentees, Abel Barnum of Danbury, sold his share to his migrating brother, Joshua Barnum. Another, Joseph Hatch of Tolland, perhaps too elderly for the move, conveyed his share to his migrating son, Barnabus. Or perhaps in some instances the migrant sought out the proprietor. When Azariah Pratt of Colchester decided to join the Colchester party moving to Kent, he may have sought out the stay-at-home Colchester citizen, Jonathan Dunham. At any rate, many shares did pass from the absentees to the Kent settlers.[28]

The General Assembly also deserves much credit for preventing absenteeism. The Act of October, 1737 provided:

Every purchaser shall be obliged within two [29] years next after their purchase, to build and furnish a house of eighteen feet square and seven feet stud and to subdue and fence at least six acres of land . . . where he is a settler or hath fixed his agent; and no person shall have any benefit of his purchase but shall be liable to forfeit the same unless by himself or his agent he performs all duties, pay-taxes . . . as shall be enjoined.[30]

These settlement provisions were highly respected. As the two-year deadline came due, the absentee proprietors sold out. Two, Ebenezer Bishop and Samuel Benedict, had disposed of their shares shortly after the auction, but others waited as long as possible. Then between May 5, 1739 and April 4, 1740 (the last day!) eighteen of the twenty-three remaining absentees sold their shares.

The five who did not sell out apparently had relatives serving as their agents, utilizing the land, and paying taxes.[31]

Further indication that the settlement of Kent was not impeded by absenteeism appears in a sort of "progress report" dated September 19, 1739.

> We most humbly showeth . . . [we] are endeavoring to plant and settle . . . and are got so far forward therein as at present there are now dwelling and living in the same thirty-two proprietors, twenty-two of which are there with their families . . . two proprietors being single men . . . and the generality of the rest of the proprietors are daily in preparation to settle there by themselves or by their agents.[32]

The optimism of the petition was justified. Other proprietors did arrive, the population grew rapidly (there were 120 adult male residents in 1750 and 321 in 1777), and absenteeism remained inconsequential.

Absence of Proprietor Delinquency at Kent

Closely related to the problem of absenteeism was that of proprietor delinquency. Historians have observed that where proprietors remained absent from the new towns, there was a tendency for them to neglect those responsibilities (road building, schools, etc.) that proprietors traditionally performed. Attitudes of proprietors were attributed to pecuniary greed (why go to expense in a distant town if such costs could be avoided?) or selfish indifference.[33] Again the situation at Kent differed substantially from this standard picture.

The Kent records reveal no complaints over delays or inadequate performance on the part of the proprietors. Roads and bridges were built, saw and gristmills were erected, and schools were provided. Roads received attention as soon as the body of proprietors came into being. At the first meeting in Windham on March 8, 1738, (on the day following the auction), the proprietors voted "to lay out highways." [34] At most meetings of proprietors thereafter highway business was transacted, although most of it was concerned with compensation for individuals through whose property the roads were to pass.[35] By 1740 the proprietors had "laid out" some thirty different highways ranging in size from the "twenty-rod highway up the mountain to the iron pots" to the "four-rod highway that leadeth from the town to the river."[36]

The proprietors were equally concerned about saw and gristmills. On May 3, 1738, at their second meeting following the sale they voted: "That Ebenezer Barnum shall take the 49th lot or share in this division on condition he build a sawmill by the last of December next and also a gristmill in two years." [37] Minutes of proprietors' meetings contain numerous similar proposals for other projects at Kent. The proprietors laid out a "common field" on September 21, arranged for a "burying place" on September 30, and provided for a "cornmill" on December 6, 1738.[38]

The first mention of a school in the proprietors' meetings occurred in May, 1739. Reference was made to the highway between "Slosson's house and the school." Frequent references to schools appear in early town meetings. On January 2, 1740 it was voted to "build a school house sixteen feet square on the twelve-rod highway between Fuller's and Morgan's." [39] Schools were built and supported by proceeds from the sale of the "school right," one of the fifty-three shares into which the town had been divided. In their divisions the proprietors always assigned one lot to the school, a second to the minister, and a third to the Church. In September, 1740 the town meeting voted: "The people that live on the mountain can have their own school and draw their proportion of school money annually according to their list." [40]

The absence of proprietor delinquency at Kent may be attributed to two factors. First was the desire of the proprietors to encourage settlement so as to enhance the value of their shares; second was the speedy incorporation of the town in 1739.

The selling price of a proprietary share at Kent was closely related to the progress of settlement. Until secure settlement and an influx of settlers were certain, the prices of proprietary shares did not climb much above their costs at the Windham auction. Once settlement was secure, once an increasingly large body of customer settlers poured in to buy land and proprietary shares, prices and profits rose many fold. By 1741 a first division lot brought a higher price than the original cost of the entire share. Clearly it was in the interest of the proprietors to encourage the all-important influx of settlers. One gathers that the last thing in the minds of proprietors was to be delinquent and to oppress or frighten away settlers and prospective customers.[41]

The second and more important reason for an absence of proprietor delinquency was that proprietor responsibilities were transferred to the town as soon as the town was incorporated, that is, received so-called town privileges.[42] At Kent and other Connecticut towns founded in the eighteenth century important functions were performed by town officers, directed by town selectman, voted by town meetings, and financed by a town rate. After Kent's incorporation in October, 1739, the Kent proprietors had nothing to do with roads, bridges, schools, Church, town defense, or even supervision of the common field. The proprietors met to survey and divide their own lands and for virtually no other reasons.[43] During settlement there was little time for delinquency even if the proprietors had been so inclined. Kent and her sister towns were settled and incorporated as shown in Table 4.[44]

TABLE 4

THE SETTLEMENT AND INCORPORATION OF THE AUCTION TOWNSHIPS

Town	Settlers Arrived	Incorporated
Canaan	1739	October, 1739
Goshen	1739	October, 1739
Kent	1739	October, 1739
Sharon	1739	October, 1739
Cornwall	1739	May, 1740
Salisbury	1739	October, 1741
Norfolk	1755	October, 1758

In each of these towns, except possibly Norfolk, a settler had no sooner arrived than he received, through the granting of town incorporation, the right to demand and obtain traditional town services through the medium of the democratic town meeting.

Settlement: Political Control on the Frontier

We have examined the speculative impulses toward settlement and found that Kent featured the same "land mongering" that appeared elsewhere in New England. We have examined the workings of the proprietor system of Kent and found that problems of settlement reported in other towns did not materialize here. A final question on which Kent's settlement sheds light pertains to the nature of political control over this frontier settlement. Again the situation in Kent was far different from that described in other towns.

It has been suggested by historians of the New England frontier that an important aspect of settlement was the effort of eastern capital to secure political control of the frontier towns.[45] Such control was secured and held by absentee proprietors in some settlements like the often mentioned Westminster, Massachusetts. The crux of the question, the pivot on which absentee or local political control hung, was the timing of town incorporation. Before incorporation, the political structure was such that absentees might dominate; after incorporation, absentees were powerless.[46]

Kent was incorporated on October 13, 1739 by act of the Connecticut General Assembly.[47] Before this date the only authority exercising local control in Kent was the body of proprietors. The rights, duties, and legal procedures of proprietors had been settled by various acts of the General Assembly, most notably the acts of 1723 and 1727.[48] According to these acts, proprietors' decisions were to be made by "major vote of said proprietors in legally warned meetings." Authority between meetings rested with standing committees on highways, on mills, or on land surveys. The proprietors were permitted to tax themselves, such rates being based on the number of shares held. For example, on December 6, 1738, the proprietors voted a tax of 36 shillings per right. Thus resident proprietor Abel Wright with three shares paid 108 shillings; absentee Proprietor William Burnham paid 36 shillings for his single share; and a nonproprietor such as Gideon Root paid nothing.[49]

The Kent proprietors initiated the end of this form of government by meeting at Joshua Barnum's house in Kent on September 19, 1739. A majority voted to direct Samuel Lewis, the proprietors' clerk, to prepare a petition for incorporation and to designate Timothy Hatch an expediting agent to "go to the Court." [50] It would be interesting to know who favored and who opposed incorporation. The records reveal no names and no opposition at

Kent. There is no record of opposition when the grant of "town privileges" was approved by the General Assembly a month later. Kent's six sister towns also were incorporated shortly after their settlement, also on the basis of petitions from their respective bodies of proprietors, and also without recorded opposition.

The Kent petition as submitted by Samuel Lewis made three requests. First was the plea for town privileges:

But our being without religious and civil rights . . . is discouraging to us . . . therefore, grant to us, the proprietors aforesaid, to be a town with the immunities, privileges, and authority of a town as is found in other towns of this government.[51]

Second, was a request for authorization to tax:

We request . . . that for support of a minister that you would grant a tax of four pence upon the acre for four years to be raised upon the divided land and paid by the owners thereof.

Third, was a warning about their need for a justice of the peace:

And inasmuch as our situation is at a great distance from persons in authority in the county and also is such that the people are very much tempted to, and some accordingly do, transgress the Lord by trading in liquors with the neighboring Indians, and also in other things to the great distraction of the peace and yet with impunity for want of proper officers.[52]

Petitions from the proprietors of the other towns in the Western Lands made the same requests in almost the same language.[53]

Three groups of men were concerned by the decision to incorporate: the resident proprietors, the absentee proprietors, and the resident nonproprietors. From the nature of the requests contained in the petitions, it is possible to assign motives to each group.

The resident proprietors of Kent had much to gain from all three requests, and so they may well have voted en masse for the petition of September 19, 1739. They undoubtedly preferred a town government with authority far exceeding that of the proprietary body. Just as they constituted a majority of the proprietors, so they constituted a majority of the town[54] and could fill the offices that were created under the new town government. As selectmen they could serve as town administrators; as deacons they could guide the church; as justices of the peace, grand jurors, and constables they could enforce law and order; as listers, collectors, and tithingmen they could handle tax affairs; and finally as fence viewers, highway surveyors, pound keepers, and haywards they could perform necessary functions for the welfare of the town.

As land speculators the resident proprietors would favor incorporation. A well organized, well governed town would attract more settler customers and thus push land prices higher. As tax payers the resident proprietors would again be pleased. Before incorporation nonproprietors paid nothing; after incorporation they had to help support the town by the "common list" and the special tax on all divided land.

The absentee proprietors could be expected to view incorporation with mixed feelings. On the one hand, an organized town with church and civil rights would mean higher land prices and profits. On the other hand, their taxes would rise sharply. Prior to incorporation there was no meetinghouse to build or minister to pay. After incorporation the new tax of four pence per acre on all divided lands bore as heavily on the absentees as on the residents who had the benefit of the minister and meetinghouse.

The resident nonproprietors may also have had mixed feelings. Incorporation meant religion, law, and order. It also meant labor on highways and land taxes from which these men had been free prior to the granting of town privileges. The change did permit the nonproprietors a share in the running of the town. After incorporation they voted in town meetings and held town offices neither of which were possible when only proprietors had held authority.

At neither Kent nor any of the settlements of the Western Lands was there absentee political control. The dominant group in all seven towns was the resident proprietors. This group wanted incorporation quickly and secured it. This accomplishment brought town government, in which all local men participated and from which all absentees were excluded.

Role of the Central Government

Harmonious towns like Kent and her sister settlements of the Western Lands possessed much in common with communities in Massachusetts that seemed steeped in controversy. Both featured avid land speculation and a proprietor system. A basic difference may have been in the roles of the respective central governments. The Connecticut General Assembly did not lose control.[55] Connecticut legislatures had gained wisdom from dealing with earlier problems of speculation, absenteeism, and proprietor control. By the 1730s the General Assembly had enacted and enforced laws to minimize previous iniquities. The Connecticut auctions of 1738 do not represent the completion of a growing and evil transition to land mongering and absentee-proprietor control. The towns of the Western Lands were sold impartially and fairly; the proceeds were effectively utilized for the support of education; absenteeism was minimized; and the new towns were rapidly incorporated and thus placed under political control of the settlers themselves. Kent was settled successfully and harmoniously by speculative proprietors under the watchful eyes of the General Assembly.

PART II

Economic Opportunity
in Kent

Kent was settled by versatile and ambitious men who sought economic opportunity in the new town. Having examined certain economic and political problems affecting the original settlement of Kent in 1738 and 1739, we now turn to the town's entire period of growth and development in the eighteenth century.[1] Parts II, III, and IV will examine the nature of economic opportunity, political democracy, and social democracy. The study of economic opportunity provides a necessary foundation for the subsequent treatment of political democracy (property qualifications for voting) and of social democracy (prestige associated with wealth).

Historical material relating to Kent and her sister towns along the Connecticut frontier indicates three main conclusions about economic opportunity in that region. The first point emphasizes the drive for profits. The average Kent inhabitant does not appear to have been content with a subsistence way of life ("the happy yeoman"). On the contrary, one is impressed with his almost frantic pursuit of a wide variety of schemes or projects. One also notes a curious moral attitude, a combination of self-righteousness and a propensity for cunning deceit.

The second principal conclusion is that Kent evidence continues as in Part I to run counter to many of the previous versions of economic hardship or oppression in the new lands. Problems described in histories of other towns arising from absentee speculation in and control of lands, harsh creditor-debtor relations, and widespread poverty are found to be less evident at Kent.

The third contention in this study of economic opportunity at Kent is that such opportunity was excellent at the town's founding and during its early years but decreased during the later decades of the eighteenth century, finally producing conditions which would make Shaysite agitation explicable. There are insufficient economic data available for a definitive explanation of worsening conditions. Kent evidence suggests, however, that some historians may have been following a false scent in stressing class-struggle aspects such as speculation, absenteeism, and debtor-creditor relationships. The present writer leans toward a far simpler explanation for hard times: pressure of an increasing population on the available supply of local land.

3

THE DRIVE FOR PROFITS

The New England pioneers present two faces to the reading public. By far the most familiar face emerges idealized and sentimentalized from the pages of poetry, local history, and some popular history. Many tend to envision our typical settler of western Connecticut, Massachusetts, or Vermont striding with flintlock in hand through the trackless forests in quest of fertile acres, a clear spring, and a homesite where his wife might transplant the lilac shoots carried tenderly from the former home. We picture the clearing of the forest, the repulse of a few Indian raids, and the emergence of a rigorous, subsistence way of life. Sons, grandsons, and great-grandsons live out contented lives drinking the clear spring water (or cider from their apple orchard), eating the produce of their own fields, and dressing in garments made beneath the home roof.[1]

The second face, familiar to readers of the works of James Truslow Adams or to college students reading the standard texts by Curtis Nettels or Oliver Chitwood, has been described above in Chapter 2. This is the face of a nascent Shaysite rebel, a humble frontiersman oppressed by eastern capitalists, the face, in Adams's words, of a slave condemned to toil for his master.[2]

In the present chapter we do not propose to quarrel over the details of the first, or sentimentalized, portrayal of the New England settler but will suggest that much remains to be added. At Kent one is impressed not so much with the contented, subsistence way of life as with the drive for profits.[3] This drive is reflected in the large number of farms that produced saleable surpluses; it is apparent from the high percentage of men who sought profits in mills, mines, and other nonagricultural enterprise; it is most obvious in the ferment of speculation by local men in local lands; and finally, it is discernible in the restlessness of the town population, a mobility wherein the average Kent resident remained only five years before moving on. This is not to suggest that Kent was filled exclusively with "carpetbaggers" participating in a hectic bonanza. The subsistence way of life was indeed present, and some families established semipermanent homesteads complete with beloved

TABLE 5
KENT FARM HOMESTEADS, 1796

	Oxen	Cows	Horses	Plow-land (acres)	Meadow (acres)
Class I					
(7 members)					
Nathaniel Hatch	4	18	7	56	36
Jeremiah Fuller	4	26	3	24	46
Nathan Skiff	8	18	2	35	30
Nathaniel Berry, Jr.	4	17	4	35	20
Joseph Pratt	2	11	6	28	24
Ebenezer Berry	4	11	3	28	17
Peter Mills	2	9	5	37	26
Class II					
(23 members)					
Jacob Bull	2	7	4	20	20
Class III					
(33 members)					
Ezra Geer	2	5	2	10	9
Class IV					
(33 members)					
Jedediah Hubbel, Jr.		3	2	8	6
John Berry		2	1	3	3
Class V					
(7 members)					
David Gilbert		2	1		
Zachary Winegar		2	1		
Samuel F——?		2	1	1	1
John Smith			1		
Gideon Tuttle			1	1	
Joshua Staunton		1			2
Elon Stone		1		1	

ᵃ To convert to pounds divide dollars by 3⅓.

lilacs and clear-running springs. What is desired is to produce a blended picture by stressing the drive for profits that has heretofore been too much ignored.

We are disposed to question the second version which emphasizes the oppressive features of the economy in the Western Lands. It seems appropriate to suggest that economic goals seemed attainable on the grounds that such a high percentage of inhabi-

Bogey Meadow (acres)	Clear Pasture (acres)	Bush Pasture (acres)	Timber-land (acres)	Total List in dollars [a] (less polls)	Total Stock	Total Farm Acreage Less Timberland
4	74	77	200	496	39	247
	15	70	230	390	33	155
6	15	35	59	377	28	121
	25	40	120	339	25	120
	20	30	100	313	19	102
3	6	80	18	294	18	134
5	6	30	93	275	16	104
	12	55	45	187	10	107
	2	10	64	116	9	95
	18	2	122	101	5	34
	3	15	3	34	2	24
				25	3	0
				25	3	0
				25	3	2
		6	5	15	1	6
		4		15	1	5
	1	2	9	12	1	5
				10	1	1

tants sought them. Comments of contemporary observers nearly
all report favorably on the prosperity and opportunity in the
region.

The Farming Pattern at Kent: Saleable Surpluses

During the latter half of the eighteenth century Kent contained about 100 dwelling houses. In 1796 the 209 adult males
dwelt beneath 103 roofs. Almost all of these were farm homesteads
possessing sufficient land for some crops, livestock, and gardens.
It should be enlightening to explore the nature of these farm
homesteads and to determine as accurately as possible the numbers and percentages, first, of those that produced saleable surpluses and, second, of those that produced at least a sufficiency for
their occupants.[4]

The 103 homesteads scattered through the township of Kent
in 1796 may be appropriately broken down into five groups or
classes as follows:

Class	Value: Total[6] of "Common List" 1796 (in dollars)	Value (in pounds)	Number of Farms in Class
I	500–250	150–75	7
II	250–175	75–52	23
III	175–100	52–30	33
IV	100–25	30–7.5	33
V	25–0	7.5–0	7

Representative holdings of inhabitants in each class are shown in
Table 5. Possessions for all men in Class I and Class V are shown,
while for the more numerous Classes II, III, and IV only one or
two representative individuals are shown for each.

We find that the seven wealthiest farmers in Class I possessed
sufficient farming resources to obtain considerable surplus and
presumable profit from the sale of this excess produce.[7] Similarly
the twenty-three members of Class II and the thirty-three of
Class III, though less productive, would still be capable of producing a saleable surplus. Thus surpluses were obtainable from
sixty-three of the 103 homesteads (61 percent). Class IV con-

tained thirty-three homeowners whose holdings would produce a subsistence but no more. Finally, the seven men in Class V were all dependent on food sources other than their own land.

The seven farmers in Class I are at the top of the scale on the basis of their highest property listings on the tax work sheets of 1796. Their farms, listed from $275 up to $496, had, on the average, fifteen cows and forty acres of arable land for production of grain crops. Unquestionably they all had considerable farming surpluses. Jeremiah Fuller with twenty-six cows was doubtless one who contributed to the reputation of Litchfield County as a supplier of cheese. Peter Mills was a licensed tavern keeper and so his surplus in grain may have been used here. The rest must have sold dairy products, wheat, and corn either locally or possibly to neighboring merchants. The original generation of settler proprietors prospered at Kent. Timothy Hatch, Joseph Fuller, Benjamin Skiff (a proprietor but not until 1750), Nathaniel Berry, Joseph Pratt, and John Mills bought shares at Windham in 1738 and moved to Kent by 1739. Each member of Class I is a son of one of these "firstcomers." Each inherited a sizable estate, though only a fifth or so as large as the original, and then augmented that estate by speculating in lands and profiting from the surplus of farming operations.

The twenty-three farmers in Class II possessed property valued on the tax list from $175 to $275 and all appeared capable of producing a surplus. They averaged six cows (eight men with eleven cows and five with only four); and most had five oxen or horses. Twenty acres of plowland and 125 acres in other categories of land were average.

Jacob Bull was a typical member of this group in point of property. His difficulties with authorities over alleged Tory sympathies produced documents which give us a better than average insight into his economic status. In 1796 Bull's list (property plus $60 poll tax) was $247. Converting this to pounds, we get £74.[8] His tax record over the years was as follows:

1770	£50	1776	£55	1781	£81
1773	49	1777	64	1791	72
1775	50	1780	81	1796	74

Jacob Bull's family was smaller than the average. He had married Mary Washburn in 1762 and the children, Ruth, Jemina, Betsy, Isaac, and Jacob, had come along between 1763 and 1772. Four children had been stillborn in these years. From Bull's petitions to the General Assembly in 1778, we see that he was operating an inn for teamsters during the Revolution. In defending his patriotism, he wrote in part:

I have helped officers and soldiers by victualling them to the number of 900. I gave 100 meals to distressed soldiers, kept teams night and day, and never did turn none away, money or no money.[9]

Despite all these "gift meals," Bull prospered during the Revolution, as is shown by the steady rise in his list. At this time he was buying more land and probably more stock. Later he seems to have dropped his inn business but did purchase a dam and sawmill in 1789. Clearly Bull was not a subsistence farmer. Like many others he appears to have enjoyed a surplus and to have cast about for money-making ventures.

Class III contains the names of thirty-three farmers whose property was listed between $100 and $150 and who comprised the middle or average group in Kent. In this group the average number of cows per farm was five and all members had in addition either horses or oxen. The average number of these draft animals was four. In plowland acreage the average was fourteen with practically all farmers owning between ten and sixteen acres. The average farm in Class III also possessed seventy-five additional acres in other categories.

Ezra Geer,[10] the Class III farmer selected for analysis, possessed sufficient resources to feed his family of twelve children and still have a small surplus in grain.[11] Since his listing of $116 puts him near the bottom of Class III and inasmuch as the four men beneath him had smaller families, it may be stated that members of Class III could sell at least some surplus from their farms.

Class IV contained thirty-three farm homesteads listed at $30 to $100. Each was small but probably adequate for subsistence if not burdened with too many mouths to feed. The majority of occupants were third-generation descendants of original settlers, but they did not necessarily remain long in Kent themselves. The average number of cows owned by this group was three. The highest number was five and only the poorest, John Berry, showed but one. Twenty had either a pair of oxen or horses but thirteen listed no draft animals. (Hogs and sheep would not show on the tax lists). On the average they owned five acres of plowland and thirty-five acres in other categories. None of the farmers of this class could have produced any substantial surplus.

Typical of the class was Jedediah Hubbel, Jr. His three cows, two horses, and thirty-four-acre farm indicate an adequate sub-sistence freehold. There is no record that he married or had any children in Kent, and like many in Class IV, he had moved on by 1800. The Hubbels were a prominent and relatively wealthy Kent family. Jedediah, Senior, had been born in Fairfield in 1731 and had come to Kent with his father, Ephraim, an original settler, proprietor, and town leader. Jedediah, Senior, father of our Class IV farmer, was himself a second-generation town leader. It was he who represented Kent at the convention in Hartford in 1788 and voted "Yes" on ratification of the Constitution. However, the Hubbel progeny soon became so numerous that pickings became thin for the third generation. Jedediah, Junior, was born in 1773, one of thirteen children born of Jedediah Hubbel and Lucy Noble.

Class V, seven homesteads listed between $10 and $30, completes the roster of Kent homes and seems significant for its small-ness. The occupants of these homes could not live off the produce of their own acres; indeed, two showed no acreage and none reached the total deemed necessary to support a person. But it is notable that a visitor to Kent in the late eighteenth century would not find numerous nonfarm homes for housing hired hands, artisans, mechanics, and other workers. Such individuals in Kent lived for the most part with brothers or parents on relatively sub-stantial farms. Only seven dwellings out of 103 housed workers who had to buy their food. An examination of the seven owners of these poorest homesteads sheds some light on the subject of economic opportunity. For each there is some explanation for the apparent rock-bottom status, an explanation which precludes the use of these seven as a nucleus for an oppressed proletariat.

Elon Stone was a younger son in the large Stone family at

Kent. His brother, Levi, had fifty-five acres, two cows, and a horse—*but no house*. Possibly Elon's house and Levi's acreage constituted the same farm. Elon first appeared on a tax list in 1795. He became a freeman of Kent in 1799 and voted "Yes" on the new Connecticut constitution in 1818. There is no evidence that Elon or the other Stones followed any vocation except farming.

Joshua Staunton was an old Kent resident living in New Preston Society. He married Sarah Beeman in 1775, became a freeman in 1777, and also took the "Oath of Fidelity" in 1777. He had several children in the 1780s and was still in Kent in 1818, at which time his list had climbed to $98.

Gideon Tuttle was a transient, here today and gone tomorrow. He differed from the many other transients only in that he had his own house (two fireplaces). He first appeared in the Kent records in 1793 and was gone by 1797.

John Smith was a carpenter, or joiner, who lived in Kent for many years. He married Hannah Swift in 1794 and had many children. He became a freeman in 1800 and was still listed as a carpenter in 1818 (at which time his list was up to $148). Like Elon Stone he may have contributed the house while a brother Stephen Smith furnished land and stock. Stephen Smith had no house but owned six head of stock and forty-nine acres of farm land.

Samuel F— is a mystery. Perhaps he worked as a hired hand either on a neighbor's farm or in a mill or ironworks.

Zachary Winegar was one of several sons of Hendrick Winegar, who had come to Kent in 1777 from Amenia. The Winegars were substantial citizens and occasionally sued their townsmen for unpaid debts (for example, Solomon Chase in 1787). Their interest seemed to be entirely in ironworks, with Winegar's Forge prominent in the early nineteenth century. None had farming land or stock. Zachariah became a freeman in 1804 and voted "No" on the state constitution in 1818. At that time he was worth $173 on the "Common List."

David Gilbert is the last of our seven Class V homeowners. He was a shoemaker and tanner and so presumably earned enough money from this trade to buy his food. He first reached Kent in 1795, became a freeman in 1799, and was still present in 1804 but not in 1818.

In summary it should be noted that of 103 Kent farms or home-steads only seven lacked sufficient land or stock to support the occupants. Of these seven, two were probably part of brothers' farms; three housed men who earned their living by carpentry, shoemaking, or iron forging; one was probably occupied by a hired hand; one was lived in by a transient; and the last was owned by a man whose name is torn off at the corner of the 1796 tax list and cannot be identified.

Contemporary Opinion on Farming in the Western Lands

The opinions of contemporary travelers who have recorded their views on western Connecticut tend to bear out the impression of prosperity and plenty suggested by the analysis of Kent's 103 farm homesteads. For example, the author of *American Husbandry*, when referring to rural Connecticut, noted:

The face of the country has a cheerful prospect . . . the farm houses are well and substantially built and stand thick . . . . All the inhabitants of the country appear to be well fed, clothed, and lodged . . . . New settlers enter at once into the class of freeholders.[12]

Dr. William Douglass's *Summary*, published in 1750, was equally enthusiastic about the Connecticut countryside. Douglass noted:

Connecticut is a good country as to soil and climate. Any country is happy when the meaner inhabitants are plentifully and wholesomely fed; warmly and decently clothed, and thus it is in Connecticut.[13]

Timothy Dwight, though critical of farming methods, was enthusiastic about Goshen, Kent's immediate neighbor to the northeast.

It is perhaps the best grazing ground in the state: and the inhabitants are probably more wealthy than any other collection of farmers in New England . . . . The inhabitants are distinguished for industry, sobriety, good order, and good morals.[14]

While Dwight praised the established farmers in Connecticut's Western Lands, the Marquis de Chastellux marveled at how quickly humble men could become "comfortable planters." On November 18, 1780, Chastellux, an aide to General Rochambeau, passed through Kent and crossed Bull's Bridge into New York

State. His eyewitness account of the settlement and farming patterns at Kent provides a colorful complement to the technical details furnished by land, tax, and probate records.[15]

Chastellux was impressed by the spread of settlement. At Kent third-generation sons were coming of age around the time of Chastellux's visit and many were clearing new farms.

Four years ago one might have traveled ten miles in the woods I traversed without seeing a single habitation . . . . [Today] I have never traveled three miles without meeting a new settlement [a single homestead].[16]

Only a small capital of £25 was necessary to start "a settlement," and most of that was borrowed according to Chastellux. The new settler brought "a cow, some pigs, and two or three indifferent horses." After clearing and building with the ever-present aid of neighbors,

The grass grows rapidly. There is pasturage for the cattle the very first year; after which they are left to increase or fresh ones are bought, and they are employed in tilling a piece of ground which yields the enormous increase of 20 or 30 fold.[17]

Kent records suggest that at least half the farm homesteads produced a saleable surplus. Chastellux concluded on an ever more optimistic note:

At the end of two years the planter has wherewithal to subsist and even sends some articles to market. At the end of four or five years he completes the payment of his land and finds himself a comfortable planter.[18]

At Kent, farming was the principal occupation and virtually all inhabitants lived on farms. Agriculture furnished a subsistence base for the economy. Where farmers sought profits above subsistence needs, many could obtain such gains by means of their husbandry.

Nonagricultural Enterprise

The quest for profits did not always end when the Kent settler had developed his farm to a level capable of producing a salable surplus. A large number of inhabitants supplemented their farming incomes by engaging in various nonagricultural enterprises. Ironworks or ore mining attracted many of the local men. Saw, grist, and fulling mills sprang up at the falls of the streams. Finally, Kent was dotted with shops, stores, taverns, and such miscellaneous establishments as brickyards, tanneries, dyehouses, and distilleries. The presence of such establishments in Kent is hardly noteworthy, for they could be found in most New England towns. What may be significant is the high percentage of local men involved in their operation. A study of the owners or operators of the town industries emphasizes the energy, versatility, and acquisitiveness of the eighteenth-century Kent settler.

IRON

Of the first forty-five adult male inhabitants of Kent, eight became involved in iron property and three more became charter members of a copper mine company.[19] A large number of the second generation became owners of ironworks. Between 1739 and 1800 no fewer than 102 men were owners of iron property. The list of "iron men" looks like the social register of early Kent.[20]

The principal ironworks during the early history of the town were three operated by the Barnums, Morgans, and Bulls respectively. The first two went through bankruptcy but that of the Bulls remained solvent. Other ironworks came and went. The Land Records refer to Bates's Forge, Converse Forge, Holley's Ironworks, Titus's Forge, and Winegar's Forge. In his 1812 history of Kent, Barzillai Slosson reported that Kent had six forges for making iron and that they made annually from thirty to forty tons each. "This iron when delivered at the slitting mills at Canaan or Washington has generally been worth about $100 a ton." [21] Slosson also noted that the iron ore and charcoal came mostly from Kent.

Kent's forges and ironworks were less important and less well known than her iron ore mine in Ore Hill three miles east of the Housatonic and a half mile north of the New Milford border. Evidence indicates that in the eighteenth century this was Connecticut's second largest source of iron ore. (Salisbury, in first place, had ore that was superior in quality and quantity but most of this was exported to New York.)[22] Slosson gives Kent's iron ore mine an early date when he writes: "This mine was discovered at an early period and has been constantly worked since the first settlement of the town." [23]

The iron industry at Kent in the eighteenth century was not always profitable but appears to have been an irresistible lure for townsmen with surplus capital. Virtually every family had some member involved as operator or part owner of an ironworks. The 102 men who owned shares in the six forges and the ore mine provide evidence that many settlers were not satisfied with a subsistence way of life but were avidly casting about for profits.

WATER-POWERED MILLS

Kent, with its gouged-out Housatonic Valley and steep mountainsides, abounds with swift streams and waterfalls. The first settlers were quick to utilize Mill Brook (now called Kent Falls Brook) in the north, Sanford Brook (modern Cobble Brook) in the west, Aspetuck River in the east, and Sandpit Brook (now called Womenshenuk Brook) in the south. Near the first waterfalls in each stream a visitor in 1750 would encounter dams and mills with their water wheels operating slow-moving vertical saws, the grinding wheels of gristmills, the hammers of forges and fulling mills, or the bellows of ironworks. In the Housatonic itself one would find two picturesque spots where the swift current was utilized.

The settlers who used these streams, Barnums, Beebes, Comstocks, Fullers, Hatches, Millses, Morgans, Pratts, Ransoms, Rowlees, and Swifts, were leading men of Kent. They were neither full-time specialists in mill operation nor mere share owners. They were hybrids. On the one hand, John Ransom could roll up his sleeves and work in his fulling mill beside his son.[24] On the other hand, Ransom was a successful farmer, land speculator, justice of the peace, and deputy to the General Assembly. John Mills was drowned in 1760 while working at the dam by Bull's Bridge. At that time he was operating one of Kent's largest farms, was speculating heavily in land, and was lending money at interest to a majority of townsmen. Thirty Kent men were part owners of sawmills at various times. Twenty-nine owned shares in gristmills and five in fulling mills.[25] Such a number of men attempting to utilize water power for profit reemphasizes the idea that Kent settlers were seeking more than a subsistence way of life.

WORKS, STORES, AND TAVERNS

Less picturesque than the water-powered mills but still economically important were the tanneries, brickworks, potash works, dye works, and stills.[26] The first reference to a tannery or shoemaker's shop was the permission granted to Daniel Comstock to build one at the side of his house in 1750.[27] By 1800 ten men were or had been operating tanneries, including sons of original proprietors John Raymond and Matthew Judd. According to Slosson's history, Kent clay was excellent for brickmaking, and Hoyts, Clarks, Berrys, and Campbells practiced this trade. Nathaniel Berry ran a potash works. Timber, however, was scarce at Kent, barely sufficing for fuel, fences, houses, and charcoal, so potash production was never important.[28] Samuel Beers ran a dye works and there was one still for making spirits operated by proprietors' clerk Julius Caswell.

According to legend, Daniel Comstock was Kent's first storekeeper, and the dwelling he erected in 1739 served as trading post and meetinghouse.[29] By the 1770s Kent had four or five general stores all acting as brokers between the farmer and his market.[30] These stores bought the farmer's surplus and in return supplied all he wished to buy. Transactions were conducted on a credit basis with settlement once a year.[31]

When Kent storekeeper Abel Wright died in 1770, the executor of his estate prepared an inventory which offers insight into the operations of a general store. Wright had been selling two categories of goods: first, local farm produce such as sheep's wool, flour, wheat, cider, butter, and cheese; second, luxury goods imported from New York merchants. Wright owed £61 to his twenty-six suppliers. His records indicated a total of 140 Kent customers who owed him £229.

Some argument has developed among historians as to the extent to which frontiersmen ran up debts by their extravagant purchases of imported goods. Wright's inventory indicates that Kent customers in 1770 could buy some hundred different items including knee and shoe buckles, red garters, fans, and white shammy gloves. Eight varieties of imported cloth carried exotic labels: blue Russell, brown shalloon, green calimenco, light calimenco, silk, spotted durant, black camblet, osnabruck (linen).[32]

Kent taverns were operated by some of the town's most respected and affluent men. The first tavern keeper was Joshua Lassell, a selectman, an agent to the General Assembly, and the most active land speculator in the town's history. By 1795 Kent had seven taverns, most of which were owned by wealthy men. Peter Mills, son of John Mills, had a large farm in addition to his tavern (17 cattle and 300 acres). Tavern keepers John Pain, Hezekiah Reed, and Abraham Fuller had similar-sized farms and were all worth over $300 on the 1796 tax list.

Altogether, 209 men were investors in nonagricultural enterprise at Kent between 1739 and 1800.[33] Of the original forty-five adult male settlers, twenty-two, or almost half, became part owners of works, mills, or shops. In each area of economic investigation one encounters some of the original settler proprietors or their descendants. The most significant aspect of this enterprise at Kent would seem to be the magnitude of profit-seeking activity.

Land Speculators at Kent

Recent historians have been impressed with the orgy of land speculation during the eighteenth century.[34] They have directed attention to the prominent, eastern aristocrats who were speculating as absentees in the lands of the numerous new frontier towns. Still to be studied is the extent to which the settlers themselves participated in this speculative mania. The present writer has found that the principal speculators at Kent were, indeed, the local settlers.[35] Not only were their speculative ventures impressive in number but they suggest the prevalence of a peculiar moral code. When the leading citizens of Kent sought land profits, they became, at best, resourceful opportunists and, at worst, conniving dissemblers.

The way Kent farmers made land deals among themselves is astonishing. The first division [36] naturally contained the best land for farming and home-building. The fifty-three lots of this division lay on both sides of the "twelve-rod highway to Cornwall" (now

U.S. Route 7). This choice land came into the hands of the settlers almost immediately; [37] but instead of remaining stable and inactive, the first division lots were bought and sold more than any other plots in Kent. For example, lot 46 was drawn by proprietor-settler Thomas Beeman at the first division in 1738. By 1748 this farm lot had reached Jethro Hatch after changing hands seven times. A glance at its gyrations in between Beeman and Hatch, as shown in Table 6, is instructive.

TABLE 6
SALES OF LOT 46

Year	Transaction	
1738	To Thomas Beeman, by draw, at first division of lands.	
	Western Section of Lot	*Eastern Section of Lot*
1739	Thomas Beeman to Ebenezer Barnum, Sr. No price.	Thomas Beeman to Nathaniel Robards, £ 114
1741		Nathaniel Robards to Ebenezer Barnum, Jr., £ 162
1743	Ebenezer Barnum, Sr., to Johnathan and Samuel Skeels, £ 100	
	Jonathan and Samuel Skeels to Ebenezer Barnum, Jr., £ 120	
1745	Ebenezer Barnum, Jr., to Amos Barnum, £ 413	
	Amos Barnum to Ephraim Fisher, £ 452	
1746	Ephraim Fisher to John Beeman (brother of original owner, Thomas). No price.	
1748	John Beeman to Jethro Hatch. No price.[a]	

[a] Kent, Land, III, 261. Usually a price is given but occasionally it is hidden behind the phrase "valuable consideration."

Every man listed in Table 6 was a local settler. These same settlers, and almost all others in Kent, were dealing in similar fashion with other first division lots. Lot 6 changed hands seven times, lots 22 and 29 changed hands ten times each, and lots 26 and 46 changed eight times each. The average turnover for all fifty-three lots during the period 1738–1760 was four, this being reduced by seven lots for which their is no record of any sales. It seems hardly an exaggeration to say that each pioneer wanted a piece of five or six other homelots. Abel Wright owned at various times parts of eleven first division lots; Nathaniel Berry held in ten, John Mills in seven, Joseph Pratt in six, and Reuben Swift in five. The Barnums collectively were in sixteen of the lots and the Comstocks, Hatches, Hubbels, and Fullers were almost as widespread.

Since all these men were settlers, it might be reasoned that the trading represented an effort to consolidate holdings. However, evidence indicates that only a small percentage of purchases were for this purpose. One need only establish the homelot of an individual and then look to see where he did his buying. Usually he bought on the other side of town or in some inexplicable, crazy-quilt pattern.[38] The writer has studied some of these most frequently traded lots to see if some special feature might account for their popularity. For the most part, there was nothing unusual about them such as iron-ore land, water-power land, or a good crossroad site for a tavern. The deed descriptions and present day inspection show merely good farming lots. One may then conclude that most of these purchases were purely speculative. Here was a steadily growing town with a considerable population turnover. Land was easy to buy, easy to sell; and, best of all, prices were steadily rising.[39]

After 1742 as the settlement survived and flourished, prices rose to the point where a single lot brought more than the original cost of the entire proprietary share. By 1755 good land was bringing two to three pounds per acre and the early divisions had bestowed fine, 100-acre lots on the holders of proprietary shares. A proprietor who held his share through all divisions and then sold his accumulated lots and pitches could realize almost a ten-fold increase over his original investment. No proprietor followed this precise course. The Kent resident proprietors not only held on pretty well to the end but in addition engaged in much trading among themselves, with newcomers, and with absentees. As land prices continued to rise (they are said to have increased fourfold between 1750 and 1812),[40] these local proprietors apparently reaped a harvest of bonanza proportions.

Many of the Kent settlers were not content with the profits stemming from the proprietary divisions and the rising price of land. The records reveal numerous schemes or contests involving large tracts of land. Jonathan Rowlee, Junior contested for a portion of the Great Plain.[41] Moses Rowlee was accused of deceiving the General Assembly into granting him an oversized tract.[42] The Skeelses devised plans for acquiring a large tract of colony land, and the Barnums sold sixty-four shares in a "silver mine" (actually iron ore) to neighbors and inhabitants of nearby towns.

THE FULLER-LASSELL TRACT

One revealing episode concerned the efforts of Joseph Fuller and Joshua Lassell to acquire nearly 5,000 acres of colony land west of the Housatonic River. The transaction was exceedingly complex involving petitions, investigations, and legislative hearings over a ten-year period, 1743–53.[43] However, once the story is pieced together from materials available at Kent and in the Connecticut Archives, several major points emerge. First, one is impressed with the leadership status of Fuller and Lassell in Kent. We obtain some insight into the economic morality of the time when we note the practices of a church deacon, practices apparently considered normal and acceptable by fellow townsmen. Second, there emerges a reinforced impression of the versatility and energy of such opportunists as Fuller and Lassell. Most interesting and revealing are the many petitions Fuller and Lassell submitted to the General Assembly. These are misleading in tone, (the writers picture themselves as humble yeomen), and fairly bristle with calculated inaccuracies, omissions, and misstatements. Finally, one is impressed with the caution and fairness of the General Assembly. If a researcher judged the case on the material available at Hartford, he might understandably conclude that here was one more example of a callous, eastern governing elite rejecting the entreaties of humble frontiersmen. Only when data available at Kent is added, does this different and more complete version appear.

An account of the Fuller-Lassell affair should begin with a brief introduction of the participants. Joseph Fuller has already been mentioned as one of the Colchester delegation to Kent. He was born in 1699 at East Haddam, Connecticut, and moved to Colchester where he first married Lydia Day and then Zerviah

Noble of New Milford. After buying his Kent proprietary share at the Windham auction, this respected pioneer moved with his large family to Kent. His sons, Joseph, Zachariah, Jeremiah, Abraham, Jacob, and Isaac, all married Kent girls and fathered Kent families of their own. Abraham commanded a Kent militia company during the Revolution. Of Joseph's daughters, Rachel married proprietor Samuel Bates, Grace married proprietor John Cahoon, Lydia married proprietor Thomas Hatch, and Mindwell married settler Asa Parrish, these husbands all being Kent men. Only daughter Ruth left town to marry Job Gould of Sharon.[44] At Kent Joseph Fuller was one of the two deacons of the First Society Church. He was the first town treasurer and served three times as selectman in the 1740s. He died in 1755 probably in his home by Fuller Pond on Fuller Mountain.[45]

Joshua Lassell came to Kent in 1743 from Windham and has previously been introduced as Kent's principal tavernkeeper. He was twice a selectman (1744 and 1755), and also served as highway surveyor, tithingman, and grand juror. Family data is lacking though a Joshua Lassell, Junior was on the scene briefly in Kent. The Lassells moved on to Amenia, New York, in 1755.[46]

Fuller and Lassell were not only respected town leaders but were versatile and energetic to a surprising degree. Page after page of the Kent Land Records of the 1740s and 1750s record their speculative ventures. Minutes of town meetings show their appointments as special agents or reveal their services on special committees. The Litchfield County Court Records suggest that in any spare time when these men were not hatching schemes in Kent or petitioning the General Assembly, they were serving as plaintiffs or defendants in local debt suits. Before one is through with the career of Lassell, nothing he undertakes comes as a surprise. While conducting his campaign to acquire the 4820–acre tract from the General Assembly he was: (1) working a farm in Kent and (2) operating a tavern. To further his land-acquisition scheme he (3) cleared more land and built a house in the tract he was seeking and (4) engineered and constructed a bridge across the Housatonic, "Lassell's Bridge."

The petitions in the Fuller-Lassell case abound with tricks and deceptions. In essence this land problem hinged on the title to a narrow strip of land between Kent, as originally laid out, and the New York border. This strip of colony land was located on the western bank of the Housatonic River, contained about 11,000 acres, and was annexed to Kent late in 1743. Fuller and Lassell claimed 4820 acres, or nearly half of the total. Before and after annexation to the town of Kent, title resided basically with the General Assembly, although some Indian claims of questionable validity appeared to exist. Settlers were ordered to keep out, and "such persons as pretended to purchase Indian titles and then sold to innocent third parties" became liable to a £50 fine and triple damages.[47] Fuller and Lassell ignored these legal hurdles and bought an Indian title. For ten years they argued that by "extinguishing the Indian title and protecting the government's claim" they had performed a valuable service for Connecticut and that their reward should be the tract in question.

Throughout the petitions, Fuller and Lassell pictured themselves as small farmers.

The said Joshua Lassell, having only a farm fit for grazing and little or no plowland, thought proper to look out for some land suitable for the plow. He learned that the tract aforesaid was suitable for the purpose.[48]

When he was writing these words, Lassell was the largest land owner in Kent and the town's most active speculator. He bought and sold more "plowland" in a single year than a dozen men could use. The petitions also stress the idea that these small farmers were acting not so much for themselves but out of colony patriotism. Their perseverance with the Indian owners, they would have the General Assembly believe, was "so that the government's title might be cleared up."

Specific omissions or factual misstatements are numerous. In early petitions Fuller and Lassell gave the government no clue as to the size of the "tract aforesaid." Undoubtedly they hoped that the government would assume it was "just a bit of plowland" and thus casually confirm title to Fuller and Lassell. By 1745 the government suspected that a sizable tract was involved, and therefore in that year's petition, Fuller and Lassell conceded that the tract contained 2000 acres. (This was true, of course. It did indeed contain 2000 acres, but a lot more besides). Not until their petition of October, 1752, did these opportunists finally admit the true acreage total of 4820. Whereas they underestimated the acreage, they overestimated their cost and financial sacrifices. Again, as the investigating committees learned more, the cost figure was lowered. Whereas the actual cost of acquisition of the Indian title had been £350, Lassell and Fuller originally called it £1000 and later £600. Again the wording was tricky. If today one paid $10,000 for a house that had changed hands five times during the year at that price and then stated "$50,000 went into the purchase of my house," he would be following the Fuller-Lassell technique.

The petitions sounded bitter about the government's action:

We have been dealt with more severely than any other person in this colony. We have done nothing to draw down the resentment of the honorable Assembly but have purchased our right of a stranger at dear rates.[49]

Actually, the government was not ungenerous. Because Fuller and Lassell had indeed paid money for an Indian title, the government did make grants to each of about 100 acres. Joseph Fuller accepted this settlement as final. "Fuller's Grant" of 100 acres shows on the proprietor's map next to Fuller Pond on Fuller Mountain. His great land adventures over, Joseph Fuller and his descendants continued to enlarge their farm lands by clearing and purchase, continued to serve Kent as selectmen and deacons, and continued to contribute an ever-growing Fuller progeny to America.

Lassell petitioned on his own in 1753. Clinging to his self-portrait as a humble farmer, he protested that "never doubting that he would get a considerable portion of said land . . . he had broke up and fenced some forty acres and built a house and barn." The lot given him did not include these improvements nor "did it accomodate him in that he can conveniently subject it as a farmer." The General Assembly, reasonably enough, was agreeable to his *buying* the land he wanted. A committee set a price of £50, but this proposition failed to interest Lassell. After 1753 Joshua Lassell petitioned no more. He sold his tavern, disposed of his speculative land holdings, and ceased to serve the town as agent or selectman.

In 1755 this aggressive opportunist left Kent for Amenia, New York. One hopes he found his plowland there.

THE MERRYALL BOUNDRY DISPUTE

Like the Fuller-Lassell scheme, the Merryall controversy featured town leaders and respected citizens dissembling and conniving to gain possession of a large tract of land. Indeed, this Merryall deception involved all the Kent proprietors. Because this case too is complex, involving disputed survey lines and different groups of petitioning inhabitants, only a summary will be attempted here.[50]

It will be recalled that under the New England land system employed in the seventeenth and eighteenth centuries the proprietors of a town became the grantees of virtually all the land within the town boundaries. What boundaries? If there were any uncertainty, the proprietors could be counted on to clamour for that interpretation or survey giving the town (and thus the individual proprietors), the most extensive acreage. It may also be recalled that the Kent proprietors who purchased their shares at the Windham auction in 1738 secured tentative land titles only. Final titles were contingent upon completion of payments for the shares and upon the fulfillment of settlement conditions (clearing land, building and occupying dwellings, etc.). The last definitive step under the Connecticut land system was the issuance of a patent by the General Assembly. This patent would define town boundaries and give the proprietors a final and perfected title.

The southern boundary of Kent was cluttered with a number of vaguely defined grants made earlier by the General Assembly. "Fairweather's Purchase," the New Milford "North Purchase," and "Waramaug's Reserve" all figured in the tangle. These tracts along the southern boundary were known collectively as Merryall. This southern boundary had been rather vague at the time of the auction sale of Kent in Windham on March 7, 1738. A survey made in 1731 (to become important later), had run a line that would have included all Merryall in Kent, but the legal status of this 1731 survey was in doubt. On May 3, 1738, shortly after the auction, the new proprietors held their second meeting and voted "their instruction to their agent to the General Assembly that he prefer a memorial to . . . ascertain the south bound." [51]

In response to this request of the proprietors, the General Assembly immediately authorized a survey by Edmund Lewis and, following its completion, passed an act on September 30, 1738, permanently fixing the Lewis line as the southern boundary. Although this Lewis line excluded Merryall from Kent, there is no evidence of proprietor objections at this time. The problem appeared to be settled, and no questions were raised for the next eight years.

At a Kent proprietors' meeting on April 10, 1746, it was voted to prepare a memorial to the General Assembly asking for a patent for the township of Kent. Having fulfilled settlement conditions, the proprietors wanted their final, perfected titles. The affair dragged on for a year during which time three Kent agents, deacon Joseph Fuller, selectman Joshua Lassell, and selectman Timothy Hatch pressed for the patent. It is important to note that these Kent agents themselves drafted the patent.[52] They "prayed for a patent according to the draft herewith presented." They wrote the lengthy descriptions of the town boundaries: descriptions filled with references to white stones, large oak trees, and forks of streams; descriptions so complex and obscure that only a surveyor or local expert would find them meaningful.

This draft of the patent prepared in Kent ignored the official Lewis line but returned to the obscure 1731 survey which included Merryall within Kent. It seems safe to conclude that the Kent proprietors (or as many as were aware of the scheme in their behalf), were deceiving the General Assembly. Apparently they hoped that approval of the patent would be casual and routine, and thus they would have their enlarged township as a sort of *fait accompli* with which to frustrate any Merryall inhabitants objecting to their transfer to Kent.

The plan worked in its initial stage. Kent's patent, accepted by both houses of the Connecticut legislature and signed by Governor Jonathan Law, became official in May, 1747.[53] For two years the Kent Proprietors were busy surveying their new windfall of Merryall. But they underestimated the wrath of the Merryall citizens whose petitions to the General Assembly led to the following resolution passed in May, 1749:

Whereas this Assembly has been informed that there is a large tract of land contained in the patent that has been made to the proprietors of the town of Kent and lying on the south side of the land contained in said patent, which tract of land was never granted nor intended to be granted by this Assembly, and this Assembly was deceived in ordering said patent to be executed: Resolved, that the King's Attorney in the County of Hartford shall enquire into the matter aforesaid . . . The patentees to appear before this Assembly . . . to show by what right they hold the lands in said patent . . . and why their patent should not be declared void.[54]

Unfortunately the key records of subsequent arguments and decisions are missing. However, a number of technical reasons make it clear that there was a compromise settlement.[55] The Kent proprietors were denied any title to Merryall. However, the disputed tract did become part of the town of Kent, its residents becoming Kent inhabitants and taxpayers.

In essence, then, the Merryall boundary dispute arose out of a scheme to switch surveyed lines in a patent. The idea originated with the town leaders and since no objections are recorded, one may assume that many Kent inhabitants acquiesced in what was attempted. The plan, opportunistic and aggressive, seems to have been part and parcel of the spirit of Kent on Connecticut's eighteenth-century frontier.

We have completed one phase of our examination of economic opportunity at Kent. The town was settled by versatile and ambitious men who sought economic opportunity in many areas. Many produced salable surpluses from their farms, a surprising number sought profits in nonagricultural enterprise, and virtually every early settler was an avid land speculator. One sees in certain of the Kent settlers not so much the contented yeoman, certainly not the "slave" toiling for his master, but perhaps the embryo John D. Rockefeller. These frontiersmen displayed economic daring plus a propensity for deceit. The Barnums at Kent did not say "There's a sucker born every minute" but they acted as if they believed it. The Comstocks at Kent did not discover the Comstock Lode, but they were looking for it. John Mills, father of clergymen and missionaries, was the town's richest man and its most noted charger of usurious interest rates. Deacon Joseph Fuller was co-engineer of an attempted 5000-acre land grab. And the whole town tried to steal Merryall from New Milford.

These aggressive opportunists generally found the economic openings they sought in Kent. Today the stately white houses crowning various hilltops testify to the prosperity their builders enjoyed. Some houses suggest farming profits, a few were built with "iron money," and others reflect gains from mills, stores, or taverns. The finest homes, those of John Mills, Eliphalet Comstock, Joseph Pratt, and Nathaniel Slosson, were built from the profits of land speculation.

4

THREATS TO ECONOMIC OPPORTUNITY: LAND SPECULATION AND ABSENTEEISM

Thus far in our study of economic opportunity at Kent we have found abundant lands for farming, ore deposits and swift streams for industry, and a free market for land speculation. If the activities of settlers reported so far were the whole story, this essay might have been appropriately titled "Prosperity Town" or "Connecticut's Bonanza Frontier." However, a balanced picture of economic opportunity in the town requires study of other features. The following three chapters, therefore, will examine threats to economic opportunity at Kent.

There are two main contentions in these chapters. Most important, we are impressed with the failure of Kent evidence to support the standard version on the nature and effect of threats to economic opportunity in the new towns of western New England. According to this version, later radicalism (Shaysite agitation, etc.), was a legacy of such early agrarian problems as land speculation and absenteeism.

Such districts . . . where radicalism was much in evidence were exactly those districts where disputed land titles, difficulties with speculators, absenteeism, and other agrarian troubles were most in evidence.[1]

At Kent there was heavy speculation and some absenteeism but no conceivable relationship between these activities and later radicalism. Before Kent is written off as a mere exception, it should be noted again that surface evidence (from petitions to the General Assembly), concerning Kent is similar to that in other communities; indeed Kent petition writers were second to none in groaning over their oppression. "Greater difficulty and disasters than was ever known have attended our settlement." It is the more obscure evidence at Kent that refutes the petition version.

The second purpose of the following chapters is to modify any idea that Kent was a roaring bonanza. Although at Kent limitations on economic opportunity do not appear to have followed the pattern usually reported, they were present none the less, particularly where population tended to overcrowd the available land.

Land Speculation and Absenteeism

During the period 1738–60 a total of 872 different men bought and sold Kent land.[2] Virtually every acre in the town was sold and resold in the 6000 transactions of this twenty-two year period. Among the 872 land speculators were William Samuel Johnson, Elisha Williams, William Williams, Jared Eliot, Benjaman Gale, Richard Jackson, and Zephaniah Swift, all prominent Connecticut men of affairs. Thus at first glance, the Kent picture would seem to substantiate the standard version, which has stressed speculation and absenteeism in the new towns of the eighteenth century.

In most respects, however, Kent fails to conform to the usual picture of absenteeism. First, whereas standard accounts have attributed all land mongering to absentees, most speculation in Kent land was conducted by local men. Second, while standard versions have written of absentee land control or even monopoly, at Kent the settlers owned most acreage. Finally, although historians have stressed class differences and antagonism between absentee and local settler, such hostility was negligible at Kent.

The investigator of absentee-resident relationships would like to know three things: first, a numerical breakdown between absentee and resident (what percentage of all property owners were absentee?); second, profits gained (who were the active traders and profiteers?); and third, a comparison of actual acreage owned (what percentage of total acreage did absentees hold at any one time?).

Of the 772 persons who owned land in Kent between 1738 and 1760, 474, or 61 percent, took up residence in Kent. As to the

298 absentees (39 percent), one finds they do not comprise a hostile or separate class from the Kent settlers. Rather, they will be grouped forthwith into relatives, neighbors, combination relative-neighbors, small investors, and finally land jobbers.

A well-known phenomenon of the time illustrated effectively at Kent was the large family, often with ten or more children. At Kent it seemed that the leading members of a family, or clan, had migrated together leaving behind a scattering of less-energetic brothers. The frontiersman at Kent could hardly be called a class antagonist of the absentee speculator when the latter was his own father, son, or brother. Of the Swifts, who came from Sandwich, Massachusetts, it was the vigorous, resourceful, and prosperous Jabez, Nathaniel, and Reuben who led the way and left behind absentee land owners Zephania and Jira Swift.[3] With the Hatches of Tolland, the Hubbels of Newtown, and the Barnums of Danbury, it was not the ne'er-do-wells who moved to Kent; again it was the substantial family leaders who started the procession to the new town. The Barnums helped fill Kent with Amos, David, Ebenezer, Ebenezer Junior, Gideon, Gideon Junior, Jehiel, Joshua, and Richard. Left behind in Danbury were Abel, Epharm, and Nathaniel. Similarly during the 1738–60 period there were eight adult Beemans at Kent, ten Fullers, fourteen Rowlees, and over twenty families with four or more adult male members in Kent.

Of the 298 absentees, 109, or 37 percent, were stay-at-home members of Kent families.[4] They represented all levels of the social and financial scale and were connected to Kent through a variety of relationships. But they had one thing in common. They avoided the stigma of callous, absentee land jobber. At the top of the scale Jared Eliot, the famous Killingsworth pastor-scientist-essayist, owned valuable Kent lands. Ezra Stiles noted of Eliot: "Dr. Eliot bo't 600 acres in Kent for 240 pounds, now worth several thousand proc." [5] This sort of reference is typical of the writings of Stiles, who was an absentee land jobber himself with holdings in Cornwall. Although men of this type were a minority, their writings have become a highly available source. The full story, that Eliot gave the land to three sons who were settlers in Kent, has gone unnoticed. Eliot's sons, Jared Junior, Nathan, and

Wathernon were prominent in the Kent community, and their descendants remained until the 1840s.

Philip Cavarly of Colchester might appear to conform to the standard caricature. However, he gave his lands to daughter Abigail, who was the wife of Josiah Strong of Colchester. By 1756 the Cavarly lands were owned and farmed by Philip's grandsons, Philip and Julian Strong. One of the most active absentee traders was James Lassell of Windham. He was a proprietor who engaged in thirty-nine separate land deals in Kent. But his brother, Joshua Lassell, was even more active on the scene at Kent.

The group of 119 relative-absentees takes a substantial bite from the total of 298 absentees. A second group of 42 absentees, or 14 percent, takes a second bite on the grounds that its members were immediate neighbors of Kent. These Kent land owners had their homes mostly in New Milford to the south and Sharon to the northwest, with a scattering in Cornwall. Some Kent land was also owned by New Yorkers from the Oblong, Dover, and Amenia. Inasmuch as these neighbors farmed the same soil and endured the same hardships as the Kent settlers, they obviously were not a class apart. In some cases, notably Benoi Pack of Cornwall, their Kent lands lay on the border and were part of the home farm. Absentee Pack lived closer to the Kent meetinghouse than did many occupants of the eastern part of the town.[6]

Most neighbors, however, owned Kent property for speculative rather than farming purposes. In 1754 the Barnums sold shares in a mine they owned above present day Kent Falls (seventh division, pitch 32). They sold 128 shares, which brought about £5 apiece. There were twenty-six purchasers of these shares who came from neighboring towns (mostly Sharon), thus accounting for over half the neighbor group. Without exception these neighbors were obscure persons making small purchases.[7]

A third group of nineteen absentees, 6 percent, is furthest of all from the standard concept. This is a combination relative-neighbor group whose members would be eligible for but have not been counted in either of the groups discussed above. It seemed that as large families moved into Kent, they would drop off a few brothers or sons in the neighboring towns. The Swifts left Jabez' son, Heman, (a Revolutionary general), in Cornwall. All the while Heman owned a parcel of Kent land. Several Sanfords came to Kent but brother Elihu never got beyond New Milford. And so it went with Hamilton, Strong, Sealey, Brownson, and other families. They had family members close by living the same sort of life but remaining absentee through the technicality of owning Kent land while residing just over the border.

With the fourth group of "small-investor absentees" we come closer to the usual picture of an eighteenth-century land speculator. This group of 91, or 30 percent, includes Kent land owners who had no known ties with Kent either through relatives using their land or their own proximity to the town. The men comprising this group fail, however, to support the thesis of class conflict and absentee control of land because of the utter insignificance of their holdings. None held more than £150 worth of Kent land at any one time. The average for the group was under £30 and the average length of ownership was less than three years. One suspects that these "little fellows" from distant Hartford, Lebanon, Windham, and New London were valued customers rather than antagonists of the Kent settlers. There was no harm done if Nat Baker, John Alford, or Peleg Brewster bought a mountain lot for £70 and sold it three years later for £110.

For the most part, these ninety-one small purchasers were customers of the big absentees in their respective towns. Wherever an absentee proprietor was located, there appeared a cluster of small fry purchasers to take the assorted lots and pitches off his hands. Twenty-seven absentees, mostly small, lived in Windham alone. This concentration can be attributed to the dealings of such Windham proprietors as James Lassell and David Ripley. Proprietors John Marsh and Ebenezer Davis had their circle of humble customers in Litchfield, and the Silsbeys sought Lebanon buyers. This tendency for absentees to trade with absentees may have kept some blocks of land out of cultivation and thus the situation lends some support to the standard contention on evils of absenteeism. At Kent, however, there is no evidence of resentment. Enough settlers did buy from absentees to suggest that there was a wide-open market and a rapid turnover. The picture is certainly not one of good land being held off the market with frustrated settlers struggling to wrest ownership from a group of wealthy absentees.

Of the 298 absentees, 261, or 87 percent, have been discussed above and more or less eliminated from the wealthy, land-jobber category. Some of the remaining thirty-seven names can be characterized as the sort of speculators that Akagi, Turner, Nettels, and others have written about. In this group are some of Connecticut's prominent aristocrats to whom Kent was just a wilderness corner where land profits might be made. On the other hand, over half the thirty-seven "large investors" made the large list only because their holdings exceeded an arbitrary dividing line (£150) between large and small.

It seems significant, therefore, that out of the grand total of 872 persons owning Kent land between 1738 and 1760, only thirty-seven, or 5 percent, were the type around which so much of the history of land policy has been written.

The second point under consideration, comparison of transactions of residents with those of absentees, helps confirm the relative insignificance of the absentee speculators. For judging speculative activity the writer has compared the eighty resident proprietors with the forty-six absentees.[8] An arbitrary scoring system has been set up wherein each man is rated according to the number of lots he received in divisions (reflecting how many proprietary shares he had and how long he held them), and his total number of ordinary transactions (reflecting his interest, activity, and profit taking).[9]

On the basis of this system local settler Joshua Lassell was the clear leader with 137 points. He was followed by three more Kent citizens, John Mills, Ebenezer Barnum, and Nathaniel Berry. The first absentee, William Samuel Johnson, was number five in the ranking with 102 points. In the top ten, Johnson was the only absentee. In the top twenty-five there were but three absentees and in the top fifty, but nine.

As for profits, the same pattern appears to hold as with trading activity. The local settlers were the big profiteers while the absentees sold out too early for their own good. This statement applies most strongly to the twenty-five absentees who became original proprietors when they bought shares at the Windham auction in 1738. In Chapter 2 we noted that a vigilant General Assembly had inserted strict settlement conditions in the purchase deeds so as to prevent absenteeism. The crucial stipulation required the proprietor or his agent to settle in Kent within two years. As a result, all but five of the original twenty-five sold out and those five had relatives serving as their agents in Kent.

The real land boom in Kent occurred after the absentee proprietors had disposed of their holdings. In selling their shares, the absentees made an average profit of only £30, or 15 percent; this in contrast to the tenfold gains reaped by some residents. Absentee proprietor Elisha Williams profited the most by buying his share at Windham for £193 and selling for £250. Jacob Wanzer gained the least, indeed he sold out for the same price he had paid two years earlier.[10]

It would be helpful to know the total acreage owned by residents and the total owned by absentees at any given time after settlement. However, it appears virtually impossible to make a precise determination in Connecticut prior to 1779 when absentee lands were first included in the common list.[11] By 1750 Kent was a patchwork of perhaps 1500 separate slices of land each of which had been bought and sold an average of three times. These slices were sold to absentees one year and bought back by local men the next, sold in multiple transactions, and sold under descriptive conditions (piles of stones, white oak trees), that are meaningless today. It would make a life's work to assemble the crazy quilt of lots and produce precise figures.

Probably the best systematic method for comparing resident and absentee holdings is to take the early divisions containing the best land and to trace the ownership, lot by lot. As already mentioned, there was a spectacular turnover of lots, some changing hands ten times within twenty years. But when the dust settled, local pioneers were in possession. When the first division was completed in 1738, twenty-eight of the fifty lots went to residents and twenty-two to absentees. By 1739 seven of the absentees had sold out to residents leaving fifteen absentee lots. By the next year eight more had sold out (this was the year the settlement really got underway), and by 1745 three more sold to local men. Of the last four absentees holding first division lots, one sold to a resident in 1755; a second, Richard Hubbel, was a member of the large Kent Hubbel family; and the last two left no record of any kind. Their lots, 39 and 43, simply disappear, and the Land Records do not reveal when they were ever bought or sold in the eighteenth century.

The fifty lots of the fourth division tell a similar story. The division was made in 1739 to thirty-eight local owners and twelve absentees. By 1745 three of the absentees had sold to residents, by 1750 four more, and by 1760 one more. Four lots remained in the hands of absentees until late in the century.

We may summarize with the following generalizations: the absentees made small purchases and held them for short periods of time; they dealt in the less desirable lands; and their ownership of Kent lands probably did not amount to more than 10 percent of the total acreage at any given time after 1742. Adding these determinations to the earlier conclusions that only 5 percent of the land owners were the prominent, absentee aristocrats of the sort usually described, and that their profits were insignificant when compared to those of the locals, one may conclude that Kent offers a notable exception to the standard picture.

The Settlers' Petitions Against Absentees

The foregoing account was based on a study of the status of each settler who lived in Kent between 1738 and 1760 as revealed by his land transactions and his tax list. Whereas these statistics produced a picture of economic opportunity and harmony at Kent, an entirely different scene emerges when one turns to the settlers' own complaints. If the Kent petitions to the General Assembly of May, 1741 and May, 1742 are accepted as true, then Kent's settlement was "attended with greater difficulty and distress than was ever known." [12]

On the subject of absenteeism, the Kent proprietors made the following complaint:

We humbly observe that there were many of the first purchasers who have made merchandise of their rights to their great advantage and there are many large tracts in our towns belonging to nonsettlers or nonresident proprietors. And those bearing little or no burden amongst us but have the value of their lands equally increasing with ours, costs a double burden upon us in respect to the settlement of a minister and building a meeting house. We . . . [urge] . . . that the lands of such nonsettlers be taxed double to the lands of the settlers.[13]

The General Assembly was not won over by this argument and the plea for a double tax on absentee lands was rejected. Not only was Kent turned down twice but similar requests from Canaan, Goshen, Cornwall, Salisbury, and Sharon were also denied.[14] Indeed, the General Assembly continued to "negative" any appeals for special taxation of absentees throughout the rest of the century.[15]

Such petition controversies have helped shape opinion about the nature of New England frontier settlement during the eighteenth century. Many historians have accepted the word of the settlers and concluded that the absentee problem was as serious as indicated in the petitions. Such historians have implied that the assemblies were "callous" or were controlled by "eastern interests" antagonistic to the settlers.[16] An evaluation of the appeal submitted by the Kent settlers suggests that for at least this one town the complaints against absenteeism were exaggerated and the request for double taxation was inequitable and thus properly rejected.

When the Kent proprietors complained of absenteeism in the spring of 1741, they were talking about twelve proprietary shares (out of fifty) that were still owned by absentees.[17] Each of the absentee owners was represented by an agent, who lived on the property in Kent and fulfilled the required settlement conditions. Jedediah Hubbel, for example, was agent for proprietor Richard Hubbel of Newtown. Stephan Pain was the local agent who fulfilled the settlement conditions for William Burnham of Farmington.[18] Undoubtedly the Kent proprietors desired the migration to Kent of an absentee like Burnham and would have found him a more useful neighbor than his less affluent representative, Stephen Pain. However, a comparison of the services to the town of a typical agent, say Pain, with those of a typical resident proprietor, say John Beebe,[19] will show that the difference was trifling.

Table 7 suggests that Kent would have felt little change if Burnham had dismissed Pain and come himself to the town. Even

TABLE 7

COMPARATIVE SERVICES TO TOWN: ABSENTEE PROPRIETOR AND AGENT
VERSUS RESIDENT PROPRIETOR

	Agent (Stephen Pain) and Absentee Proprietor (William Burnham)	*Resident Proprietor (John Beebe)*
Political services		
1. Town officeholder	highway surveyor	constable
2. Town meeting voter	yes	yes
3. Freeman (colony elections)	no	admitted, 1740
Economic and social services		
1. Church membership	admitted, 1743	admitted, 1742
2. Militia	yes	yes
3. Highway labor	yes	yes
4. Productive facilities	small farm	sawmill
5. Special work	drive back "foreign" cattle	swept meeting-house
6. Miscellaneous: barn-raising, etc.	yes ª	yes
Financial services: taxes paid, 1740		
1. "Common list"	£20 (Pain)	£39
Town rate: 2 pence		
Church rate: 3 pence		
School rate: 2 pence		
Total: 7 pence per pound	£0-11-8 (Pain)	£1-3-7
2. Proprietors taxes:	£1-13-0 (Burnham)	£1-13-0
33 shillings per share for		
expense of 3d Division		
3. Special land tax:	£5-16-8 (Burnham)	£5-16-8
4 pence per acre (Proprietors		
had received 350 acres)		
Total	£8-1-4	£8-13-3

ª John Mills rewarded Pain's general services by a gift of land. "I John Mills, for the consideration of the difficulty and hardships undergone by Stephen Pain in his first settling in said Kent and benefit it was for the proprietors to have a family settled here, have given 20 acres." Kent, Land, II, 262.

though agent Pain's "common list" was only £20, the Pain-Burnham tax contribution was 90 percent that of Beebe, the median resident tax payer. Under such circumstances, the General Assembly may have seen no reason to punish the likes of Burnham for harmless absenteeism. To have granted the Kent petition would have been to raise Burnham's tax from £8–1–4 to £13–18–0, or to a point almost 40 percent higher than that of Beebe. Assessing Burnham and his fellow absentees with a double tax would have raised the total Kent tax receipts from about £650 to £775, an increase of 16 percent. The General Assembly may well have felt that this additional income was less essential to the town than the hardship petitions implied.

Evidence of absenteeism at Kent suggests that the proprietors of this town were not exploited by nonresidents. Instead, the local economic scene continued to feature a group of aggressive opportunists eager to capitalize on any chance for more land, more profit, or a decreased tax burden. The Kent proprietors would have been delighted at a £125 windfall in the form of a double tax on absentees; and this prize was well worth one or two petitions. The Kent petitions, and scores of similar complaints from other towns, are readily available at the State Library in Hartford or in other central archives. According to such petitions, economic democracy was seriously threatened. The other side of the coin, what the petitioners were actually doing while airing their grievances, is revealed only in obscure town records.

5

THREATS TO ECONOMIC OPPORTUNITY: DEBT
AT KENT AND HER NEIGHBORING TOWNS

The early residents of Kent filled ten volumes of land records with their speculative transactions (three pages of the index are devoted to the Barnums alone); and their tax records show farms, mills and stores constantly increasing in size and number. However, such a picture of economic opportunity derived from land and tax records may need to be balanced by a study of indebtedness. Conceivably, opportunity at Kent was inhibited by a number of factors arising from the debtor status of its inhabitants.

A study of debtors, creditors, and court actions in northwestern Connecticut may also throw light on the larger problems of relationships between an eastern, mercantile, creditor class and an agrarian debtor group. Historians have studied such a class controversy in Massachusetts and some have stated or implied that conflicts elsewhere in New England, though less severe, were basically similar.[1] Should we discover that numerous court suits, harsh property attachments, and imprisonment for debt were absent on the Connecticut frontier, such a finding would not affect conclusions about Shaysite counties immediately to the north. However, such evidence would help round out a picture of frontier debt in New England and would warn against generalizing too broadly from the debtor-creditor patterns of Massachusetts.

The Widespread Nature of Indebtedness

The Kent records reveal an astonishing amount of debt.[2] In 1760 when an original resident proprietor, John Mills, was drowned in an accident at Bull's dam, he left historians a probate inventory that showed the financial operations of a money lender.[3] The inventory of his estate, dated August 6, 1760, lists the names of men owing him money and the amount for each. "The notes under here are all upon interest from the date save those marked." There follow 116 names and amounts! And this is not the end. A second list is headed "Notes for wheat reckoned at four shillings per bushel." Fourteen men are on this list. Then comes "Notes for sheep and wool" with sixteen men listed. Finally, we reach "Notes of Hand" with five men listed. John Mills was thus owed £3215 in 151 separate debts.

One may state that almost every man in town owed John Mills money (there were about 140 adult males in Kent in 1760). The debts so listed were mostly contracted in 1760 with no debt earlier than 1757. About half were under £5 with the other half scattered between £5 and £66. Nineteen fortunate men had the "no-interest" mark after their names, some of them being relatives.

Other Kent inhabitants were loaning money in similar fashion though probably on a smaller scale. When Abel Wright died, he was owed £149 by twenty-one men. Jabez Swift, Joseph Fuller, Nathaniel Berry, and Daniel Church were occasionally plaintiffs in debt suits, which fact suggests they may have been conducting money-lending operations like Mills.

If the probate records reveal surprising activity by the Mills-type lenders, they are even more revealing on the amount of borrowing. As the smallpox[4] raged at Kent between 1773 and 1778, seventy people died in the East Greenwich Society alone. Of these, twenty-seven were adult males with the remainder women and minor children. Table 8 below indicates the remarkable number of debts each man had contracted.[5]

These debts were owed to a variety of men. Book debts were owed to tavern keepers, storekeepers, blacksmiths, tanners, and carpenters. Numerous small sums (notes of hand), were owed to the various money lenders of Kent. Men owed tax money to three or more rate collectors.

TABLE 8

DEBTS OF KENT MEN DYING BETWEEN 1773 AND 1777

Name	Number of Creditors	Amount of Debt (in pounds)
Thomas Carter, Jr.	68	?
John Beeman	56	116
John Taylor	38	52
Samuel Chappel *	36	?
William Castle	33	150
Jonathan Sackett	27	76
Thomas Palmer *	27	57
Elizur Price *	20	30
Christopher Beeman	17	32
Moses Case	16	24
Zenas Finney	7	14

* Insolvent.

The account book of John Converse, town blacksmith, shows over 100 citizens owing him money in 1778.[6] It also indicates the irregular nature of payments. The account of Solomon Chase increased for ten years between 1775 and 1785 until an entry finally read: "Received and settled all accounts and made even on both sides. I am to pay for plastering that Damon had of Chase." Abraham Fuller paid £6 in 1783 and next paid £3 in 1788. Wealthy Lewis Mills (son of John), ran from 1775 to 1782 before finally paying his £10 debt.[7]

One might expect to find land heavily mortgaged; however, there is little evidence of debt of this type. As already indicated, the original proprietors acquired their shares by a promise to pay within a time limit or forfeit their lands. In general, these payments seem to have been cleared up by 1746.[8] Each year or so the Kent land records show one or two mortgages, but these total only thirty-three for the entire period between 1740 and 1796.[9]

It would appear from Probate Records and account books that the economy of Kent was a vast tangle of debts. On the basis of the men who left inventories during the years 1773–1777 it might be estimated that the average adult male had at least twenty creditors. If we multiplied Kent's adult male population by this twenty-debt figure, we would find that Kent had 2500 debts in 1751, 6500 in 1777, and 6370 in 1796.

Debt Settlements Out of Court

Having noted the volume of borrowing at Kent, we may turn next to the question of debt settlement. It will become apparent that on this question, the towns of western Connecticut differed from those in western Massachusetts. Whereas in the "Shaysite" counties of Massachusetts the courts appear to have become surfeited with suits brought by creditors against their debtors, in Kent and her sister towns the vast majority of debt transactions were settled without recourse to law.[10]

In 1752, the first full year for the Litchfield County Court, there were 160 debt cases and Kent furnished more than her share with twenty-five. Such figures suggest a mixed verdict. For as many as twenty-five Kent men (20 percent of the adult male population) to go to law over debts in one year would be unheard of today. On the other hand, if the twenty-five Kent debt transactions that ended in court are contrasted with the 2600 debts that were cleared up without litigation,[11] then one can be impressed with the amicability of settlements. From 1752 to 1786 debt litigation decreased relatively in Litchfield County. In 1764 the number of cases was 389; and in 1774 when the county population was 26,905, debt cases reached a peak of 535. In 1786, on the eve of Shays' Rebellion, the county population was up to 33,127, but the debt cases had dropped back to 447. At Kent in 1786 only six men (3 percent), were defendants in debt suits. Thus the contrast with Berkshire County, Massachusetts where many men, perhaps a majority, "were haled to the hated Court of Common Pleas for non-payment of debt,"[12] was striking.

One reason for the small number of court suits at Kent may have been a tolerant or casual spirit among the creditors. For example, probate inventories classify debts into these "likely to be collected" and those "not likely to be collected." Elizur Price owed sums to twenty men when he died of smallpox in 1777, but seven-

teen men owed him money. Of these, "nine persons are not likely
to be collected." One gathers, then, that many debts were quietly
dropped without court action. Also indicative of casualness and
leniency was the tendency to let book debts run beyond seven
years. Technically such debts "were not pleadable on the debtor's
death." [13] Yet the account book of Kent's blacksmith, John Converse, shows such debts frequently running as long as ten years.

Such problems of debt collection may have tended to raise
interest rates. However, a debtor might find protection in the
Courts against "usurious rates of interest." John Mills haled his
debtors, Ebenezer and Jehiel Barnum, into court in 1752. The
Barnums protested to the court that Mills' note was "usurious and
oppressive" and "prayed the court to inquire into the case as a
court of equity." The court found "the said note to be usurious
whereupon it is considered that the plaintiff recover not his demanded £120 but the sum of £36 old tenor." [14]

Debtors and Creditors in Court

Further light on the general problem of indebtedness at Kent
and her sister towns may be shed by a study of cases which were
not settled amicably but did reach the Litchfield County Court.
It will be helpful to investigate the extent to which privileged
gentry sued humble yeomen and to which eastern merchants were
demanding payments from western farmers. [15]

At Kent and in other western towns of Connecticut a clear
pattern of gentry suing poor farmers is not apparent. A study of
Table 9 below suggests two conclusions about the Kent debtors
who were defendants in court suits in 1752. Most noticeable is
the high percentage of prominent men being sued. For example,
John Ransom, Esquire, was justice of the peace, town deputy to
the General Assembly, and town selectman. Ebenezer Barnum,
John Beebe, Matthew Beals, and Joshua Lassell all served as town
selectmen and were important in local affairs. If five of the seventeen debtors were leaders of the town, eight others could be classified as "officeholders." Such men as Jehiel and Richard Barnum
or John Beebe's son, Hezekiah, were younger men but of medium

TABLE 9

KENT DEBTORS AND CREDITORS AT LITCHFIELD COUNTY COURT, 1752 AND 1786 [a]

Debtor	Social Status	Economic Status	Creditor	Amount of Debt
		1752		
Ebenezer Barnum, Jr.	leader	speculator	John Mills	£ 36
Jehiel Barnum	officeholder	speculator		
Richard Barnum	officeholder	small farmer	Daniel Church	13
Matthew Beals	leader	large farmer	(Greenwich)	15
John Beebe	leader	speculator	Abel Wright	30
John Beebe			(Sheffield, Mass.)	45
John Beebe ⎫ John Silby ⎬	officeholder	small farmer	Abel Wright	220
Hezekiah Beebe	officeholder	speculator	Daniel Church	220
Daniel Church	officeholder	speculator	Abel Wright	100
Daniel Church			(Boston)	800
Daniel Church			(Boston)	788
				(Old Tenor)
Jacob Galusha	obscure	small farmer	(New Milford)	18
William Jones	obscure	hired hand	(Litchfield)	16-10
Joshua Lassell	leader	speculator	(Canaan)	525
Daniel Moss	officeholder	speculator	(Sharon)	52
Pereg Partridge	obscure	small farmer	Joshua Lassell	6
John Ransom	leader	speculator	(Sharon)	98
John Ransom			(Sharon)	£ 90
Jonathan Rowlee, Jr.	officeholder	speculator	(Litchfield)	120
Caleb Reede	officeholder	speculator	Joseph Fuller	
William Bostwick of New Milford			Jabez Swift	220
			Nathaniel Berry	
Daniel Worden	obscure	speculator	(Derby)	220
(New Milford)			Joseph Beeman	£ 16
(Litchfield)			John Cahoon	300
(Windham)			John Finney	200
(Fairfield)			James Lake	62
(Reading)			Joshua Lassell	60
(Stratford)			Daniel Worden	130
		1786		
John DeWitt	obscure	speculator	(New York City)	£ 140
Dr. Oliver Fuller	leader	town physician	Henry Delano	22
Dr. Oliver Fuller			(Branford)	15
Phinias Lewis	obscure	speculator	(New Milford)	35
Daniel Moss	officeholder	speculator	(New Milford)	47

TABLE 9 (CONT.)

Debtor	Social Status	Economic Status	Creditor	Amount of Debt
John Ransom, Jr.	leader	speculator	(New York City)	100
Asher Ross	obscure	small farmer	Simeon Ross	£100
(Colchester)			Benjamin Ashley	10
(New Milford)			Rachel Beeman	20
(New Haven)			John DeWitt	65
(New Milford)			Darius Kent	6
(Washington)			Peter Pratt	20

ᵃ Where a Kent creditor or debtor was involved, his name is listed; where an absentee was a party, his residence is given in parentheses.

A "leader" was a man who held such offices as selectman, justice of the peace, deacon, militia officer, or was frequently a town agent or moderator in town meetings. An "officeholder" was an individual who held such subordinate town posts as constable, grand juror, lister, or highway surveyor.

A "speculator" engaged in large land deals unrelated to his home farm. A "large farmer" showed property on the common list exceeding £50; a "small farmer" showed property between £30 and £50; and a "hired hand" showed property under £30. All sums of money are in "lawful money (pounds) of Conecticut" unless otherwise indicated.

prominence. They held such offices as tithingman or grand juror, served on committees, and were generally active in the community. The four remaining men labeled "obscure" took no recorded part in town affairs. Galusha and Partridge, owners of small farms in the East Greenwich Society, lived in Kent for many years but never became freemen. William Jones was on the Kent tax list for 1752 only and showed no ownership of property. Worden kept himself out of all Kent records except those of the County Court. His appearance as debtor for £200 in one suit and as creditor for £130 in another suggests that he was a promoter or speculator.

A second conclusion is perhaps more significant. Most of the debtors involved in litigation were speculators. Joshua Lassell, the Barnums, Jonathan Rowlee, Junior and others were men who kept their fingers in many pies. We have called them aggressive opportunists. Their sharp dealings and complex transactions were of a type to keep them in court, suing as often as sued. Of the seventeen debtors, we have classified twelve as speculators on the strength of their numerous land transactions and their promotion of nonagricultural enterprises. We cannot be certain what the other five debtors were doing, but Kent records suggest that most were farmers who did not become involved in outside transactions.

The line-up of debtors and creditors in 1786 as shown in Table 9 above seems most significant for what it does not show. Although the handful of debt cases for that year is too small to establish any positive pattern, it is notable that yeoman farmers were keeping out of court. One also observes that the aggressive opportunists had largely disappeared. Daniel Moss, sued in 1752, was sued again in 1786. John De Witt, both creditor and debtor, may have been carrying on the tradition of a Joshua Lassell. But the old days of speculative ferment were gone and Oliver Fuller was but a faint shadow of his grandfather, Joseph Fuller. One gathers that John Ransom, Junior confined his interest to the fulling mill which for his father had been only one of numerous prospects.

It is interesting to note that occasionally the rival litigants in the Litchfield County Court were close relatives. Indeed, some of the most oppressive executions were those levied by father on son or brother on brother. Eleazer Chamberlain was a son of the prominent Peleg Chamberlain. Peleg had come from Colchester with sons Peleg Junior, and Eleazer in 1754 and bought several large tracts of colony land west of the Housatonic. All three Chamberlains were office holders and freemen. Peleg's list was £80 with the sons showing about £35. Peleg gave Kent land to both his sons. By 1765 Peleg had moved to Spencertown, Massachusetts, and Eleazer had moved to parts unknown. Peleg launched an angry suit and attachment against his son, whom he called "an absconding person." Four other Kent citizens also attached the remaining lands of Eleazer.

The most oppressive act recorded at Kent was the execution Simeon Ross secured against his brother, Asher. Both brothers had been rivals for the hand of the same "heiress," one Clarina. (She was an heiress at least to the extent of owning a house and farm). Asher won Clarina, married her, and settled down in her house, all

the while owing Simeon £100. Simeon's chance came in 1786
when the time limit expired on Asher's debt to him. Simeon obtained judgment in Litchfield Court in September wherein the
bride's house, land, and barn were transferred to him.[16] Nothing
was said in the attachment about Clarina but one hopes she learned
this lesson: when choosing between two brothers, pick the creditor
for a husband, not the debtor.

Just as a class struggle fails to emerge in the debt litigation at
Kent, so any east-west pattern in creditor-debtor relationships is
also lacking. The writer has tabulated all court cases in the four
sister towns of Kent, Cornwall, Sharon, and Salisbury for the
years 1752 and 1786. About one fourth of the cases pit local versus
local: a money lender like John Mills of Kent sues his neighbors,
the Barnums. In another fourth of the cases the local money
lender is suing an absentee debtor, almost always a debtor from
a neighboring town.[17] About half the cases reveal locals being
sued by absentees, thus offering some support to the usual picture.
In 1766, for example, "big," eastern creditor Roger Sherman of
New Haven (the founding father), sued "little" Noah Pain of
Kent and collected £3-2-5 by attachment. Most absentees, however, were not from the "east" but were from neighboring towns.
The settlers apparently borrowed as close to home as possible.

Property Seizures: Misleading Writs of Attachment

An analysis of all recorded attachments, executions, or property seizures in Kent, Cornwall, Sharon, and Salisbury between
1752 and 1786 reveals a surprisingly low total and a remarkable
lack of severity in light of what has been reported in Massachusetts.[18] Documents at Kent also suggest that some legal procedures
and terminology can be quite misleading in that they suggest far
more numerous and oppressive attachments than actually took
place.

At Kent, when the time limit on a debt expired and the creditor felt compelled to take legal action, his first step was to go to
the office of a local justice of the peace and there assist in the
preparation of an original writ. These writs gave details of the
debt transaction. After 1770 in Kent all original writs were on

printed forms with blanks left for dates and amounts. The original
writ also assigned date and place for trial. If the amount in dispute
was less than 48 shillings, trial was assigned to another justice of
the peace (never to the justice preparing the writ). If the debt
was over 48 shillings, the case was assigned to the County Court.[19]
A major purpose of the writ was to order a constable to attach the
property of the defendant.

On the back of the original writ of attachment the sheriff or
constable always recorded his response. He listed precisely the
property attached. There are ten writs for 1773 at Kent and they
are listed in Table 10 in order to show the apparent severity of
these attachments.

TABLE 10

DEBTS AND ATTACHMENTS, KENT, 1773

Debtor	Original Debt (in pounds)	Amount of Attachment (in pounds)	Details of Attachment
Uriah Sharp	5	10	Land, haystack, grain on ground
Asa Parish	30	60	All land, all improvements that fell to his wife by Isaac Fuller, his dwelling house, shop, tools, and other moveables
Mathias Beeman	7-19-9	16	House and land in East Greenwich
Parker Wilson	6	12	All land and one smith's shop
Asa Parish	60	120	All lands, all improvements of wife's land, dwelling house, shop, tools, moveables
Parker Wilson	12	30	Smith's shop and all land owned
Asa Parish	2-11-0	5-2	All buildings, lands, and moveables
Samuel White	16	32	55 acres
Joseph Beeman	11-10	22	Two pieces of land
Christopher Beeman	16	32	12 acres and dwelling house

Ten such property seizures in a single year would represent
serious economic oppression *if they had taken place.* But they did
not. These sheriff's attachments were preliminary and tentative,
and title to property did not change as a result. These writs and

sheriffs' responses represent a dangerous pitfall for the historian who stumbles onto them and fails to realize that their bark was worse than their bite.[20]

Of the ten cases listed above, eight were settled in court where the sums owed by the debtor were paid in cash. For these eight no attachments of property took place. Asa Parish, for example, faced three suits totaling £91. There is no record of his losing any property. Parish seems to have been a substantial citizen except for his debt troubles. He had been a freeman since 1751. He married Mindwell Fuller (daughter of Joseph), in 1752 and had nine children born in Kent. His tax list 1774 through 1777 showed £28, 40, 38 and 41. He was still in Kent in 1787 getting sued for unpaid debts again. Like Parish, the other debtors, Sharp, White, and Joseph Beeman, paid their debts and avoided the sheriff. Mathias Beeman lost his suit, still failed to pay, so faced the visit of the sheriff. But whereas the original attachment was for £16 and took house and land, the final execution took only fourteen acres and no house. This settlement appears in both the Litchfield County Court Records and the Kent Land Records. Mathias Beeman left Kent at this time.

The other debtor who played out the string to the end was Parker Wilson, branded "an absconding person." Whereas the preliminary attachment against him was for all land and a smith's shop, the final attachment was for seven acres only.

Property Seizures: Their Relative Scarcity and Nonoppressive Nature

During the year 1752, although there were between two and three thousand individual loans to Kent's 130 adult males, only seventeen Kent debtors were sued in court, and all of these settled with their creditors so that no attachments occurred in Kent that year. More often there were one or two property seizures in a given year. Altogether there were forty-seven attachments between 1752 and 1786. In the four western towns of Kent, Cornwall, Sharon, and Salisbury the total was only 145 for the thirty-four year span.

In the great majority of these attachments, the constables took only land and ignored dwellings, barns, tools, stock, and personal property. Of the 145 attachments in the four towns between 1752 and 1786, only twenty-four, or 16 percent, involved seizures of property other than land.[21] In case after case the sheriff or constable "went to the usual place of abode" and found no debtor or personal property. The creditor then pointed out a tract of land that might be attached. Three appraisers (one selected by the creditor, a second by the constable, and a third by the debtor, if present, otherwise by the constable), fixed on a fair amount of land to discharge the debt and court costs.

At first glance it might seem surprising that so many absconding debtors possessed so much land. This land possession was the obvious aftermath of the land speculation boom in which virtually all settlers appear to have participated. Ebenezer Barnum, Junior, who was sued by John Mills, never rose higher than his original 1740 common-list figure of £27. However, he was a Kent proprietor, who acquired five lots from his share and who made nineteen additional land purchases. This land was not utilized or taxed in the common list (Barnum's main activity was his ironworks). It was just lying about in scattered tracts. Other debtors who depended on their home farms for a livelihood also had spare lots and pitches scattered about the town. It appears that they might surrender some of these scattered tracts without suffering any particular pinch on their principal economic activity.

Attachments were not spread evenly among the debtors but were levied over and over again on the same individuals. Of the forty-seven attachments levied against Kent property, ten can be ignored here because they were against the property of absentee land speculators, men who had never lived in Kent. The thirty-seven remaining attachments all piled up on the heads of only sixteen Kent residents. Eleazer Chamberlain, branded "an absconding person" was the Kent champion with five attachments. Noah Pain and Jonathan Morgan each had four. Cornwall produced some champion debtors in William Chichester, whose property was attached fifteen times, and Joseph Mather, who heard the sheriff's knock on eight occasions. On the one hand, this hardship of a

Chamberlain, Chichester, or a Mather is grist for the mills of agrarian sympathizers; on the other hand, a handful of men are accounting for all the attachments, leaving the bulk of the citizenry undisturbed by sheriffs. A total of sixteen Kent residents suffered attachments in thirty-four years for an average of only one person every other year.

Property Seizures: Types of Men Suffering Attachments

It was noted earlier that a majority of the Kent debtors who lost their suits in 1752 were not humble subsistence farmers but seemed to be economic adventurers. They were able to settle with their creditors and avoid attachments. Before concluding this analysis, we should look briefly at the sixteen men who, between 1752 and 1786, seemed unable to pay their creditors and defaulted or absconded instead. It should be helpful to know how many were relatively prosperous citizens sacrificing land in preference to paying a debt, how many were aggressive opportunists, and how many were obscure yeomen caught by insufficient income.

Seven of the sixteen were men who suffered only the one attachment, yielded a bit of land, and continued on in Kent with status unchanged. Asa Parish, described above, was typical. In no case was there a drop in "common list" to indicate their economic potential had been curtailed.

On the other hand, nine of the sixteen were attached more than once, and each of these departed "for parts unknown." Six of them were town officeholders and speculators. Two were a step nearer an "oppressed class" and one, at last, was a humble man: poor, underprivileged, and harassed by attachments.

First of the six speculators was David Bates, who came to Kent from Coventry around 1752. He was probably related to original settler proprietor Samuel Bates, also from Coventry. David engaged in ten Kent land deals, one for £1500, and had a "list" of £60. He was neither a freeman nor an officeholder. His own attachments came in 1755 presumably after he had left the town.

They were small. Local creditor Jonathan Morgan (one of the oppressed nine himself) got £14 worth of land. Joseph Pratt got land worth £5. From what the record tells us, Bates rates little sympathy. An adventurer, he swept into and out of Kent leaving his debts behind with just enough land to cover them.

Gideon Barnum, an original proprietor, settler, and freeman and one of the most active speculators, met his Waterloo in 1761. He had made some sixty speculative transactions, mostly in iron properties, and had served the town as grand juror and highway surveyor. His ironworks may have pulled him down or he may have lost out on the Barnum silver-mine fiasco. He left town, and creditors Jonathan Morgan (again!) and John Griffis of Sharon took his dwelling house and "the bellows that belong to the iron works." Barnum's tax list rose and fell reaching £112 in 1744 and falling to £29 in 1752.

John Bliss was still another speculator. He came to Kent in 1752 and departed ahead of the sheriff in 1762. While in Kent he engaged in thirty land deals and slowly advanced on the tax list from £37 in 1754 to £52 in 1760. He was a freeman but held no town offices. Levi Brownson and Josiah Finney, both Kent neighbors, brought suit and attached £16 worth of land in two proceedings. The small size of the debts compared to Bliss's list and land transactions suggest that here again was a relatively prosperous individual who moved on and left some loose ends behind.

Jonathan Morgan was an original proprietor, settler, and freeman who obtained lots and pitches from his proprietary share and made some thirty other speculative purchases and sales. Originally a sawmill operator, he later turned to iron works. His tax list reached £91, and he was frequently the creditor in debt litigation. His versatility was reflected in the town offices that he held: pound keeper, brander of horses, fence viewer, and lister. Three attachments in 1763 and one in 1764 followed his departure. The last was for £243 owed to Daniel Brown of New York and this attachment swept up his house as well as his lands.

Eleazer Chamberlain, described earlier, and Noah Pain were officeholders and speculators. The latter departed in 1766 with

three small attachments in his wake. Pain had twelve land transactions and a tax list of £69 in 1753. He was a freeman and held
the office of highway surveyor.

Two men, Timothy Buel and Samuel Chappel, come closer to
the standard picture of the back-country debtor. Buel arrived in
1759 and was gone when the sheriff reached his abode with two
attachment writs in 1765. One writ arose from a suit brought by
Simeon Fuller of Kent for £5. The other was for £5 owed to
Samuel Jackson of Woodbury. Buel was a freeman, his tax list
reached £39 in 1759, but he was not a land speculator. (Only
two Buel transactions are recorded).

Chappel was not a freeman but did hold the office of highway
surveyor. There are only four entries for him in the land records,
but his list was surprisingly high: £48 for his first year, 1750; and
£62 for his last, 1764. Three attachments were levied on his property arising from suits won by Benjamin Birge of Woodbury
(£10), William Drinkwater of New Milford (£5), and John
Merwin of New Haven (£65). He was described by the sheriff
as "late of Kent. Not an inhabitant of this government." Again we
wonder whether the attachments were a mere "clean up" after a
casual departure or whether he was ruined and his debts drove
him away. As always, there seemed to be ample land in Kent to
satisfy the creditors.

At last, one man, Michael Lyon, appears to fit the debtor
stereotype. None of the four Lyon brothers in Kent (Nathaniel,
Moses, Hezekiah, and Michael), were rated over £40 on the tax
list. Michael had ten land transactions but all were with his brothers. None of the brothers appear to have been freemen or office
holders and Moses was an indigent town pauper. The three attachments against Michael were brought by outsiders (£62, 12, and
1) but his land sufficed to satisfy their demands.

Imprisonment for Debt

Much of the formal language of the final sheriffs' writs of attachment had been handed down from medieval times and was
not expected to apply to Connecticut. For example, each writ

spoke of taking "the body of said —— and commit unto the keeper of the Gaol in Litchfield County aforesaid." This threat of imprisonment was not carried out in any of the 145 attachment cases in the four towns. One Salisbury man, George Caldwell, was threatened with imprisonment in 1771, but even he did not spoil the no-prison-for-debt record. Caldwell, incidentally, was not a humble farmer. The petition for his exemption from arrest spoke of his great "fondness for new projects in trade and manufacturing." He was granted exemption from arrest but ordered to pay by means of other property.[22]

Many accounts suggest that a debtor was imprisoned when he lacked ability to pay. Indeed, the writs produce this impression. However, the writer believes a more complete study of this question is needed. Contrary to the standard view, the Connecticut Code of 1750 operated on the principle that jail was to be used only as a weapon against debtors who had property which they refused to surrender. The Code states: "Provided also that no man's person shall be kept in prison for debt but when he hath some estate which he will not produce or present.[23]

The problem was complicated by a debtor's trickiness in transferring his property to friends or to his wife. Acts of 1763, 1764, 1765, 1766, and 1777 attempted to plug such loopholes but tended to bog down in complexity. The present writer has happened upon only one jailed debtor in all Litchfield County (a systematic search turned up none for the western towns). Benjamin Hawley of Woodbury was in the Litchfield jail in 1784. His petition for release stated that he had no property but admitted that his wife did. He was held, he claimed, "with the hope she will pay the debt." It seemed she would not pay the debt and would not even secure for him "the liberty of the jail yard." His petition was negatived and Hawley's end must remain unknown.[24]

It should also be noted that the practice of "binding out" debtors for services had practically vanished in Litchfield County.[25] The only debtor put to service in Kent was an Indian named David Sherman who had wounded his brother in 1775. By 1776 "he had fled." [26]

In our examination of economic democracy at Kent we have

studied debtor-creditor relationships. Our conclusion is that whereas problems of indebtedness might have been serious obstacles to economic opportunity in Massachusetts, they were unrealized threats at Kent. Borrowing was extensive; however, relatively few debts reached court, and most of these were settled without recourse to attachments. Even the few attachments were mild. At Kent no widespread pattern of eastern creditors suing local debtors was apparent, nor was there a pronounced tendency for creditors to be wealthier or more prominent than debtors. For the most part, debt litigation on Connecticut's western frontier was the province of the aggressive opportunist. Suing and being sued in turn, the active speculator or promoter was a familiar figure in court. Most of these men emerged from their court suits without mortal wounds and continued their prosperous ventures. The few Jonathan Morgans or Gideon Barnums who fell by the wayside had not lacked opportunity but perhaps had enjoyed too much. Opportunity in some newer town may have beckoned irresistibly or perhaps they had taken one gamble too many.

6

THREATS TO ECONOMIC OPPORTUNITY: POVERTY AT KENT

In our study of Kent we have noted that neither absenteeism nor widespread indebtedness constituted a threat to economic opportunity. In the present chapter we shall continue to examine factors which might indicate limited opportunity within the community. Many historians have been impressed with the extent of frontier poverty. Concern has been expressed over the plight of the early settlers, of the squatters, of the public charges, and of the propertyless hired hands.[1] Where records show the presence of such unfortunate men in Kent, it will be helpful to note their numbers, status, and prospects.

Historians have tended to form impressions about frontier poverty in part from the hardship petitions of the settlers. Although such sources can be valuable, they can also be misleading. A study of poverty at Kent offers a further opportunity to test the reliability of the local petitions.

Poverty among the Original Settler-Proprietors

The first inhabitants of Kent and of the other new towns in the Western Lands sent a number of petitions to the General Assembly in 1741 and 1742. Parts of these petitions have been quoted above to show the settlers' complaints about absenteeism. Actually, the petitions had one primary purpose. The time had expired for proprietors to pay for the shares they had bought at the auctions, and the various towns to which the proprietors' bonds had been assigned were trying to collect their money. The proprietors wanted an extension of the due date and the elimination of interest payments. Thus the major emphasis in the petitions was on how poor they were. The following excerpts are typical:

We are crowded upon by some of those towns to which your honors have divided our bonds. Some will have the principal instantly, some will wait a year and no more on lawful interest, and others will not wait at all for less than 10 percent; and for that unlawful interest which some have required, they will not wait more than a year. Some indeed will wait a year for 8 percent but that is more than we in our sorry state are able to give.

We have paid a very high price for this wilderness land. We have proceeded with resolution, have not been discouraged . . . although greater difficulty and distress than was ever known have attended our settlement . . . .

Yet when we have so remarkably suffered famine and pestilence, now we die and continually drop by writ or execution upon our bonds to the government. Some of us are new and some of us are pioneers and not a man of us now able to take up our bonds without being racked in our estate, some torn, others quite broken, so that not three-quarters of us can have above half our home lots and pay our purchase. Neither can we maintain our minister or build our meetinghouse but must quit the place or become tenants, we and our children to neighboring rich merchants who are seeking our land—but that at their own price.[2]

Local records indicate that no Kent proprietor ever lost his share through inability to pay his bond. Abel Wright, author of the 1742 petition from Kent, had obtained three proprietary shares at Windham and had obligated himself to the amount of £564-13. On the credit side he had accumulated twelve lots through the first four divisions. Their market value (and it was a very active market), at the time he wrote the petition was between £3300 and £4000. During the same year he was protesting inability to pay, he was purchasing nineteen other parcels of land in Kent at a cost of some £3000. He was also selling land (twenty-one sales), and all the while seeking profit through adroit speculation in a rising market.

We have already indicated the extent to which most of the settlers were speculating. We should stress here that much of this speculative activity was taking place in the midst of the so-called hardship period. Between 1739 and 1742 the original thirty-six proprietor settlers made 227 sales and 234 purchases for an average of better than twelve deals per man. Ebenezer Barnum sold thirty-three lots in this period and bought seventeen. Samuel Lewis had

forty-four deals and Nathaniel Berry, twenty-nine. Average proprietors like the Comstocks, Morgans, and Hatches made from
twelve to twenty deals apiece. The average was reduced by such
proprietors as the Porters or William Roberts who left early in
1740.[3]

Understandably the General Assembly was not impressed with
the hardship petitions from the western towns. Both houses "negatived" the 1741 petitions. The renewed petitions of 1742 brought
a relief proposal that called for two interest-free loans to each
petitioning town. A loan-fund of £500 was to help needy proprietors pay their purchase debts. (This would have taken care
of only two proprietors). Also £200 was to be made available for
loans to needy families. The upper house balked at this trickle of
help. A conference ensued and assistants James Wadsworth and
Nathanial Stanley finally agreed to permit just the £200 loan for
the needy.[4] Thus the petition fiasco ended. Kent proprietors got
nothing, and if local evidence is trustworthy, they deserved nothing.

Minutes of town and proprietors' meetings suggest that Kent
inhabitants could become thoroughly aroused when justice was
on their side (the bridge dispute), or when they thought they had
a chance to win, (The Merryall boundary dispute). However,
the miuntes of their meetings do not reveal expectation, anger, or
even interest in the hardship petitions. The proprietors did vote to
make Timothy Hatch their agent in May, 1741,[5] but they did not
even bother to meet in 1742. The town meetings made no references to the affair. Kent had one meeting in May, 1742, when the
fate of their petition was being debated in Hartford. The two
items of business were: "We will provide six gallons of rum for
the raising of our Meetinghouse." and "We will have a rate of
£50 for it." [6]

Squatters

In versions of colonial history that stress poverty and conflict
on the frontier there are frequent allusions to squatters. Absentee
proprietors, for example, "wage war on squatters." [7] There were
squatters at Kent and a scholar using the Connecticut Archives

may encounter their petitions and those of their opponents. Such petitions furnish abundant material for anyone interested in evidence to bolster a class-conflict presentation. These sources are important, for quite obviously there were examples of hardship and conflict. However, the controversies should be viewed in proper perspective. It is important to know how many squatters there were, and how many of these were genuine "little people" rather than aggressive opportunists. One also wonders about the opponents of the squatters and whether they were rich absentees or local inhabitants. Finally, the settlements the squatters received are important in an estimate of economic hardship.

A squatter was a person who occupied and utilized land to which he had no legal title. The safest generalization about a squatter is that he tended to be an unknown or shadowy figure because of his rapid movement and extralegal status beyond the reach of recording town clerks and tax listers. At Kent one suspects that there were relatively few squatters and even fewer at other western Connecticut towns. The basis for this statement is the belief that most squatters (certainly most near Kent) were squatting, not because they were poverty stricken and had no alternative, but rather because they were seeking land profits. Squatting seemed to be one way of obtaining an inside track on undeveloped, colony land.

If this hypothesis is true, we would expect no squatters in Kent proper. Every foot of land was surveyed, and titles were recorded in the Kent Land Records. A squatter in Kent would know that he was on the land of, say, absentee David Lassell. Such an intruder had no future prospects. Even if David's agent in Kent left the squatter alone, the latter could expect no peace from the town government. Authorities would be after him for payment of taxes, labor on highways, and service in the militia. Kent evidence does reveal evictions over boundary disputes and encroachments of various kinds, but the parties to such disputes were established property owners. There is no evidence in Kent proper of disputes between proprietors on the one hand and squatters on the other.

At Kent the ideal situation for squatting was at hand in that just across the river was a large tract of 11,000 acres of ungranted colony lands. An examination of these lands throws considerable light on the squatter problem.

Squatters occupied these lands early, possibly even before the settlement of the town in 1738. They came under the attack of the first Kent settlers, and a petition of the "Kent inhabitants" was presented to the General Assembly in May, 1743.

There are some inhabitants upon colony land who are not under any town nor within limits of any society . . . . [They are] . . . well situated to make an addition to our parish and town meeting . . . . There is danger of its being overstocked with very unwholesome inhabitants who in all probability will be a vexation to us and a charge to the government. Therefore, [award] the land to us . . . so the inhabitants may pay their due as to supporting the commonwealth and that we may have the liberty of keeping bad inhabitants therefrom.[8]

The above petition might create a picture in the reader's mind of a throng of humble squatters about to lose their freedom and land to the town of Kent. However, the Kent settlers repeatedly demonstrated an ability to write deceptive petitions. It was to their advantage to convey an impression of numbers. Only then would the government, distressed at anarchy and untaxed inhabitants, grant the desired land annexation. Actually, the petition says "some inhabitants" are there. This could mean as few as three (though it probably meant six to twelve). The crowd of unruly squatters was "expected." As indicated below, an investigating committee in 1744 found the land virtually deserted. Indeed, it seems probable that the Kent inhabitants cared far less about squatter unruliness then they did about acquiring the land for division among themselves. The General Assembly suspected this motive and ordered that "the land be annexed to the town only with reference to town privileges and without any passing of the fee of the land thereby."[9]

These so-called "Colony Lands" thus came under Kent's jurisdiction in 1743. They were not surveyed until 1752 when Roger Sherman was appointed surveyor by the General Assembly. He and two chainmen took seventeen days to divide the 11,000 acres into twenty-eight lots. Later an Act of October, 1753, ordered the sale of these lots at auction.[10]

During the ten-year interval between Kent's acquisition of

legal jurisdiction and the government's final sale of the land, the General Assembly sent out two investigating committees. The first committee, that of 1744, reported: "Some persons were said to have entered but we found no improvements save two small houses, but not inhabited at present." [11] However, reports kept reaching the government about trespassers. A complaint in 1748 stated that one Robert Watson had purchased Indian titles and had convinced his customers (the trespassers) that this land was actually in New York beyond Connecticut jurisdiction. The trespassers were "destroying and wasting timber and making improvements in the hope the Assembly wouldn't remove them." [12] In 1751 the second investigating committee visited the scene and reported to the Assembly:

A great part of the most valuable land was under improvement by several persons which we warned off the land excepting two or three which lived toward the southward part whom we could not get to account the difficulty of the season. But those we did warn not being willing to give up their possessions, we offered them leases . . . to which all save one consented. [13] The land so leased was 412 acres. [14]

These trespassers, or squatters, thus had leases forced on them in 1752 and then faced the survey and sale of the land in 1753. Under this pressure they submitted individual petitions to the General Assembly. There are petitions from eight men: Charles Buckley, Jonathan Rowlee, Jonathan Rowlee, Junior, Stephen MacIntyre, David MacIntyre, Moses Rowlee, Joshua Lassell, and Joseph Fuller. The petitioners wrote of their good faith and how they thought their Indian titles were good. They referred to their "need of plowland," their "payment of town rates," their "laying out their whole substance thereon," and their "feeling of safety till October last when the Assembly ordered our eviction." Altogether, the petitions produce a pathetic picture. It is easy to visualize humble men being oppressed. Further examination of local records alters this impression, however.

Charles Bulkley was not a humble man. He was from Colchester, a member of one of Connecticut's leading families, and himself a Colchester deputy from 1744 to 1750. Other members of his family were assistants, agents to England, and Superior

Court judges. Bulkley apparently went ahead and purchased the land on which he had "squatted." [15]

The Jonathan Rowlees, father and son, were members of Kent's largest family (fourteen adult Rowlees in Kent during the 1750s). They were office holders and freemen of Kent but relatively humble as to tax list status. We could perhaps put them down as oppressed squatters were it not for a letter from Jonathan, Junior to Thomas Seymour, an attorney and deputy for Hartford. Rowlee wrote:

Father is too infirm and I am too busy so please handle our affairs at the General Assembly. The contest over the plain 'tween self and John Mills continues. Mills hath made some attempts to improve upon the land but I have hitherto kept him off so he hath got no possession. If it should happen so that Minor and Williams should be at the Assembly to get the grant established, I would have you to do as you shall think most proper in the affair. Times and seasons are so difficult that I have not got old tenor at this present to send you, but take good care of my business and old tenor should not be wanting.[16]

The Jonathan Rowlees, then, sound much less like "little men" than they do like aggressive opportunists.

Moses Rowlee may also have been playing for big stakes. He bought his tract in unauthorized fashion from Robert Walker in 1748 and built a sawmill on Macedonia Brook near the present-day Heathcote Woolsey home. Somehow the surveyors missed him, and "his land" was not sold along with the rest in 1753–54. However, in 1769 he received an eviction order and petitioned plaintively against it. His eviction "would make him a public charge." [17] A committee investigated and satisfied itself that what Rowlee alleged was true. They recommended that he receive a grant to include his sawmill and thus produce a happy ending for Moses. The General Assembly approved and the grant was formalized in 1769.[18]

The story of Moses Rowlee does not end here, however. A storm broke in 1771 when it was charged that Moses had deceived the Assembly and "that the land granted to him had been represented to be small in comparison to what it really is." [19] After two more investigations, Moses was ordered to appear in New Haven "to say why the grant should not be declared void." No further material is available among the General Assembly records. Kent records show, however, that Moses Rowlee did become a public charge in 1771, so it seems probable that his grant was rescinded.[20] Documentation is too scanty to appraise the justice of the General Assembly's action. Rowlee admitted to 900 acres. If this was much smaller than the actual grant, he was indeed playing for large stakes. Even though he ended as a public charge, he does not conform to the "little-man" stereotype.

Fuller and Lassell have been discussed earlier. One who reads only their petitions and ignores their activities in Kent might be touched by their "need for plowland." Actually, their effort to acquire a 4820-acre tract seemed to typify the speculative, venturesome, opportunistic spirit of the Kent settler proprietors. The final settlement (they each received small grants), reveals the government as an intelligent policeman, neither blind nor merciless.

The two MacIntyres, Stephen and James, seem closer to the squatter caricature. Stephen's petition, received by the General Assembly in May, 1764, noted that he had bought a tract from the Scatacook Indians north of the Ten-Mille River and built his home there. He had thought he was safe until warned by the committee. He requested permission to buy the 26th lot with a committee to set the price.[21] Unlike the "squatters" described above, he was not a prominent, longtime Kent resident. He appeared on the tax list for 1752 ($£25$) and 1753 ($£13$) only. The latter figure suggests he was an absentee in 1753 as the £18 poll tax is obviously missing. Furthermore, Stephen was illiterate.[22] His purchase from the Indians and his willingness to buy lot 26 suggests a touch of the speculator. On the other hand, if this was a speculative venture, it was certainly on a small scale.

James MacIntyre (a brother?) appears in an eviction order. In 1756 he was reported holding land without right. Roger Sherman was appointed as the agent to eject him, and there is no further evidence on what transpired.[23] There is no record at Kent of any James MacIntyre. Perhaps here at last we have the true, shadowy squatter.

The eight men described above comprise the total squatter-roster of Kent as far as petition literature is concerned. Perhaps there were squatters on these colony lands whose names we missed because they avoided any petition efforts. Some may have slipped away when the General Assembly applied the pressure. However, it seems unlikely that we missed many, for the reports of the investigating committees indicate that there were probably only eight inhabitants on the land and no more than twelve at most.[24] And we have accounted for eight. Even if we have missed three or four squatters, the pattern suggests that their motives may have been similar to the eight we have described. Like our eight, any such undiscovered squatters were probably men who purchased Indian titles and made improvements with the hope that they might secure firm title from the General Assembly by outright grants or at substantially reduced prices.

The questions posed at the start of the examination of squatters may now be answered. At Kent there were between eight and twelve squatters. The majority were not refugees from an overcrowded east but were land speculators hopeful of turning a handsome profit. Their opponents were not absentee proprietors but were usually committees of the General Assembly and, occasionally, the town of Kent. The treatment meted out to the squatters seemed equitable; indeed, considering their activities, it could be called overly solicitous.

Public Charges

A full picture of poverty at Kent requires examination of public charges: paupers including widows, orphans, senile men, and transients.[25] In Connecticut the town selectmen were responsible for the relief of these poor persons.[26] They were to draw on the town treasury up to £5 per person for food, clothes, and firewood. They had authority to "bind out the poor, idle, or children." They could warn out transients likely to become public charges. However, if a transient managed to stay three months, he became eligible for relief.[27]

Unfortunately there were no special books in which selectmen entered their actions. Unlike land, tax, court, and church records, which were kept in large volumes, the selectmen's records were kept on easily scattered sheets of paper. Much of their activity might be found in justice court records, but for Kent the justice court records are missing. What one does have at Kent is a scattering of papers, orders of selectmen literally swept up off the floor and deposited in packing cases. The writer has found and sorted out enough of these papers to show the type of activity in which Kent selectmen were engaged.[28]

Senile men received brusque but efficient treatment. The case of Moses Rowlee showed how the selectmen could take the initiative and secure endorsement for their action from a justice of the peace.

Whereas the subscribers, selectmen of the town of Kent . . . have inspected into the affairs of Moses Rowlee of Kent and find he is guilty of poor husbandry and great mismanagement in his business and is thereby in great danger of wasting his estate, we do therefore appoint Abraham Fuller to be overseer over said Moses Rowlee to order and direct him in the management of his business until the selectmen of Kent aforesaid shall give further order . . . .

25 February, 1771

Nehemiah Sturdevant was similarly taken in hand by the selectmen. It was found "he spends his time to no good purpose and his family will likely be reduced to want." Nathaniel Swift became his overseer and all persons were forbidden to trade with him. Ebenezer Peck was declared guilty of "poor husbandry and mismanagement of business." In 1766 John Ransom was made his overseer. This sort of procedure seems a far cry from our present standards of freedom and individualism. It seems especially out of place on the frontier if the frontier is to be considered the haven and breeding ground for the rugged individualist. On the other hand, paternalistic overseeing was grounded in long standing tradition.[29] Also, it should be borne in mind that the selectmen who initiated the supervision were democratically elected each year.

That the selectmen and their delegated overseers were not considered oppressors [30] was made evident by cases where individuals voluntarily applied for supervision.

Whereas Jabez Rowlee by reason of age and indigent circumstances has made application to said town of Kent and is in such needy condition that he is not able to care for himself, family, or estate, he hereby puts himself under the care of the selectmen.

On the basis of this information, justice-of-the-peace Jedediah Hubbel issued a writ and Constable Peter Mills took possession of the house, barn, and one cow of Jabez Rowlee.

Some cases did not involve property. The problem might be the care of widows, children, or handicapped men who lacked means of support. Such aid was often voted in town meetings. For example, in April, 1772, it was voted:

Daniel Averill [a selectman] to have twenty pounds lawful money to care for Amos Whittelsey one year provided that said Daniel provide suitable clothing, meat, drink, washing, and lodging for said Amos.[31]

Again at the same meeting it was voted:

That Samuel Averill shall make provision for Robert Dickerson during his present sickness and bring his account to the town for the same.

Also:

The selectmen shall provide for John Lake, the daughters of Silvia Barnum, and Samuel Barnum's little girl as they did last year.[32]

The selectmen appear in their harshest light when dealing with the problem of transients. Obviously charity cases were expensive, and we encounter occasional efforts to send transients back to the towns whence they came. In May, 1786, Phineas Palmer was ordered back to Woodbury. On the bottom of the writ was a certification from Woodbury selectmen: "This may certify that Phineas Palmer was a Legal Inhabitant of Woodbury in the year 1785." [33]

If the Selectmen could order a Phineas Palmer to "depart the limits of Kent," they also had to receive back their own Kent wanderers.

Whereas Rhoda Clark, an impotent person and inhabitant of Kent transferred to Wallingford in an illegal manner, we command you to carry her back to Kent.

This writ bears the writing of Amos Clark on the bottom noting that "I took her and delivered her to Moses Averill, Kent Selectman." [34]

The system was not inflexible. If a pauper from New Milford

could secure employment in Kent, the Kent selectmen might hesitate to keep him for fear that after three months he would become their responsibility. It is interesting to note the following solution to such a problem in 1776.

These certify that whereas David Cogswell, an inhabitant of New Milford, has moved himself and family into the town of Kent and having not gained a residence by purchase of freehold estate nor any other means, and considering his circumstances being poor and judging that he can better support his family if suffered to reside in Kent than in the town of New Milford, and the selectmen of Kent not being willing that he, the said Cogswell, should reside there: therefore, the said Cogswell applies to the subscribers, the selectmen of New Milford . . . . Therefore, these certify that the said Cogswell is an inhabitant of New Milford and if suffered to reside in the said town of Kent, will not gain a residence there . . . . If the said Cogswell should not be able to support himself and family in Kent without the assistance of the selectmen of Kent, the selectmen of Kent will notify the selectmen of New Milford as soon as may be.[35]

These ten cases offer a picture of the nature of poverty and of the steps taken by the town to meet various problems. However, the cases tell us nothing of the extent of economic misfortune. The instances above comprise the total known instances of such actions by selectmen in Kent during the eighteenth century, but we have no way of knowing the true number of such cases.

Hired Hands

In our examination of poverty at Kent we have looked at the original farm owners but found them generally prosperous. Next we turned to squatters and public charges. The squatters turned out to be speculators, and the public charges were mostly women, children, transients, or senile men. Finally, we turn our attention to those adult men without houses or farms of their own and with little or no property shown on the tax list. Presumably these men are hired hands working on farms, in mills, or in ironworks. They are the most important group in any study of economic opportunity on the frontier. A community in which such individuals comprised a large, permanent proletariat would be lacking in economic opportunity. On the other hand, a town where propertyless men were few and where such status was temporary would be enjoying a relatively unhampered economic status.

We have no descriptive evidence concerning these Kent hired hands. They wrote no petitions, they kept surprisingly free of law courts, and they seem to have been ignored by contemporary observers.[36] However, they all appear in the Kent records. We can watch their comings and goings in the tax, land, and church documents. We can obtain a quantitative picture that answers more questions about Kent society and economic opportunity than either petitions or narrative accounts.

A major part of the work of this essay has been the compilation of data for all adult male inhabitants of Kent for five particular years: 1740, 1745, 1751, 1777, and 1796.[37]

Table 11 summarizes economic data on Kent inhabitants for the five key years.

Boundaries between economic classes are seldom precise and the selection of £49 and £30 as dividing lines was of necessity somewhat arbitrary. The £30 figure separating middle-class farm owners from "poor" hired hands, or proletarians, is especially important. Choice of these figures was based on the following percentages derived from an analysis of Kent tax figures and corresponding property ownership in 1796.[38]

Adult male residents rated between these figures: [39]	Percentage who possessed subsistence farm freeholds and who qualified for freemanship [40]
£49 and up	100
£30 through £48	90
£24 through £29	50
£21 through £23	10
£18 through £20	0

The men showing less than £30 on the tax list have been labelled "Poor" and were mostly hired hands with little or no property. Some with tax figures in the upper twenties remained hired hands but might possess a horse, a cow, and one or two acres to serve as garden and pasture. There would be a few under £30 who were not hired hands but belonged to the poorest class of

TABLE 11

ECONOMIC CLASSES AT KENT, 1740–1796

	1740	1745	1751	1777	1796
Total Resident Adult Males	42	67	129	321	209
Upper Middle Class					
($£$ 49 and up)					
Number	14	31	58	146	73
Percent	33	46	46	46	35
Lower Middle Class					
($£$ 30 to $£$ 48)					
Number	14	17	37	91	50
Percent	33	25	29	29	24
Poor Class					
($£$ 29 and below)					
Number	14	19	34	83	86
Percent	33	29	25	25	42
No. of "Poor Transients"	6	2	3	53	43
Their percentage of all adult males	14	3	4	12	20
Their percentage of "Poor Class"	43	11	9	65	50
No. of "Poor Climbers"	7	15	28	16	22
Their percentage of all adult males	17	22	22	4	11
Their percentage of "Poor Class"	50	79	82	19	25
No. of "Permanent Proletarians"	1	2	3	14	22
Their percentage of all adult males	2	3	4	3	11
Their percentage of "Poor Class"	7	11	9	16	25

subsistence farmers. However, in the final totals, these would be offset by the handful of nonfreeholders whose tax lists crept over $£$ 30.

Table 11 shows interesting fluctuations in the percentage of poor. The figures show the poor comprising 33 percent of the adult male population at the time of the town's founding in 1740. By 1745 the percentage had dropped to 29 percent; in 1751 it had reached a semi-permanent plateau of 25 percent (a figure which was the same in 1777); but a sharp rise occurred between 1777 and 1796 such that the percentage of poor had climbed to 42 percent of the population.

More important than the numbers was the composition of this poor class. Some of its members were youthful sons of prosperous families, men just starting their climb to a higher economic status.

A number were transients, or drifters, men whose restlessness drove them out of Kent before they really tested the economic opportunities within the town. Others were part of a permanently depressed group, men who had little property and seemed unable to obtain more. For purposes of statistical comparison, men who remained in Kent, climbed over the £30 mark, and thus apparently left the hired-hand class by acquiring farm property of their own have been labeled "climbers." These men were often the sons of established farmers but others were newcomers who started low and found the means for economic advancement. Men who remained at Kent five years or over but failed to reach £30 have been classified "permanent proletarians."

The outstanding fact about the composition of the poor (climbers, transients, or permanent proletarians), would seem to be that for the middle-period, 1740–1777, opportunity, not oppression, was the key word. In 1751, for example, of the thirty-four poor, twenty-eight would remain in Kent and prove to be climbers. Only three were transients, and three were permanent proletarians.

Something was happening to the economy after 1777. Although in this year the relatively low percentages of poor still held at 25 percent, this "poor" group was far different in composition. In 1751 it had been composed of climbers but in 1777 it was composed of transients. In 1751 the poor hired hands liked what they saw in Kent and stayed. In 1777 Kent appeared relatively less attractive and they moved out.

As if confirming the foresight of the "poor transients" of 1777, the economic picture at Kent turned darker. By 1796 not only had the percentage of poor climbed from its long-time plateau of 25 percent to 42 percent, but for the first time there emerged a significant number of men destined to remain poor. In 1796 there were twenty-two permanent proletarians in Kent, comprising 11 percent of the adult male population. This number represented a considerable increase over the earlier figures.

The most obvious conclusions about the "hired-hand poor" would seem to be these: from 1740 to 1777 they were temporary poor, temporary hired hands. The greater part of them stayed in

Kent [41] and soon saved or borrowed enough to buy a farm of their own. After 1777 only one fourth of them became farm owners with the rest either moving on or remaining as a permanent propertyless class.

Poverty and the Pressure of Population

The picture of economic opportunity at Kent, bright in 1751, had turned relatively dark by 1796. Kent society, predominantly middle-class in 1751, included a growing class of propertyless men by 1796. In this final section on the Kent economy we will seek the principal cause for this change.

Evidence at Kent does not support the concept that dislocations of the "Critical Period" were of primary importance. Neither high taxes, nor a deflationary price trend, nor commercial stagnation can explain the increase in local poverty. Connecticut state taxes were not heavy during the 1780s. In 1784 the rate was only 1 pence on the pound; in 1785, 1½ pence; in 1786, 1½ pence; and in 1787, 3 pence.[42] If the deflation of the 1780s had been serious in western Connecticut, we should have seen the same sort of increase in creditor-debtor litigation that occurred in Massachusetts. However, as shown in Chapter 5, the Litchfield County Court had fewer cases in the 1780s than in previous decades. Many historians have suggested that during the 1780s commerce was strangled by barriers between state and state. At this time the *entrepot* for Kent may have been Poughkeepsie, New York, and that state was famous for her imposts. However, Merrill Jensen has pointed out that only foreign goods were affected and that during these years "Connecticut trade with New York did grow rapidly." [43]

Having discounted the factors usually brought forward to explain poorer times in the 1780s and 1790s, we should proceed to advance our own explanation. This must take the form of a suggested hypothesis because there are insufficient data for definitive conclusions. Our suggestion is that increased poverty stemmed from the pressure of a population swollen by a fantastic birthrate against a limited amount of land. The land may have seemed inexhaustible to the first generation in 1740, ample to the second generation in the 1750s and 1760s, but it appeared quite limited to the third generation after 1780.

The first settlers who came to Kent were remarkably uniform. They were prosperous enough to buy proprietary shares and to accumulate large amounts of land. They were in the prime of life, their average age being in the upper thirties.[44] One of the oldest, Daniel Comstock, had an adult son with him who was also a proprietor and may be rated "first generation." The rest had sons and daughters who would come of age in the 1740s and 1750s.

During the forties and fifties at Kent the population was augmented first by offspring of the original settlers, young Beebes (John, Junior had been thirteen, Daniel eleven, and Hezekiah nine when John Beebe settled in Kent in 1739), young Fullers, young Hatches, young Comstocks, etc.; and second by new families of similar substance that came in and participated in the land boom. Swifts, Skiffs, Geers, Carters, Sacketts, Bulls, and many others arrived five to fifteen years after the town's first settlement but many of them bought proprietary shares and caught at least part of the land profits.

By 1751 the adult males had increased from the original 42 to 129. This was one of Kent's best years as first generation, second generation, and newcomers spread out over abundant land. But also in 1751 a wave of marriages and births of third-generation children heralded a population increase of ever expanding proportions. The vital statistics are astonishing as family after family produced from eight to fourteen children.

In 1777 the town was literally flooded with members of the third generation just coming of age. The adult male population was 321 for 1777, but if we count all adult males who lived in Kent between 1774 and 1777, the total is 525. Obviously there was a considerable turnover in those years with about fifty men moving out of Kent each year.[45]

The writer has compiled an alphabetical file of the 525 adult males who appeared in Kent as residents during the four-year span, 1774–77. The vast majority of men were in family groups. Among the "Bs," for example, were four Bardsleys, seven Barneses, seven Barnums, eight Bateses, sixteen Beemans, five Benedicts, nine Berrys, three Blisses, four Brownsons, and six Bulls. In each family group we find departees, mostly young men who were on the tax list one or two years and then vanished. The Beemans, descendants of original settler-proprietor Thomas Beeman, illustrated what was happening to the third generation:

TABLE 12

THIRD GENERATION OF BEEMANS

Name (all Beeman)	Age in 1777	Tax List (in pounds)	Remarks
Abel	31	38	
Christopher	30	31	died, 1777
Daniel, Jr.	20	19	married and left, 1779
Ebenezer	60	44	
Ebenezer, Jr.	30	29	
Ezekiel	15		
Friend	27	25	left, 1775
Isaac	21	21	left, 1776
John, Jr.	18		died, 1776
Joseph	18	7	left, 1774 (to Albany Co., N.Y.)
Park	40	23	left, 1776
Thomas, 3d	28	48	
Thomas, Jr.	49	46	
Timothy	26	23	left, 1774
Truman	17		
William	21	18	

Of the sixteen Beemans, six left Kent in the seventies. Their ages were 20, 27, 21, 18, 40 and 26. In each case their tax list figure put them in the "Poor Category" of Table 11. This same pattern of large numbers of third-generation men coming of age in the seventies could be shown in family after family.

There was insufficient land for the third generation. Some stayed and remained in a poorer status than that of their fathers and much poorer than that of their grandfathers. Others left at the rate of about fifty a year.

The Fuller family was similar to the Beemans although on a higher economic scale. The economic status of three generations of Fullers suggests how the original holdings of proprietor settler Joseph Fuller were spread thinner and thinner. Where possible, dates and highest tax ratings are shown in Table 13.

TABLE 13
DIMINISHING PROPERTY: THREE GENERATIONS OF FULLERS

Name	Dates	Highest Tax List (in pounds)
First Generation		
Joseph	(1699–1775)	203
Second Generation		
Joseph, Jr.	b. 1723	42
Zachariah	b. 1725	103
Jeremiah	b. 1728	147
Nathaniel	?	67
Adijah	?	46
Simeon	?	49
Abraham	b. 1737	136
Jacob	b. 1738	59
Isaac	b. 1741	7
Third Generation		
Abel	?	40
Abraham, Jr.	?	50
Asahel	b. 1770	48
Benajah	b. 1757	32
Daniel	b. 1749	65
Ephraim	b. 1760	100
Howard	b. 1750	28
James	b. 1770	40
John	b. 1760	?
Oliver	b. 1747	50
Revilo	b. 1770	35
Samuel	?	14

Here again the drop in farm property as recorded on the tax list is steady as the land was divided and redivided. The average for the first generation was £203; for the second it was £81, and for the third, £49.

This hypothesis based on over-crowding might appear to be weakened by the fact of population mobility. Admittedly the numerous third-generation sons poured out of Kent, often as many as fifty emigrating in a single year. When the time came for a given farm to pass from one, second-generation family to six, third-generation sons, the economic interests of the sons dictated the migration of five and the continuance of only one on the family farm. However, we do suggest that there was a stickiness in the process. In practice, we suspect, economic interests were sometimes outweighed by psychological factors. Instead of five sons migrating, two or three might ignore the lure of outside adventure and prefer poverty amid familiar surroundings and friendly neighbors. Whatever the reasons, psychological or other, we do know that although many sons migrated, so many others remained that the land was divided and subdivided, leaving far less for individuals of the third and fourth generations.

The pattern of economic rise and fall at Kent can be summarized by noting the following steps:

(1) 1739 Substantial, middle class settlers found town.

(2) 1740–50 Original founders and "early-comers" speculate their way to sizable holdings.

(3) 1750–70 Second-generation sons inherit sizable stake but have less land than fathers. Most remain in Kent.

(4) 1770–1800 Third-generation sons inherit smaller slices. Overcrowded. Majority leaves. Poverty more widespread among remainder.

It would be presumptuous to suggest that evidence on economic democracy in a single town such as Kent now explains or reconciles the differences between such an historian as Robert Brown, who stresses opportunity and prosperity on the frontier, and his numerous opponents, who emphasize frontier depression and east-west conflict. One might, however, use Kent evidence to suggest a tentative hypothesis, one which could be subjected to the necessary test of expanded research in local land, tax, and probate records of other towns along the New England frontier. If such expanded research should indicate patterns similar to those at Kent, then a substantial modification of the present version of settlement might be in order.

If Kent were established as typical, then Brown's "middle class democracy" would be characteristic of the early stages of a new settlement. Settler grievances expressed in petitions against absenteeism, speculation, and general hardship would be regarded more as examples of the agressive opportunists' technique than as reliable descriptions of economic conditions. On the other hand, Brown's prosperity would disappear, and the depressed conditions described by a Nettels or an Adams would creep in at a later date. However, such conditions would not be a legacy of class conflict at the towns' original settlement. Rather they would emerge mainly from the pressure of population on a limited supply of land.

PART III

Political Democracy at Kent

An appraisal of political democracy at Kent during the eighteenth century requires answers to a number of questions. Most important is the problem of how many adult males were freemen and thus could participate in colony affairs by voting or holding office. Historians have not only differed on this question but have tended to set up their battle flags at the furthest possible extremities.[1] We may learn the extent of the colony (freeman) franchise in at least one town, Kent, by counting the men who met the property qualifications and comparing them with the freemen's lists and the total adult male population. Kent evidence on this problem of the colony franchise fails to support extremists on the nature of colonial democracy. The numbers and percentages of Kent freemen indicate that in this town democracy was incomplete but more widespread than is often suggested.

In addition to knowing the numbers and percentages of freemen, we should find it helpful to learn their relationships and attitudes toward nonfreemen. Whereas some historians have pictured the latter as an underprivileged, excluded "class apart," Kent evidence offers a contrary picture. In this town the nonfreemen were often apathetic citizens who had sufficient property to qualify but insufficient inclination. Or, more frequently, they were sons or younger brothers of freemen, men who were in no sense a class apart but would soon acquire more property and join the freemen group.

A more elusive question deals with the role of the freeman in colony government. It has been argued by some authorities that, regardless of the number of freemen, the system was still undemocratic. The underrepresentation of the frontier and the monopolization of elective offices in Connecticut by members of a few "eastern families" have suggested that the freemen were mere automatons acting out electoral procedures that were rigged in favor of the ruling cliques. Kent evidence does not sharply refute this concept but does reveal other factors influencing the situation. Kent was not underrepresented in the General Assembly. Kent inhabitants had close kinship ties with the "ruling hierarchy." Above all, this hierarchy appeared to govern in the best interests of the Kent citizen, thus suggesting that tenure in office was based partly on meritorious service.

Turning from colony government to local government, we again find disagreement among authorities on numbers and percentages of adult males who could vote in town meetings. While college history texts and general surveys have tended to follow the traditional idea that the town-meeting form of government was indeed democratic and the local franchise broad, such students of the Connecticut town franchise as McKinley, Gipson, and Zeichner have suggested that only a small minority could vote and participate in town government. The present writer believes on the basis of Kent evidence, the pertinent statutes, and his interpretation of contemporary opinion that these scholars are incorrect. An argument will be developed to indicate that in the western towns, and probably throughout all Connecticut during the eighteenth century, virtually all adult male inhabitants were eligible for full participation in town government.

Finally, there arises the problem of the operation of town government and the location of the true seat of government. Whereas some authors have stressed the importance of the appointed justices of the peace, Kent was apparently directed by democratically elected town officials.

7

THE FREEMEN AT KENT

There were many types of franchise in colonial Connecticut. Freemen voted for deputies (town representatives to the General Assembly) and for colony officials (governor, deputy governor, assistants, etc.). "Town-meeting voters" participated in town meetings and elected town officials. Proprietors voted in proprietors' meetings, church members voted in church meetings, and militiamen voted to elect their officers.[1] Of these types of electors, we need concern ourselves only with the first two, freemen and town meeting voters.

Connecticut Statutes: The Freeman Qualification

There is no need here to retrace the evolution of the statutes relating to freemanship. Albert E. McKinley has produced a definitive work on this subject, commenting on the many changes in the seventeenth century.[2] It should suffice to note that basic acts were passed in 1689, 1702, 1709, and 1729. The act of 1689 was most important. This established the familiar and traditional English forty-shilling freehold. An inhabitant might qualify for the freemanship if he possessed a freehold which would yield an annual income of forty shillings.[3]

There was a second method for qualifying. Possession of a certain amount of personal property provided an alternate path to the freemanship. In 1702 the legal code set the permanent figure at "forty pounds personal estate."[4]

A crucial act was passed by the General Assembly in 1709. It was ordered that the value of freehold as well as of personal property should be taken from the tax lists.[5] The practice in the eighteenth century thus became one in which specific "annual-income" figures were assigned to land and livestock, these values varying with type, age, and location. In the code of 1750, for example, meadowland in Hartford County was to be listed at 15 shillings per acre; upland pasture was 8 shillings per acre, etc. A person owning five acres of upland pasture thus met the forty-shilling freehold requirement.[6] Tying the forty-shilling freehold requirement to the tax list made qualification by this route quite simple. To own real property was virtually to qualify.

On the other hand, tying personal property to the tax list may have practically removed this avenue of qualification. Scholars who have examined the problem closely assume that in Connecticut most ordinary personal property was useless to an applicant for freemanship.[7] The wording of the statutes stated that to qualify for the forty-pound route one must have "forty pounds personal estate in the General List of Estates." [8] Prior to 1771 the only items of personal estate that could have counted were horses, oxen, and cows. After 1771 a few luxury items (coaches, clocks, watches, and silver plate) were included in the common list; but furniture, tools, clothes, and miscellaneous possessions never appeared on the list and were thus ineligible as credit toward the forty-pound goal.[9] Under these conditions the forty-pound personal property route was virtually a blind alley.[10] Anyone who could qualify by this personal property route would be over the top tenfold by the forty-shilling freehold route. It would take fourteen cows to reach £40. But a fourteen-cow farm would have at least forty acres of plowland, ten times more plow acreage than the four needed to qualify as a forty-shilling freeholder.

The last decisive statute date was 1729, at which time the General Assembly turned over to the towns the task of screening and accepting candidates for the freemanship.[11] The present writer feels that before this time, when freemanship was conferred only by the General Assembly or special commissions, freemen may have been as scarce as Adams, Gipson, and Zeichner claim.[12] They would have been scarce not because of their inability to qualify but simply because of distance, laziness, or general inertia. After 1729, when "open freemen's meetings" did the admitting on the spot, the simplified procedure may have encouraged many more qualified settlers to take the last step and become legal freemen.[18]

Unfortunately the statutes do not spell out the details of this simplified procedure for admitting freemen by the towns after 1729. The best description the present writer has found is that of Edward Kendall written in 1807. Unfortunately Kendall does not cite his sources. What he describes was undoubtedly the practice in 1807; and since there were few if any changes in freemanship practice after 1729, it seems reasonably safe to push Kendall's generalizations back into the eighteenth century. Kendall stated that "the duty of certifying a freeman was formerly confided to the selectmen only; and they were liable to a fine if they granted a certificate to an unqualified person." [14] Kendall pictured the selectmen gathering beforehand at the site of a prospective freemen's meeting. Before the opening of the meeting ("not afterwards") they would examine applications for admission to the privileges of the freemanship. When satisfied, the selectmen would certify in writing an applicant's admission. He would take the freeman's oath then and there prior to the meeting.[15]

Usually the "Open Freemen's Meetings" or the selectmen appear to have conferred freemanship in accordance with the legal property requirements. It seems doubtful that they would be overly strict with applicants close to the line. Such strictness would have surely lead to protests; and although Kent records abound with quarrels, no disputes over freemanship have come to light. In 1796 and 1797 young Gardner Geer showed no property, as only his $60 poll tax appeared on the common list. He was made a freeman in 1800. In this year his list was combined with his father's and showed "Ezra and Gardner Geer . . . $198." More difficult to explain was the admission of Lewis St. John in 1804 when his list was the bare poll-tax figure of $60. In the same year Alpheus Fuller was admitted on a $75 list. Assuming a $60 poll tax, we find $15 worth of property was at best a close squeeze. Perhaps the party politics of the time were involved here.

Before we conclude with freeman qualifications, the non-property requirements should be observed. These were:

(1) the applicant must be at least twenty-one years of age;
(2) he must swear the "Freeman's Oath";
(3) he should display quiet, peaceable behavior and civil conversation.

Some historians have been impressed by the apparent barriers under this last qualification. However, in Kent these appear to have been dead letters. At Kent, Abel Wright was virtually ostracized for his religious beliefs. He was expelled from the church and left town under a cloud. However, he became a freeman at the time of his troubles (Freeman Roll of 1743) and returned to Kent later, still presumably a freeman. Jacob Bull went to jail for his Tory sympathies but was a freeman before and after his troubles. Joseph Pack was haled before church meetings for drunkenness three times in the 1740s but he made the Freeman's Roll of 1751.

"Once a freeman, always a freeman" was virtually a rule in Connecticut. According to Edward Kendall, the task of disfranchising on moral grounds rested not with the towns but with the Superior Court. This court was to act on complaints. Once it disfranchised, only it could reenfranchise.[16] The present writer examined Superior Court Records between 1774 and 1776 but found no such cases for Litchfield County. The fact that only the highest court had jurisdiction emphasizes the unusual nature of such cases.

Numbers and Percentages of Freemen at Kent

Professor Chilton Williamson employed a method for determining the number and percentage of adult males (in East Guilford, Connecticut) who could qualify for the freemanship; that is, who could enjoy top political status in the colony or state. Williamson's percentage of adult males for 1800 was 65. Using the same method for Kent in 1796, the present writer arrived at a figure of

63 percent. It should be stressed that these figures, based on tax "work sheets," indicate merely what men had sufficient property to qualify, or meet the test. These "qualifiers" did not necessarily follow through and become freemen.[17]

The Kent percentages of "qualifiers" and of actual freemen from 1740 to 1796 are shown in Table 14.

TABLE 14
KENT FREEMEN

Year	No. of Adult Resident Males	Qualifiers	Percentage Qualifying	No. Who Became Freemen	Percentage of Freemen
1740	42	30	71	No Freemen's Roll	
1745	67	51	76	33	50
1751	129	100	79	66	51
1777	321	253	79	163	51
1796	209	132	63	62	30

If Kent and East Guilford were typical, then some estimates of the numbers and percentages of freemen (or of men who could qualify for the freemanship) were far too low. One cannot examine a lengthy "Enrollment of Freemen" at Kent or note the numerous freehold farms shown on the tax lists and still maintain that only a small minority could vote. On the other hand, one cannot say that Kent men enjoyed full political democracy. In any given election of town representatives and of colony officials during the eighteenth century, one man in four (later one in three) had insufficient property to participate in the government of the colony.

Potential "Qualifiers" for Freemanship

Further study of the nonvoters reveals that their inability to participate in colony government was temporary. The reader is referred again to Table 11 concerning economic classes on page 96. Of the fourteen nonqualifiers in 1740, six were transients who did not remain long enough to reach the qualification level. Seven did stay and qualify for the freemanship. Only one remained as a voteless proletarian. In 1751 Kent appeared to offer the greatest inducements to the nonqualifier to stay and climb. As Table 11 shows, of the thirty-four nonqualifiers, twenty-eight remained in Kent and all soon passed the qualification level. Only three departed early, and the last three remained voteless proletarians. In 1777 the door of opportunity seemed to be closing. Most of the eighty-three who could not qualify in that year did not wait in Kent to climb but moved on to greener pastures. Fifty-three moved, sixteen stayed and attained the freeman level, and fourteen remained as nonfreemen. Finally, in 1796 the harder conditions envisioned by the fifty-three movers of 1777 were realized. The highest number and percentage of nonqualifiers was reached as eighty-six men had estates below £30. Again a large number pulled up stakes (forty-three) while twenty-two remained and advanced into the freeman bracket. Another twenty-two men remained and seemed unable to climb.

Thus in 1796 there was for the first time a noticeable voteless class. Previously the highest percentage of such a class to the total adult male population had been 3 percent. Now in 1796, 11 percent were destined to continue living in Kent and remain unqualified for the freemanship.

"Qualifiers" Who Did Not Become Freemen

Robert Brown and others who have indicated a broad franchise in eighteenth-century New England have written in terms of men who could qualify rather than in terms of those who did actually become freemen. At Kent the percentages of freemen were substantially and consistently lower than the percentages of qualifiers. In 1745, eighteen qualified men did not bother to become freemen. In 1751 the apathetic numbered thirty-four, in 1777 there were ninety, and in 1796 there were seventy.[18]

Year	Qualifiers	Freemen	Apathetic	Percentage of Apathetic
1745	51	33	18	35
1757	100	66	34	34
1777	253	166	90	35
1796	132	62	70	53

The writer has scrutinized the ninety men who had enough property in 1777 to qualify but were not on the freemen's roll for that year. The following patterns emerge:

First, they tended to be citizens farthest removed physically from the Kent meetinghouse. Twenty-three were from New Preston Society, twelve miles away and separated from Kent proper by a mountain. Thirty-two lived on the mountain in the East Greenwich Society, present-day Warren. Thirty-five were from the "First Society," as Kent proper was called, but many of these lived in its distant corners. Comparing numbers of apathetic in each society to total population of the society, we find the following: New Preston, 30 percent apathetic; East Greenwich, 25 percent apathetic; and Kent, First Society, 20 percent apathetic.

Second, the apathetic were men who showed a continuing disinterest in public affairs. In 1777 there were eighty-four town offices to be filled. Only five of the "apathetic ninety" were among the office holders. Four of these five were from the New Preston Society and were elected to perform duties in that society.[19]

Third, the freemen's rolls suggest that men joined in family groups or when an issue stirred them. Few rushed to be certified as soon as they qualified economically. For example, Jabez Beardsley was not certified a freeman until 1800. But he had come to Kent in the 1760s, married Martha Pain in 1766, and by 1768 had acquired a large farm consisting of twelve head of stock, fifty-two acres of good farm land, and 270 acres of timber land. In 1800 four of the five new freemen could have qualified much earlier. In 1804 ten of the thirteen were propertied men of long standing. Of our group of ninety who could have been freemen in 1777 but were not, fifteen did pull themselves together and become freemen at a later date (including Jabez Beardsley).

The writer is also interested in the sharp rise in "apathy" from the mid-century plateau of 35 percent to the situation in 1796 when over half the men with sufficient property failed to obtain certification as freemen. However, the Kent evidence has not provided any certain explanation for the change. One clue might be the more rapid population turnover at this time. In times of rapid movement, stirring, and general ferment there might be less interest in civic duties and rights. Also the year 1796 may have been transitional between two political attitudes: the eighteenth-century feeling for dignity and status (it was a social honor to be a freeman); and the nineteenth-century political awakening ("the rise of the common man" or Jacksonian democracy). In 1796 the old feeling for status was dying, but a new political fever had not yet taken hold.

In any final conclusion about the nature of the colony franchise at Kent it seems advisable to avoid extreme statements about democracy. On the one hand, it would appear wrong to proclaim "middle-class democracy" when no more than half the adult males were certified as freemen at any given time. On the other hand, there is danger in envisioning an "unenfranchised mass," particularly if such a "mass" is pictured as constituting a separate and less privileged class.

At Kent the 50 percent of all adult males who assembled in freemen's meetings were not a "class"voting in their own interests against those who were debarred. The other 50 percent, the non-freemen, were not figuratively standing outside looking wistfully in at the privileged half who could raise their voices in colony affairs. Of the "outsiders," at least half were far away and could have joined the group inside had they overcome their repugnance to traveling twelve miles (one way) over a mountain on muddy April roads. The other half of the outsiders were young men, many of them sons or brothers of the freemen inside. Most knew that if they remained in Kent, within five years they too could be on the inside casting their votes for town representatives and colony officers.

8

THE ROLE OF KENT FREEMEN
IN COLONY GOVERNMENT

Twice each year the freemen of Kent met to play their role in the government of the colony. An appraisal of political democracy in this town on Connecticut's western frontier should consider the effectiveness of this role. It has been suggested that on the colonial frontier as a whole the back-country farmers were underrepresented. They might be able to vote for town representatives, but "they could do little to achieve their ends in most colonial legislatures." [1] Our first inquiry, then, should determine the extent to which Kent and her sister towns of the Western Lands were under or overrepresented.

It has also been stated that the "elective offices of Connecticut were monopolized by a small number of prominent families." [2] This clique is said to have held power because "Democracy never existed nor was it desired by Connecticut's leaders during the colonial period." [3] The relationship between the freemen of Kent and the "ruling hierarchy" also requires attention in this study of political democracy.

Representation

From 1739 (when Kent and her sister towns first received town privileges), to the late 1750s the new western towns were untaxed and unrepresented in the General Assembly. [4] Far from desiring representation (at the cost of paying colony taxes for the first time), Kent and her sister towns seemed well satisfied with the status quo. When Kent learned the honeymoon was to end, the town's immediate reaction was to call an emergency meeting (September 28, 1756), and dispatch Captain Nathaniel Swift to the General Assembly "to git the colony rate forborn." [5] At the same time the Kent petition machine was turned on. In these years when local figures indicate Kent prosperity was at its height, Nathaniel Berry complained to the government that all three Kent societies were "destitute of ministers," that the town had gone to great expense in building a bridge, and that "all we raise this year will not half satisfy our own rates." [6] The General Assembly appeared untouched by this nonsense. Kent had her taxes and her representation forced on her despite all protests.[7]

Kent and her sister towns never protested that they were underrepresented. Prior to 1757 they were content with no representatives (and no colony taxes), and after that date they were overrepresented. The population of Connecticut in 1782 was 202,577. At this time seventy-eight towns sent 155 deputies to the General Assembly. If representation had been perfectly apportioned, each deputy would have had 1300 constituents, or each town with two deputies should have had a population of 2600. Populations of the western towns (each of which had two deputies), were: Kent, 1835; Cornwall, 1144; Sharon, 2184; Salisbury, 2190.[8]

Kent and the Governing Families of Connecticut

Kent's eagerness to forego representation and the willingness of her freemen to elect the same magistrates to the highest offices year after year may surprise scholars who have become conditioned to view eighteenth-century American history in terms of factional struggles. The titles of books (*Connecticut's Years of Controversy*),[9] or sub-titles (*The Struggle for Equal Political Rights and Majority Rule during the American Revoluton*),[10] or chapter headings ("Protest and Rebellion" or "Revolution and Internal Conflict"),[11] all overpower the reader with the din of battle. The student who encounters on nearly every page such words as "strife," "struggle," or "rivalry," often modified by such adjectives as "bitter," "unequal," or "oppressive," comes to view colonial history in terms of rival factions and their relative powers.

To understand the relationship of Kent and her sister towns to the General Assembly it would seem helpful to revise one's historical vocabulary and substitute such words as "harmony," "mutual respect," and "loyalty."

The charter of the Colony of Connecticut made certain persons a "Body political and Corporate." [12] These persons were designated "the Governor and Company of the English Colony of Connecticut." [13] They formed, indeed, a sort of joint-stock company whose members were the freemen and whose purpose was to enhance the wishes or ambitions of the freemen. The freemen chose their "directors" (governor, assistants, and deputies), who were to exercise executive, legislative, and judicial power and to facilitate the orderly enjoyment of the fruits and blessings of colonial Connecticut. Just as modern, corporation directors who promote the interests of the stockholders, settle disputes tactfully, and grant reasonable requests are likely to hold their offices year after year, so the magistrates of the Connecticut Company constituted a benevolent, long-term directorate.

Historians have been most impressed by the tendency for all offices to be held by a relatively small clique of men, who, despite annual elections, always clung to their posts. Some have suggested that the longevity was made possible by the rules of the game, rather unfair rules, which permitted a privileged class to hold power and thus govern in its own interests. However, it will be suggested here that the satisfied shareholders in the Connecticut Company were far more numerous than has usually been suggested.[14]

Connecticut in 1750 was governed by about 600 officials. Reference is made here to officers above the town level. This governing clique would include governor, deputy governor, treasurer, secretary, twelve assistants, ninety-four deputies, and also judges of the Superior Court, county courts, and probate courts. There were 134 justices of the peace plus numerous auditors and comptrollers. There were also special committees, commissions, councils, and agents. Militia officers (appointed by the General Assembly on the recommendations of soldier elections), would add about 200 to the list of leading men.[15]

The 600 offices were filled by perhaps 400 men. Plural office-holding occurred at the upper levels, where most assistants served as higher court judges, and at the lower level, where town deputies were frequently justices of the peace. Agents and special commit-tees were almost always composed of officeholders.[16] If 400 men operated the governmental machinery in one year, about 900 dif-ferent men served in seven years.[17]

Over half of these 900 officeholders for the period 1744–50 were members of about 100 prominent Connecticut families. For example, among the Averys of Groton the following were prominent: Benjamin, Christopher, Ebenezer, Humphrey, James, Jonathan, and Theophilus. These Averys were deputies, justices, and militia officers; and one, Benjamin, was appointed agent to England. Humphrey was Kent's first proprietor, first moderator, and first proprietor's agent. Family after family might be termed "First Governing Families." To name the Bs only, Baldwins, Bateses, Beebes, Benedicts, Bentons, Bostwicks, Brainards, Browns, Buckinghams, Buells, Bulkeleys, Burnhams, and Burrs were all prolific producers of officeholders.[18]

While there were about 100 families producing four or more officials, another 500 families produced one or two. Thus Beach, Beeman, Berry, Blackman, Brownson, etc. with a deputy or militia officer apiece might be called "second governing families."

The present writer suggests that most inhabitants of Kent in the late 1740s were members of either first or second governing families. Few lived at Kent who did not have a father, brother, or cousin serving in the governing clique. Examining the Kent Bs in alphabetical order, we find two Baldwins, three Barneses, three Bateses, three Beaches, five Beebes, etc. All of these are first or second-class family names. The family tree for the Beebes shown in Table 15 may be instructive.

John Beebe was of only medium prominence at Kent, his highest office being constable. Although a proprietor, he was one who swept the meetinghouse for 15 shillings a year. As a debtor he lost a suit in 1752. A typical mover, he pushed on to Amenia in 1754 and again to Columbia County, New York, where he died in 1788. John Beebe, a typical Kent settler, should not be looked

TABLE 15

THE BEEBES OF CONNECTICUT

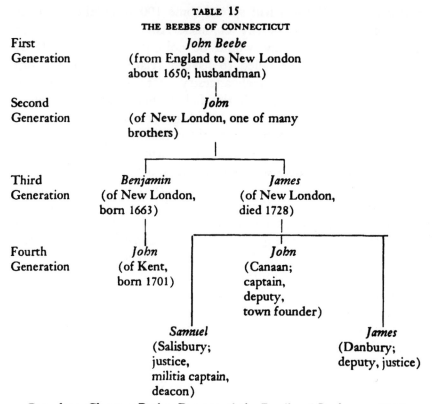

Data from Clarence Beebe, *Descent of the Family of Beebe*, pp. 22–24.

upon as an "oppressed frontiersman" excluded from the privileges of Connecticut's governing clique. On the contrary, Beebe was a freeman and thus a member of the Connecticut Company. Although he was not of the governing clique himself, his cousins James in Danbury, John in Canaan, and Samuel in Salisbury all were.

The genealogies of such Kent families as Averill, Benedict, Benton, Boardman, Bulkeley, Carter, Carey, Chamberlain, Curtis, Eaton, Fuller, Geer, Hatch, Hollister, Hubbel, Judd, Newcomb, Noble, Mills, Porter, Pratt, Ransom, Raymond, Root, Sackett, Slosson, Sprague, Swift, and Wright show relationships similar to those of the Beebes.[19] The Kent members were part of the third or fourth generations of huge families. Their fecund grandfathers

and great-grandfathers had spread some 100 namesakes throughout Connecticut and nearby colonies. Almost inevitably several
members of each family would be colony officeholders. If by
chance a Kent settler failed to have a relative among the first
governing families by his male ancestry, there was an equally good
chance by the female line. If this failed, there might be seven or
eight pretty daughters to forge a fifth-generation link.

It is not contended here that these relationships were an immediate and sure-fire guarantee of harmony throughout the
colony. Then, as always, relatives could be the bitterest of opponents. Admittedly John Beebe's squire cousins at Danbury,
Salisbury, and Canaan may have been of little help to him in his
problems at Kent. On the other hand, this widespread family stake
and participation in the government, or Company of Connecticut,
may have had a considerable underlying effect. The network of
relationships may have imparted a feeling of kinship and a sense of
class equality. Historians who have bundled colonials into warring
cliques may have neglected too much the plodding work of
genealogists, who show these family ties in all sectors of the
society of colonial Connecticut.

Benevolent Paternalism

We have suggested so far that there was in Connecticut a
general company of citizens governed by a group of company
directors. These directors appeared, at first glance, to be an exclusive clique, but study revealed that the governing families included in their outer fringes most inhabitants of Kent. We now
turn to an appraisal of how this group of directors performed its
tasks. Perhaps it was maintained in office because the company
"stockholders" were gratified at its benevolent paternalism, or possibly its tenure was based more on a stubborn, clever holding action against inroads of individualism and democracy.

Actually both of these alternatives were probably true. Historians have shown, with undoubted accuracy, the growth of
democratic spirit in the early nineteenth century, a growth that
in many instances was opposed by the old governing cliques. Too

often, however, they have failed to show that the eighteenth-century governing body did rule equitably and that its benevolence was distributed to virtually all Connecticut inhabitants. We need not mourn the passing of this paternalistic order. Neither should we deny or distort what was apparently a skillfull and popular performance.

The word paternalistic is employed to suggest that the towns did not always think for themselves but seemed closely tied to the apron strings of the General Assembly. In a bitter Kent dispute Kent's leading citizen, Timothy Hatch, spoke for the town (at least most of the townsmen signed his petition), and stated: "If the government frowns on certain men [Moravians], we all should frown on them." [20] The towns did not locate their own meeting-houses but had the General Assembly assume responsibility.[21] The Assembly set the bounds between church societies and ordered which churches the inhabitants should attend.[22] Let a good dispute develop over the location of a bridge or a road and the town would invariably turn to the government for advice and a final decision.[23]

In over sixty disputes or problems arising between 1740 and 1770 the town of Kent or its citizens looked to the General Assembly for an equitable decision. Who should pay for Bonnie's Bridge? (The entire town.) Should Tory-sympathizer Jacob Bull be released from jail to support his family? (Yes.) Should Eliphalet Comstock be reimbursed for paper money which went up in smoke when his house burned to the ground? (Yes.) Was Phoebe Finney's tragic case a miscarriage or infanticide? (It was ruled a miscarriage.) The tragic, the complex, the bizarre, and the ridiculous, all manner of cases landed in the lap of the General Assembly. This body dispatched its investigating committees, heard pertinent evidence, and after due deliberations made its decisions.

At the risk of making too subjective a judgment, the author is inclined to applaud the Assembly's work. Each decision seems to have been carefully weighed and was, by modern standards, equitable. A tendency to compromise was especially noticeable. John Woodworth would ask for £60 compensation for loss of an eye at Cape Breton and be granted £30.[24] Kent proprietors would ask indefinite postponement on payment of debts and would get two years extra. Fuller and Lassell would ask for two lots apiece and get one.

The Assembly's frequent failure to give an unqualified yes or a flat no may well have been based on a genuine interest in the petitioners. Such compromising decisions are not so much the mark of the martinet as of the troubled, conscientious arbitrator. One unfortunate effect was the consequent encouragement of the citizenry to advance all sorts of exaggerated claims. If one's judge cuts all demands in half, it is wise to make the original request extra large.

What was true of Kent's relationship to the General Assembly in the mid-eighteenth century seems true of all the Connecticut towns. The petition literature from other towns that is recorded in the *Colonial Records* from 1744 to 1750 suggests that benevolent paternalism was the key to the government's response. The General Assembly could say no but more often it said yes. Kent voters and those of other towns acquiesced in the status quo. It seems doubtful that they would have returned the same men to office year after year if they had not admired these officials and appreciated the sort of government they were furnishing.[25]

Kent and the Colony Elections

In Connecticut the freemen of Kent and all other towns met in September to choose two town representatives for the October session of the General Assembly and also to vote for nominees for governor, deputy governor, and the twelve assistants of the upper house. In April they met again to choose two representatives, this time for the May session. Also in April they voted for their choices of colony magistrates from among the twenty nominees who had received the most votes the previous fall.[26] Here was the famous Connecticut paradox. On the one hand, a numerous electorate had two chances each year to unseat their representatives or any of the twelve assistants; on the other hand, the stability of Connecticut politics was legendary. Between 1783 and 1807 only one assistant was rejected by the voters, all the others retiring voluntarily.[27] Many magistrates held office for over thirty years.[28]

As has been suggested, there were two explanations for this apparent paradox. One was the good conduct of the official: "The electoral body sits in judgment twice each year. . . . If the conduct of any one of them has been such as to deserve exclusion from office, public opinion expells him from office." [29] The other answer was Connecticut's unique nomination-election system with its special procedural "gimmick," the operation of which may be observed at Kent.[30]

At nine o'clock in the morning on the third Monday in September the Kent freemen held their nomination meeting. In 1745 the date was September 17, and at least thirty-three freemen of Kent showed up at the meeting place, Daniel Comstock's house atop Goodhill. Each man present cast twenty votes. He voted for one nominee for governor, for one nominee for deputy governor, and for eighteen nominees to contest for the twelve assistantships. The records are silent on the extent of oratory or politicking, but the uniform results of the balloting suggest that some advice was given. We do know, "each of the enrolled freemen gives his suffrage for twenty persons whom he judgeth qualified." [31]

Although the Kent freemen could have voted for each other, or for Kent's leading citizen, Timothy Hatch, they obviously considered such a practice a waste of votes. They voted for the prominent men of the colony. In practice this usually meant voting for the incumbent slate (twelve assistants plus the governor and deputy governor) and then for six more men to bring the total of nominees to twenty. About the only suspense arose over the "additional six." Most obviously one could vote for the extra six nominated but not elected the previous year. Or one could support instead a personal favorite, say Colonel Prescott, regimental commander of the unit of which the Kent trainband was a part. If one of the incumbent assistants had displeased, he could be passed by. Assistant Hezekiah Huntington, for example, was a New Light. Kent voters, staunchly Old Light, might be expected to reject Huntington but vote heavily for John Bulkeley, an equally determined Old Light.[32]

TABLE 16

CONNECTICUT ELECTIONS, 1744–1746

	A Nominees of Sept., 1744[a]	B Elected May, 1745[b]	C Kent Votes for Nominees, Sept., 1745[c]	D Winning Nominees, Sept., 1745[d]	E Elected May, 1746[e]
1.	Jonathan Law	Law	Law 32	Law	Law
2.	Roger Wolcott	Wolcott	Wolcott 32	Wolcott	Wolcott
3.	James Wadsworth	Wadsworth	Wadsworth 29	Wadsworth	Wadsworth
4.	Nathaniel Stanley	Stanley	Whiting 29	Stanley	Stanley
5.	Joseph Whiting	Whiting	O. Pitkin 28	Whiting	O. Pitkin
6.	Ozias Pitkin	Pitkin	Pierce 26	O. Pitkin	Pierce
7.	Timothy Pierce	Pierce	W. Pitkin 33	Pierce	Lynde
8.	Samuel Lynde	Lynde	Newton 24	Lynde	W. Pitkin
9.	William Pitkin	Pitkin	Fitch 27	W. Pitkin	Fitch
10.	Thomas Fitch	Fitch	Lynde 29	Fitch	Newton
11.	Roger Newton	Newton	Silliman 28	Newton	Silliman
12.	Ebenezer Silliman	Silliman	Trumbull 28	Silliman	Trumbull
13.	Jonathan Trumbull	Trumbull	Bulkeley 28	Trumbull	Bulkeley
14.	John Bulkeley	Bulkeley	Burr 30	Bulkeley	Burr
15.	Hezekiah Huntington		Chester 28	Huntington	
16.	Andrew Burr		Hill 27	Burr	
17.	John Chester		Benjamin Hall 29	Chester	
18.	Elisha Williams		John Hubbard 27	Griswold	
19.	Samuel Hill		Theodore Nichols 28	Williams	
20.	John Griswold		John Reed 23	Hall	
			Eli Tupper 1		
			John Fowler 6		
			William Preston 8		
			Robert Walker 1		
			Daniel Coit 1		
			Hezekiah Huntington 1		
			Griswold 1		

[a] *Public Conn. Col. Records*, IX, 44.
[b] *Ibid.*, IX, 103.
[c] Conn. Hist. Society, Misc. Papers.
[d] *Public Conn. Col. Records*, IX, 168.
[e] *Ibid.*, IX, 188.

Table 16 shows five columns of candidates. Column A shows the twenty men who had won nominations the previous year, September, 1744. These were the men who, when all the votes from all the towns had been counted, had the highest totals. Column B shows the fourteen men out of the twenty who were actually elected to office when the final election occurred in May,[33] 1745. Column C shows how Kent voted for nominees on this September morning in 1745. Column D looks ahead and shows which men were the successful nominees in this 1745 race. Finally, Column E completes the cycle by showing the fourteen victors the following May, 1746.

It is interesting to note that Kent went with the tide on all but Williams, Huntington, and Griswold, each of whom won nomination despite unpopularity in Kent. Kent gave rather heavy support, but to no avail, to Hubbard, Nichols, and Read. The confused order of the Kent ballot suggests that no set lists were presented or read to the voters at their nomination meeting.

The "gimmick" which seems mainly responsible for the continuity in the Connecticut electoral pattern was employed at the next freemen's meeting in April of the following year (on the Monday following the first Tuesday). When the Kent freemen assembled again, this time to elect a governor, deputy governor, and twelve assistants from the list of twenty successful nominees, a special procedure was followed.[34] After the balloting for governor, deputy governor, secretary, and treasurer had been completed, the assistants were voted on one at a time. First, the name of James Wadsworth was called out by the Kent constable, John Beebe. A Kent freeman could write "Wadsworth" on a piece of paper and step forward to give it to the teller, he could sit glowering in his seat as other Kent freemen filed past, or he could deceive his fellows by turning in a blank. As the twenty names were called, the same process was repeated for each. A freeman was permitted twelve votes for assistants.

In such a voting situation human psychology seems to have been such that the first twelve names called won the most votes for assistants. There might be variations in individual towns, but on a colony-wide basis the votes averaged out so that the top twelve nearly always came through victorious. No statute law dictated the crucial order of calling the names, but custom was unvarying. Those nominees who were presently serving in office received priority on the basis of longevity in office. The six men not in office were called out in an order determined by the number of votes they had received in the fall "nomination election." Conceivably Wadsworth might have placed twentieth from the top in the nomination contest but his length of service required that his name be called first. Even if he suffered considerable unpopularity, the advantage of his position would pull him through. On the other hand, even if there had been landslides for Burr or Huntington in the fall nomination elections, their highest attainable position was fifteenth or sixteenth in the list.[35]

In practice, then, the twelve assistants each clung to a rung of the ladder, moving up when someone ahead dropped out. John Bulkeley, a favorite of Kent freemen, illustrates the process. His name was presented to the freemen in the following orders:

1736	20th	
1737	17	
1738	17	Position determined by number
1739	18	of votes received in fall nomina-
1740	15	tion election.
1741	15	
1742	15	
1743	14	
1744	14	
1745	14	
1746	13	Position determined on basis of
1747	12	seniority among other assistants.
1748	12	
1749	11	
1750	11	

In appraising the share of the Kent freemen in colony government we faced a dilemma. We found a central government whose directors were constantly weighed by the electorate but never found wanting. We noted that one explanation for such stability was an electoral "gimmick," but we also observed that the effectiveness of the "gimmick" was never really tested. The magistrates were giving the freemen a benevolent, paternalistic rule which seemed to satisfy them. In satisfying the Kent freemen, the colony magistrates were also satisfying the Kent population as a whole for scarcely any Kent men were part of a depressed class incapable of achieving freemanship. One might say there was democracy at the colony level in that the numerous freemen did have the ultimate power. We suspect they could have "turned the rascals out" if the magistrates had ever become rascals.

9

LOCAL DEMOCRACY: THE TOWN-MEETING VOTER
AND TOWN GOVERNMENT

The colony franchise in Connecticut was not liberalized until a new constitution was adopted in 1818; but the local franchise, the right to vote in town meetings, may have become universal for men much earlier. A study of local political democracy at Kent should throw light on the extent to which men had a voice in town affairs. Furthermore, regardless of the number of voters, regardless of the popularity and efficiency of the elected officials, local democracy would be limited if real administrative power rested with *appointed* officers such as justices of the peace. A comparison of the elected selectmen and appointed justices at Kent should help to round out the picture of political democracy on Connecticut's western frontier.

The Town-Meeting Voter [1]

Although historians who have dealt with the town-meeting franchise in Connecticut have concluded that it was limited ("Only a small minority were admitted members of the towns."),[2] the present study of Kent suggests the opposite conclusion. At Kent, in the other western towns, and probably in nearly all Connecticut towns after 1740, all adult males except "strangers" could vote in town meetings. To support this statement it is necessary to classify different types of inhabitants, to trace the confused history of statutes relating to town-meeting voters, to observe actual practices at Kent, and finally to note contemporary opinion on the subject.

In colonial Connecticut the adult males (twenty-one and over) fell into four classes: [3]

Class I, Freemen: those who were eligible for any office and could vote in town and colony elections.

Class II, Town-Meeting Voters: those who could vote in town meetings. Freemen were automatically town-meeting voters.

Class III, Inhabitants: called variously "approved," "admitted," "legal," or "settled." Sons of "inhabitants" gained this status automatically.

Class IV, Strangers: also called non-inhabitants.

Of the four classess of town inhabitants listed above we have covered Class I, the freemen. We will quickly dispose of Class IV, the strangers, about whom there is no argument. They had no political privileges whatsoever. Indeed, they were liable to be whipped out of town after their thirty days for visiting were up. We have remaining to be examined *Class II,* the town-meeting voters, and *Class III,* the legal inhabitants. The crux of the problem is the question of whether Classes II and III were actually distinct. On this matter the following evolution appears to have taken place:

1660– 79   Classes II and III were the same; qualification difficult.

1679–1727   Classes II and III were distinct. Qualification for II, difficult; for III, fairly simple.

1727–1818   Classes II and III become identical in practice (not by law); qualification, simple.

In 1660 Class II, town-meeting voters, and Class III, legal inhabitants, appear to have been one and the same. The Act of May 17, 1660, provided that no one should be received as an inhabitant unless he were of honest conversation and had been admitted by the vote of the majority of the town inhabitants.[4] Nothing further was said about qualifications so apparently these admitted inhabitants could vote. This status of legal or admitted inhabitant went automatically to sons of admitted inhabitants.[5]

In 1679 Classes II and III were separated as the property qualification for town-meeting voter was added.

This Court do order that no person that is not an admitted inhabitant, a householder, and a man of sober conversation, and have at least 50 shillings freehold in the common list besides his person, shall adventure to vote . . . in the town meeting . . . provided that no freeman be hereby barred from voting.[6]

Presumably an admitted inhabitant who lacked a 50-shilling freehold remained a Class III inhabitant, whereas one who was a householder and had his 50 shillings in the common list moved up to Class II and became a town-meeting voter.

Commencing in the 1720s (or perhaps a bit earlier), a basic change seemed to be taking place. The towns tended to ignore the complex legal distinctions between Classes II and III. Whereas in, say 1700, a Class III inhabitant might have been stopped at the door of a town meeting and been turned away for failing to meet the property qualification, after the 1720s no one bothered to keep out the propertyless hired hands. The year 1727 is picked as a focal point for this gradual mixing process of Classes II and III. In that year we have the last recorded dispute over who were or who were not town-meeting voters[7] There were irregular procedures in admitting certain Voluntown town-meeting voters (or in refusing to admit them). Some disgruntled losers petitioned the General Assembly to review the whole proceeding. In response the General Assembly stated: "It is also considered that towns have the right by law to judge of the qualifications, and consequently the power of admitting their inhabitants." [8] This decision appears to have put a government stamp of approval on what the towns had probably started to do anyway: that is, admit all inhabitants to the status of town-meeting voter. From this time on the towns seemed to have done as they pleased without bothering the General Assembly.

Some Connecticut historians might well raise questions about the conflict between this version and the provisions of the Code of 1750.[9] This code indeed spelled out in precise terms the requirements for admitted inhabitants and town-meeting voters. Students of the eighteenth-century franchise in Connecticut have based their comments on the contents of this code. As to admitted inhabitants the code stated:

No person shall be received or admitted an inhabitant in any town in this colony, but such as are known to be of honest conversation and shall be accepted by the major part of the town; or by authority of the selectmen of the town.[10]

The code also set forth requirements for the town-meeting voter:

(1) To be a lawful inhabitant and householder;

(2) To possess Freehold estate rated in the common list at fifty shillings, or personal estate rated in the list at forty pounds;

(3) To be at least twenty-one years of age.

No person not meeting the above shall be allowed to vote, intermeddle, act, or deal, in any town meetings, in the choice of officers, granting of rates, or any other town affairs.[11]

A number of reasons suggest that these provisions were not followed at Kent or other Connecticut towns during the last two-thirds of the eighteenth century.

First, the so-called 1750 code was simply a compilation or digest of pertinent acts passed by the General Assembly. The five copies at the State Library in Hartford all show publication in New London in 1750, though surprisingly they all include acts not passed until the 1760s. The present writer regards the code as a rather carelessly prepared, relatively unimportant compilation of old laws. On the franchise question the old seventeenth-century statutes were displayed once again. Historians have read the 1750 preamble with great interest: "Whereas several persons of un-governed conversation have thrust themselves into the towns of this colony upon pretense of being hired servants. . . . " [12] Some historians have assumed this was happening in 1750. Actually this preamble was copied word for word from the preamble of a law of 1682.[13] Probably the committee which decided to keep the seventeenth-century preamble and laws "on the books" did so as a matter of habit. These laws may well have been a dead letter before their display in the 1750 code and perhaps remained so afterwards.

Second, there is the matter of the humble and unqualified men (by the standards of the 1750 code), who were elected to town offices in Kent. In 1739 among the twenty-seven elected Kent officers were five who could not have had enough property to qualify.[14] Of these propertyless men, Samuel Bates and Caleb Morgan were elected to the responsible post of lister, Stephen Pain became a highway surveyor, and William Porter and Samuel Wright were made haywards.[15] It might be argued that since statutes did not require town offices to be held by town-meeting voters, we should not be surprised at the election of such excluded men, particularly when the town was new and short on manpower. The present writer finds it hard to envision an ambiguous status where a Caleb Morgan could hold a highly responsible town post but could not "intermeddle in town affairs." The writer believes that propertyless Bates, Pain, Morgan, Porter, and Wright (all but Pain were sons of proprietors), attended town meetings, argued, voted, served on committees, and were elected to office.[16]

Third, the writer is impressed with the total lack of any documentation or mention of any mechanism for distinguishing Class III and Class II inhabitants. If the old seventeenth-century distinctions had really been maintained, surely the records would reveal lists of town-meeting voters or would make some mention of a distinction in minutes of town meetings.[17] Minutes of town meetings at Kent, Cornwall, and Sharon in the eighteenth century nearly always started with the words: "At a legally warned meeting of the inhabitants of Kent holden on the seventh day of March . . . etc." The language implied that all these inhabitants voted. The clerk recorded: "It was voted we will build a bridge . . ." There was never mention of legally qualified voters or any hint of distinctions among inhabitants. Most significant, the Kent town meetings decided a number of issues on which local feeling ran high. There were close votes, protests against illegal procedures, and appeals to the General Assembly to arbitrate. Amid all the wranglings and close votes, no question was ever recorded about the qualifications of the voters.[18]

In Edward Kendall's study of the Connecticut franchise, written in 1807, his comments on the freemen were detailed and supported by references to current statutes. On non-freemen or admitted inhabitants he was vague. Indeed, his only comments about them were speculations as to their role in the seventeenth century. His omission of any reference to property requirements for town-meeting voters suggests that the whole subject had become devoid of interest and importance.[19]

Fourth, as will be explained below, when Connecticut devised plans for her ratifying convention for the Federal Constitution, it was provided that delegates to the ratifying convention in Hartford were to be elected not by freemen alone but by town-meeting voters. This step tends to confirm the obsolescence of the old town-meeting-voter qualifications. If such qualifications were actually being enforced, throwing open the elections to the town-meeting voters would have been no concession to democracy. The town-meeting-voter qualifications were technically stricter than the freeman qualifications! [20] The present writer concludes that allowing town-meeting voters to participate in the election of delegates was a democratic move and was democratic because enforcement of town-meeting-voter qualifications had long since ceased.[21]

Town Government: Elected Selectmen and Appointed Justices

If all adult males except "strangers" could be town-meeting voters, it remains to be established whether or not the officials chosen in town meetings, notably the selectmen, constituted the real civil authority in the community. Some historians have suggested that *appointed* justices of the peace exercised basic administrative control.

In the new western counties [of Massachusetts] at least, the sources suggest that the administrative control which the justices exercised from the quarter-sessions bench approached tyranny . . . . the exact extent to which the county courts thwarted democratic processes needs as much careful study as Dr. Brown has given the franchise.[22]

In Connecticut the fear that appointed judges or justices might inhibit democracy would have less justification than in Massachusetts. In Connecticut these officials were appointed, but they were chosen by a government each member of which (governor, assistants, town deputies) was himself popularly elected each year.[23] The electorate thus held an indirect check. Actually such a check was seldom employed as the same justices were usually reappointed year after year. In the early years at Kent, Timothy Hatch and Ephraim Hubbel were "perpetual" justices of the peace. In the seventies and eighties John Ransom and Jedediah Hubbel had similar longevity. The reappointment of these men year after year was part and parcel of the Connecticut political arrangement of the eighteenth century. At Kent, on the matter of justices the "arrangement" appeared to work out to the advantage of all concerned.

The justices of the peace at Kent were not tyrannical and they did not "thwart democratic processes" because: (1) in administration, the justices were subordinate to the elected selectmen; (2) they possessed few legal powers which could affect democratic processes; (3) they were sparing in the use of these powers; (4) they were respected men who kept in the good graces of the majority.

The Connecticut statutes of the eighteenth century conferred the major administrative powers on the elected selectmen. The pound keeper operated a pound "erected by the selectmen." [24] The sealers of weights and measures checked all town standards by means of master weights and measures furnished by the selectmen.[25] Grand jurors shared with selectmen the responsibility for proper education of the children.[26] As indicated above, the selectmen were responsible for all problems relating to support of the poor, management of incompetents, and removal of undesirable strangers. In many of these activities the concurrence of a justice of the peace was necessary; but it was a selectman who initiated the proceeding. Of major importance, the selectmen were charged with responsibility for the admission of freemen.

In times of emergency it was the selectmen who shouldered the responsibility of government. During the Revolution the selectmen were responsible for providing arms for the militia.[27] One of the touchiest jobs during the Revolution was the requisitioning of grain for the support of the armies. In 1779, for example, Connecticut promised the Continental Army 15,000 bushels of wheat. When Kent furnished 200 bushels of wheat and twenty-five of rye, it was the selectmen who designated the farmers who must furnish the grain (with compensation). The selectmen were given the authority to seize supplies if necessary.[28] Finally, the selectmen were to help fill the soldier quotas for the Connecticut Line. An Act of 1781 provided that where any town was deficient in meeting its quota, "The selectmen, after consulting commanding officers of the several military companies, shall have liberty and authority to designate and point out soldiers to the number of their deficiencies." [29]

In comparing authority of the elected town officials with that of the appointed justices, it might be observed that constables, grand jurors, tax listers, tax collectors, tithingmen, and fence viewers were all elected annually. It would be needlessly burdensome to list all their duties. Along with the selectmen, these officials carried on the main administrative work of the town.

The justices of the peace were important men but their duties were almost entirely judicial and passive. Their main function was trying small cases in the justice courts. They also were a party to certain legal procedures. Where fence viewers, for example, found broken fences, they went to the justice for a warrant against the offender. Again, highway surveyors would report malingerers (work on highways was compulsory for adult, able-bodied males), to the town justices. All land deals were recorded by the town clerk in the presence of a justice.

In many communities leadership and executive authority go with the man rather than with the office. Undoubtedly many justices became dominant leaders in various towns, and some eighteenth-century writers were impressed. A leading jurist, Zephaniah Swift, wrote in 1785:

Justices of the peace are considered as the civil authority of the town in which they dwell and have extensive power in directing and advising about the management of the offices of the town.[30]

Edward Kendall, making a detailed study of town and state government in 1807, disagreed. Kendall stated:

The selectmen compose the real civil authority . . . . The justices of the peace, as lawful and even principal inhabitants, have unquestionably much power and influence; and the statutes occasionally join them with the selectmen, in the exercise of magisterial duties.[31]

If a justice of the peace happened to possess a tyrannical nature and happened to feel inclined to thwart democratic processes, it is difficult to see where he could find any statutory authority for his "thwarting." Town meetings could be summoned, they could enact all necessary laws and measures (by majority vote of virtually all adult males), and they could elect each year all town officials except the justices. All this could be done without let or hindrance from any justice of the peace. If we continue to envision a callous justice wishing to deal harshly with the townsmen, we must picture him in a passive role. He could strike only after an elected constable, an elected selectman, or other elected official presented him with a complaint.

The justice did appear to have one check on the electoral process. According to statutes in effect in 1807: "Any justice may set aside the town election, at his discretion on the appeal of the party elected." [32] At first glance this appears to be a formidable power. However, the justice could thwart an election only where the *winner* appealed to him. This provision did no more than offer relief to harassed townsmen who were elected to too many offices against their wishes (and were threatened by a fine for refusal to serve).

Far from being tyrants, the Kent justices appear to have been among the most respected men of the town. John Ransom was a justice continually in Kent from 1752 to 1777 and a look at his career may be instructive. He was one of the first settlers to reach Kent in 1739. Previously a resident of Colchester, he apparently became interested in the Kent venture when the group of Colchester families (Lewises, Pratts, Beebes, Fullers), moved west to help found the town.

Like the other settlers, Ransom was in the prime of life. He was thirty years old when he left Colchester for Kent in 1739 along with his wife Bethiah (sister of Samuel Lewis, Kent's first town clerk), and two children. Actually, Ransom seems always to have been in the prime of life. His first son Robert was born in 1733 and a daughter followed in 1735. He appears to have had five more children in the forties by his first wife, Bethiah, and then four more by her in the fifties. After Bethiah died in 1771, he took a deep breath and married Rebeccah Baldwin in 1775. Still full of energy, he served as a lieutenant in the Continental Army during the Revolution. His genealogist descendant, Wyth C. Ransom, credited him with eleven more children by his second wife (for a total of twenty-two). He died in 1797 at the age of eighty-eight.[33]

John Ransom, esquire, did not enjoy any privileged economic status. He was a proprietor (as were nearly all the original settlers), having bought his share from absentee Thomas Tozer of Lyme in 1739. He was one of the few settlers who lacked strong speculative inclinations. During the early years of trading ferment he made but two sales and five purchases. Accordingly, his property showing on the tax list was substantial but never impressively high. Starting at £31 in 1740, he climbed steadily by small increments to reach £143 in 1760. A series of gifts to three of his sons, Robert, John Junior, and Charles, reduced his tax list to the £60 level where it remained in the later years of his life. A son, John, Junior, showed more property than his father in the seventies and eighties. Much of John Ransom's economic interest centered around his saw, grist, and fulling mills. Writs ordering a defendant's appearance before Justice Ransom always said "At his house by his fulling mill."

Justice Ransom was deeply involved in debt procedures. He prepared original writs of attachments and conducted trials of small debtors in his Justice Court. One suspects that he may have been sympathetic to the interests of debtors, for he had been a defendant and lost debt suits himself. At the July session of the Litchfield County Court in 1752 Ransom was a losing defendant against a Sharon creditor and suffered a judgment of £98.[34] In 1789 it was necessary for him to mortgage his homelot and fulling mill. He obtained an £86 mortgage from Abraham Beecher.

The means by which such a family man, mill operator, and debtor become a justice of the peace are instructive. He climbed the ladder of elective offices and so demonstrated competence and won respect. During his first year in Kent he was elected to the minor post of "brander of horses," a position to which he was reelected four successive years. In 1741 he was elected to the additional post of fence viewer, still a minor office but more responsible in that he was to report offenders. In 1744 he was elected a highway surveyor and, more important, in this year he was first elected a grand juror. A grand juror was essentially a town prosecutor. Although such officers served on the county grand jury, their main responsibility was to "enquire after and make presentment of all misdemeanors to the justice or the county court." [35]

Presumably John Ransom's performance in these minor offices gave him increased stature in the eyes of the town electors. In 1746 he was elected constable and was reelected each year until his appointment as a justice of the peace in 1752. Finally, in 1747 he was elected to the town's highest post, selectman. He served in this office in 1747 and 1750–52. On the basis of this record, it would appear that in 1752 when the General Assembly had the task of appointing a new justice for Kent, it found in John Ransom an ideal choice. The government selected a man of medium economic status who had acquired experience as prosecutor, policeman, and administrator and in these roles had received repeated votes of confidence from the people.

Justices seldom held other town offices once they were appointed to their judicial position. However, they could and did serve as town deputies to the General Assembly. Ransom was frequently elected Kent's deputy to the General Assembly during the 1760s and 1770s, thus demonstrating that his elevation to the bench had not cost him the esteem of the town freemen. That Connecticut justices were generally popular with the freeman is evident from the fact that over half served as justice and deputy concurrently.[36]

Our only glimpses of John Ransom, esquire, in his role of justice of the peace come from the records of his justice court. We see his judicious settlement of typical town quarrels that were often picturesque and often ridiculous. Jehiel Barnum with "clubs, fists, and swords" assaulted the body of Abner Kelsey and "made him incapable of business for a long time." This assault is difficult to visualize. Presumably Ransom settled it amicably for at least no property changed hands.

Joseph Washburn appeared before Ransom with a complaint.

He had been peacefully feeding his twenty good sheep when a "spiteful dog" intruded. (One can easily visualize that spiteful dog.) The dog, owned by Nathanial Butler, scattered the sheep, "worried them," and killed one worth 15 shillings. Joseph was awarded damages but the amount is illegible.

Most picturesque was a deer hunt of 1771. Three New Yorkers (from the Oblong, just over the line), were "a hunting after deer" with two bloodhounds. The dogs drove the deer into Fuller Pond whereupon the hunters "did discharge three guns loaded with powder and lead." The deer, allegedly wounded, floundered out of the pond, plunged down the side of Fuller mountain, and swam the Housatonic River only to fall into the waiting arms of a Kent farmer, Samuel Miller. When the breathless hunters and dogs arrived, they found Miller calmly "adressin said deer." Miller, contrary to "antient custom time out of mind" refused to hand over any part of the deer. The settlement? Ransom was a Kent man and perhaps he had no love for New Yorkers, bloodhounds, or deer hunters. Miller kept all of the deer.[37]

It is necessary to move on from clubs, dogs, and deer in order to summarize Ransom's role as a justice. His cases were small affairs. They did not pit rich creditors against poor debtors but simply involved a hodgepodge of town quarrels. Since there was no discernible pattern of wealthy versus poor at Kent, it is impossible to range Ransom on either side. The idea that justices were tyrants and thwarted democracy seems untenable for this town.

It has also been suggested that there may have been thwarting of democracy by the county courts. The Litchfield County Court (if we may go by its records and the colony statutes) confined its activities to the trial of cases, 99 percent of which were debt cases. The only apparent intrusion into town affairs was to license the tavern keepers. One must conclude that for Kent, very likely for her six sister towns, and possibly for all Connecticut, town government was notably free from control by the colony judiciary.

Our final conclusion about political democracy in Kent must be a mixed one. At the local level, democracy appeared complete. Practically all adult males could participate in town government, and the annually elected town officials (rather than the appointed justices), constituted the civil authority. In practice, justices of the peace were popular men who received numerous "votes of confidence" in their frequent elections as town deputies.

Political democracy at the colony level was more complex. On the democratic side was the fact that freemanship seemed attainable eventually by nearly all adult males. The property qualifications posed but a slight barrier to an agricultural population. In 1751, 79 percent of the adult males in Kent could qualify, and most of those who were below the requirements in that year soon climbed to qualification status. Not only could most adult males vote, but their deputies enjoyed disproportionate power, for Kent and her sister towns were overrepresented in the General Assembly. Although Connecticut was governed by a clique of directors, these leaders seemed closely related to Kent men through blood ties. Their benevolent paternalism was appreciated by Kent freemen, who willingly supported the established order.

On the undemocratic side we noted that lessening economic opportunity after 1777 was tending to narrow the entryway to freemanship. In 1796, 11 percent of Kent's male inhabitants were destined to remain in Kent below the qualification level. It was also discovered that many qualifiers did not bother to become freemen. A percentage of "apathy" that was around 35 percent in mid-century rose to 50 percent by 1796.

Conservatives include a wide variety of men, but a common trait is satisfaction with existing conditions. Political democracy at Kent met the requirements of most inhabitants. Like the colony itself, Kent was a "land of steady habits" where conservatism stemmed in part from an appreciation of the political status quo.

PART IV

Social Democracy at Kent

When the Marquis de Chastellux passed through Kent in 1780, he was impressed by the number of new settlers obtaining freeholds for themselves. It is possible that he noticed the new farm of David Whittelsey and was referring to such a man when he commented on the rapidity with which young pioneers were becoming "comfortable planters." [1] Certainly this young man enjoyed economic opportunity for his tax list showed the following property:

1774	£ 18- 0-0	(poll tax only—no property)
1775	28-18-0	
1776	35- 9-0	
1777	48-10-6	(his highest rating)
1780	46- 8-0	

Similarly, Whittelsey had soon acquired political privileges. His election to the office of town lister in 1776 suggests activity in town meetings, and the presence of his name on the "Enrollment of Freemen" for 1777 informs us that he played a role in colony government. In general, our study of Kent has suggested that most of the "Whittelseys,' (if we may so designate the mass of obscure, middle-class farmers), enjoyed economic and political democracy.

David Whittelsey, however, never became a town leader. One suspects that despite his auspicious start in Kent, a further advance was blocked by certain barriers. The "Whittelseys" of Kent appear to have been "kept in their places."

In our study of social democracy at Kent we propose to examine these barriers. Many historians have attributed them to a gentry class that owed its position to "blood, wealth, and the support of the Church." [2] This elite group is said to have clung tenaciously to its privileged position.

Members of the gentry made their influence felt in every sphere of town life. At Church . . . at town meetings . . . as proprietors . . . the New England squires saw to it that the town thought as they thought and acted as they would have it act.[3]

At Kent the barriers are not so easily explained. However, if we learn who the leaders were, how they achieved power, and how they held it, we may have a better understanding of the nature of social democracy on the Connecticut frontier.

10

THE TOWN LEADERS OF KENT

Although many writers have felt that town leadership was furnished by proprietors, gentry, or squires, such privileged groups were not necessarily prominent in Kent. Perhaps the possession of considerable property was the touchstone that insured a position of authority and prestige. Or possibly ability and energy made one a leader despite lowly economic or social status. In the present chapter we will endeavor to learn who the town leaders were and how they obtained their posts.

Proprietors, Gentry, and Squires

One of the discrepancies between the standard version of an eighteenth-century town on the New England frontier and the evidence at Kent arises over the status of the town proprietors. The difficulty may be traced to Roy H. Akagi's *Town Proprietors of New England*, the definitive and only general monograph on the subject. Akagi concluded:

The proprietors constituted a privileged class through claims of blood, wealth, and influence backed by the pronounced support of the Church. Thus the bulk of the freemen, instinctively inclined to democracy, found it difficult to tolerate the existence of such a lordly gentry class within their town limits.[1]

Akagi assumed (without supporting evidence from the history of Connecticut), that a few rich "gentry" purchased shares and became a lordly, ruling class. Actually, at Kent and her sister auction towns, the majority of original settlers became proprietors. The rapid turnover of shares was part of the speculative boom in which nearly all settlers participated. Of Kent's original forty-five settlers, at least thirty-two were proprietors. Eighty different Kent residents took turns owning proprietary shares between 1740 and 1760—this with an adult male population rising from only forty-five in 1740 to only 129 in 1751. The list of proprietors at Kent is not precisely a cross section of the town population. Most of the richer men and only a few of the poorer were proprietors. But there was no evidence of class cleavage. Proprietors John Ransom and John Beebe swept the meetinghouse for fifteen shillings a year. Proprietors Philip Judd, William Roberts, and Samuel Bates had unimpressive property holdings. Proprietor Joseph Pack was the town drunk.[2]

In our examination of social democracy at Kent, in our search for badges of privilege, and in our analysis of leadership groups there is simply no place for proprietors. In the early days of the town when proprietary shares had at least a property value, possession of such shares was no distinguishing mark because so many had them. Cash was not necessary at the Windham auction. The buy-now-pay-later plan (the two years to pay were later extended), meant that virtually any man with some nerve and the energy to ride or walk to Windham could become a Kent proprietor. After 1750 the proprietors did constitute a minority group in the Kent population, but by this time most of the good land had been distributed and the shares had little value.

Just as "proprietors" fail to provide a key to an understanding of town leadership, we may be equally suspicious of "gentry" or "squirearchy." The present writer believes that these words should be used only with great caution for New England and not at all for towns in western Connecticut. A true gentry would be found where large landholdings had accumulated and were protected by primogeniture and entail. Neither condition applied in western Connecticut.[3] Moreover, with any original aristocrats producing squadrons of children, there would be a devastating diffusion of blood by the fourth generation. As suggested above, nearly every inhabitant of Kent had a "distinguished old Connecticut name."

"Gentry" will not suffice as a class label because unless a committee of historians agrees on what the term means, no one will know where to draw a line. One wonders if John Mills was "gentry." He had distinguished descendants in the clergy and was the richest man in town. Today his hilltop house remains one of the stateliest in Kent. On the other hand, he had middle-class origins and his sons included farmers, storekeepers, and a tavern-keeper. Mills' voice seems to have been negligible in town affairs and his highest honor was his appointment as a militia lieutenant. Perhaps a busybody like Joseph Cary was a member of the "gentry." In the space of three years he was a tithingman, grand juror, tax collector, tax lister (assessor), highway surveyor, and constable. He certainly did his share of running the town. However, his property, a mere £40 on the common list, rated him in the lower half of all Kent property owners. It is no wonder that historians have argued about numbers and influence of gentry. Depending on one's definition, one can enroll two-thirds of the town in the gentry class, or better yet, none at all.

"Squire," or "esquire," on the other hand, can and should be precisely defined. Despite the caution of some historians, we need not be vague about the word's meaning in Connecticut. A "squire" was any justice of the peace, any judge of a higher court, and any magistrate from assistant up to governor, but *not* a deputy. Only such positions rated the title. Deputies, selectmen, deacons, militia officers, or men of outstanding wealth were never called "squire" because of such status.[4]

Squirearchy, if used to designate the class of men who were squires, is no more useful than gentry. There were too few squires. The squirearchy at Kent for the first fourteen years comprised just Timothy Hatch and Ephraim Hubbel. These were prominent men but they stood only twenty-seventh and twenty-third in wealth; and in governmental authority they were no more than partners with such fellow-leaders as Jabez Swift, Nathaniel Berry, Joseph Fuller, Abel Wright, Joseph Pratt, and Nathaniel Swift.

Town Leaders and "Mass of Town Officers"

With "proprietors" too broad a term, "gentry" too vague, and "squirearchy" too narrow, the present writer proposes to use the prosaic but serviceable term, town leader. A town leader was simply an influential man who was entrusted with top responsibility, honored by his fellow-townsmen, and listened to with respect.

If we use the label town leader, we have the problem of definition once again. The offices held by Joseph Cary, for example, may not have been exalted enough to qualify him as a town leader. Actually, the town positions can be divided into two rather distinct categories: first, positions of honor and leadership including selectmen, justices of the peace, moderators, church deacons, militia officers, and ministers; second, the mass of town offices. In many ways the system seemed analogous to the military with its distinction between commissioned and noncommissioned officers. If selectmen and justices were the colonels or majors, then constables and grand jurors were the sergeants, and haywards were the corporals.

The writer justifies this division partly on the basis of the duties of the officers in question but mainly on the basis of the officeholding pattern at Kent. As to duties, the selectmen and justices have been discussed above in Chapter 9. Together they constituted the civil authority of the town. Moderators are included as town leaders because of their probable ability to sway town and proprietors' meetings.[5] Deacons appear to have been influential in the "hire and fire" of ministers and in the maintenance of town moral discipline. Finally, militia officers (captain, lieutenant and ensign) conducted the four militia musters held annually. More important, they alone had responsibility for calling out the trainband in the event of Indian attack or other emergency. The four sergeants in a militia company were elected by their men. Officers were similarly elected but confirmed and announced by the General Assembly.[6]

It is difficult to appraise the role of ministers as town leaders. During the seventeenth century Connecticut was a "Bible Commonwealth" in which "the civil rulers, seeking to rule in accordance with the will of God, sought counsel of the divines."[7] The minister was frequently an awe-inspiring figure[8] but his influence declined after 1700.[9] Most historians have been noncommittal about the ability of ministers to influence secular affairs in the eighteenth century. However, Ola Winslow has written: "The

country minister was close enough to his people to be their un-
official spokesman in community affairs," [10] and one suspects this
situation applied at Kent.

Kent's First Society had only two ministers during the entire
span of years from 1741 to 1812; first, Cyrus Marsh, and then Joel
Bordwell. Both were educated and propertied men. Marsh in particular appeared to possess qualities of leadership, for after leaving
the ministry he became a justice of the peace. Bordwell married
the daughter of John Mills. His house, the oldest in Kent, is said
to have been a present from his wealthy father-in-law.

Church records show instances where parishioners were dis-
ciplined, and in several cases the minister appears to have initiated
the action.[11] Perhaps the most important Kent evidence on the
subject of minister leadership is the fact that the first name on
every "Freemen's Roll" was that of the minister. Joel Bordwell
was also the leadoff signer of the "Oath of Fidelity" in 1777.

On the other hand, the record of salary wrangles in town
meetings and the demonstrated hire-and-fire power which the
town held raise doubts as to the status of the minister as a town
leader.[12] Times had changed. In the seventeenth century a minister might lead his flock to a new location in the wilderness and
guide his parishioners in the founding of their town. In the eighteenth century towns like Kent were founded by groups or fragments from several different towns none of which brought a
minister with them. Once settled and incorporated, a town like
Kent then shopped around for some available clergyman willing
to accept the meager salary offered.[13] Where a Marsh or Bordwell
had long tenures, they may well have won the hearts and respect
of the townsmen. The extent to which they utilized this respect in
governmental matters is not made clear by the records.[14]

The actual pattern of officeholding at Kent helps significantly
in distinguishing town leaders from the lower category, mass of
town officers. Both categories tended to be mutually exclusive.
Only one man, Gideon Barnum, was ever a moderator in Kent
without first having served as selectman. Only one man, John
Beebe, was ever elected and confirmed a militia officer without
having served as a selectman or justice. Town leaders did not

TABLE 17

LEADERSHIP AND PROPERTY

	"Leader" Rank	*"Leader Points"*	Selectman	Justice
Timothy Hatch	1	54	•	•
Ephraim Hubbel	2	54	•	•
Nathaniel Berry	3	52	•	
Jabez Swift	4	44	•	•
John Ransom	5	44	•	•
Joseph Fuller	6	42	•	
Abel Wright	7	42	•	
Nathaniel Swift	8	42	•	
Joshua Lassell	9	32	•	
Joseph Pratt	10	32	•	
Samuel Waller	11	32	•	
Samuel Averill	12	22	•	
Benjamin Brownson	13	22	•	
Daniel Comstock	14	22	•	
John Mills	15	22	•	
Azariah Pratt	16	22	•	
Ebenezer Barnum	17	12	•	
Matthew Beals	18	12	•	
Nathan Eliot	19	12		•
Benjamin Newcomb	20	12	•	
John Porter	21	12	•	
Abraham Raymond	22	12	•	
Gideon Barnum	23	10		
John Beebe	24	10		
Daniel Comstock, Jr.	25	10		

Barnabus Hatch
Ebenezer Washburn
Daniel Church
Stephen Noble
Reuben Swift
Benjamin Eaton
Nathaniel Slosson
Eliphalet Comstock
Jonathan Morgan

Agent	Moderator	Deacon	Militia	Property (in pounds)	Property Rank
•	•		•	93	27
•	•		•	119	19
•	•	•	•	172	4
•	•			238	1
	•		•	143	11
•	•			203	3
•	•		•	152	7
•	•		•	115	21
•	•			115	20
•	•			169	5
	•		•	144	9
•				92	28
•				103	24
		•		110	23
			•	227	2
		•		127	17
				94	26
				58	—[a]
				132	15
				65	—
				55	—
	•			91	30
				112	22
			•	131	16
		•		142	13
				161	6
				144	8
				143	10
				142	11
				141	14
				121	18
				115	21
				98	25
				91	29

[a] Beals, Newcomb, and Porter are not ranked because their low totals would place them far down in the list of all property owners, probably between 150th and 300th.

hold lower posts. Similarly the mass of town officers rotated in the lower offices. Some like John Ransom did climb into the leadership ranks but most alternated among constable, grand juror, lister, etc.

The distinction between the two groups is further emphasized by noting the men who were designated by the town to prepare special petitions or serve as agents to the General Assembly. For such missions Kent always chose town leaders. In Table 17 the author has rated town leaders by a point system. The eleven men who served as agents correspond almost precisely to the top eleven leaders.

It is important to realize that in average-sized frontier towns like Kent, Cornwall, Sharon, or Salisbury a large proportion of all adult males had to hold office. In 1739 Kent's adult population of forty-five had to fill thirty-one offices. When the adult male population reached 321 in 1777, there were eighty-four offices to be filled. Historians may use this information in three ways. First, they may ignore it or shrug it off with the implication that such officeholders were controlled by the "squirearchy." Second, they may go to the opposite extreme and find that many poor men were officials and therefore enjoyed social democracy.[15] Finally, they may take a middle course and distinguish between two categories of town office holders. This last procedure, followed by the present writer at Kent, will show that humble men could be fence viewers or highway surveyors and could thus display some mild authority in these roles. But it will also show a lack of complete social democracy. It will show a system whose operation produced a rather exclusive group—one is tempted to say clique—of town leaders who possessed the basic power and authority in the town.

Property and Office

Kent officeholders tended to show a correlation between leadership status and property. At the top level of town leaders the correlation is indicated by Table 17. This table undertakes to indicate the top twenty-five town leaders on the basis of points assigned for various leadership posts held between 1740 and 1777. Men are listed in order of their leadership rank. Two columns at the right show, for purpose of comparison, their highest property holding on the tax list and their rank among other propertied men.[16]

The twenty-five town leaders correspond generally with the top thirty property owners. It is significant that only three men, Beals, Newcomb, and Porter, held a top office without being among the property leaders. Of these, Porter does not really break the pattern for he remained in Kent only until 1740 and in that year his list of £55 was seventh highest in the town. Of the top ten leaders only Timothy Hatch and Ephriam Hubbel are moderately out of line. Berry, Swift, and Wright correspond almost perfectly on leadership and property rankings.

Not only did the town leaders tend to be among the wealthiest men, but the mass of officeholders were an economic cut above non-officeholders. In 1777 Kent had eighty-six offices to fill. The average property holding for all eighty-six officeholders was £80. Table 18 gives the breakdown by offices.[17]

TABLE 18
PROPERTY OF KENT OFFICEHOLDERS IN 1777

Office	No. of Officials	Average Property (in pounds)	High (in pounds)	Low (in pounds)
Selectmen	5	125	159	88
Provision collectors	4	114	160	50
Packers	3	105	185	41
Constables	3	103	126	67
Fence viewers	8	95	150	31
Treasurer	1	95	95	95
Grand jurors	10	82	138	21
Highway surveyors	21	74	127	31
Listers	9	69	144	21
Sealers	3	69	95	43
Key keepers	4	66	93	43
Collectors	5	63	80	36
Tithingmen	6	55	141	27
Leather sealers	3	55	72	31
Town clerk	1	50	50	50

These figures and averages do show that most officeholders were above average in wealth. The average of £80 for office-holders may be compared with the total town figures for 1777. In that year 146 men were over £48 and 174 were beneath it. Eighty-three men were in the "poor" classification (below £30) and of these, only two were officeholders. In the lower-middle-class category (£30–48) only fourteen of the ninety-one members held town offices. Finally, seventy of the office holders, or 82 percent, came from the so-called upper-middle group (£49 and up).

Attainment of Town-Leader Status

We have suggested that nearly all town positions were held by men of property, and that the top offices were filled by a small group or clique of the town's wealthiest men. However, Kent's "aristocracy" was essentially one of ability. Property and social prestige may have helped, but neither appeared to be the crucial factor in raising a man to the rank of town leader. Rather, an exceptionally able man would become a town leader on the basis of his shrewdness and ambition (for dealing with the General Assembly), his energy (for administering town affairs), and his poise and qualities of leadership (for running town meetings). Officeholding would be closely connected with property because in an era of intense land speculation and in a town where land values were soaring, those who were most shrewd, energetic, poised, and eager for power (thus becoming town leaders), were likely to be the richest men.

It is difficult to prove such an hypothesis but evidence at Kent would seem to support it. Significant, perhaps, was the practice of using selectmen or other town leaders as agents when the town wanted to win over the General Assembly. That town leaders Hatch, Hubbel, Berry, Fuller, and Swift were often picked to argue before the General Assembly would seem to indicate their undoubted ability. In an emergency like the Merryall dispute, Kent would hardly pick an agent because he lived in a large house or had an impressive social pedigree. It is notable that the best men and the town leaders were one and the same.

A number of wealthy men seemed to lack qualities of leadership. John Mills was never a moderator, never an agent, and was selectman for one year only. The Comstocks, though high in property ranking, were low on leadership. Daniel Comstock, Junior, was indeed a deacon for many years, but he may have gained this post through his frosty moral posture and his awe-inspiring (for Kent) intellectualism.[18] If these wealthy men were doubtful town leaders, then nine of the top thirty property holders establish the contention still more firmly. These nine, shown at the bottom of Table 17 on page 148, held no positions of leadership whatsoever.

Also revealing was the officeholding record of sons of the first-generation town leaders. If inherited property and social position provided the touchstone, we would expect young Hatches, Hubbels, Swifts, Berrys and Ransoms to succeed their fathers. These sons were indeed high on the tax lists in the 1770s and 1780s, but usually other and perhaps more capable men ran the town.[19]

11

"STEADY HABITS" AT KENT

In studying social democracy at Kent our aim is to determine the nature of barriers that might have kept an average inhabitant, say a David Whittelsey, "in his place," barriers that could have prevented his attaining a post higher than lister or a status above the mass of town office holders. Thus far we have shown that his advance was not blocked by proprietors, gentry, or squires. Neither was property the touchstone, for Whittelsey's wealthy neighbors (Joseph Berry, Eliphalet Comstock, Abraham Fuller, Nathaniel Hatch, and Abijah Hubbel), were likewise excluded from the inner circle of leaders. Instead, Whittelsey could look up to Kent's leading magistrate, John Ransom, esquire, and realize that ambition and sheer ability had carried him to his top town post.

At the risk of oversimplifying we may say that David Whittelsey, regardless of his ability, was barred from high office for one reason. Someone else had got there first. The top leaders of Kent such as John Ransom and Ephraim Hubbel lived on and on, and served on and on (both were in office for over forty years). With annual elections the voters could have spread the leading offices among many. Indeed, between 1740 and 1760 they could have chosen over one hundred different selectmen, fifteen different militia officers, forty deacons, sixty moderators, and forty agents or petition writers. These 255 potential posts were held by only twenty-five men, and only sixteen men held 85 percent of these. The handful of men listed as town leaders on page 275 monopolized the top posts often holding two or more concurrently.

If Whittelsey was blocked by a Ransom or a Hubbel, a final

question might be raised as to why the voters kept returning the same venerable leaders. Competent performance of duty may supply half the explanation. The other half may have arisen from the conditioned conservatism of the Kent voters. Certain institutions tended to keep them steady. The schools in Kent supported the church; the church in turn taught respect for leaders; and the leaders could capitalize on the "awe" generated in the people and complete the cycle by exercising some thought control.

Schools in Kent

The first school in Kent was built as soon as the earliest settlers arrived and is mentioned in the minutes of proprietors' meeting in May, 1739.[1] By 1812 the number of Kent schools had reached thirteen with ten in Kent proper and three in the outlying societies.[2] The presence of these primary schools in Kent could be interpreted as democratic [3] or aristocratic.[4] To be democratic, schools should be free and open to all. At Kent the records can tell us the extent of schooling and the manner of defraying its cost. On the other hand, if colonial education was designed to teach respect for authority, we would expect to find evidence of such intent in the school curriculum. Direct evidence on what was taught at Kent is missing but indirect evidence can be helpful.

All Kent children appear to have received a primary education. Connecticut laws required that towns maintain schools, "those towns containing seventy families or more to keep school eleven months of each year" and those with less than seventy to provide education for six months.[5] At Kent the minutes of town meetings suggest a veritable ferment of school building. Some twenty separate references to school construction appear during the first ten years. In the December meeting in 1745, for example, it was voted:

We will build three school houses or more: one near the spring between Jabez Swift and Reuben Swift; one in the best place near Timothy Hatch; and finish the one between Daniel Comstock, Junior and Jehiel Benton.[6]

The locations were always carefully specified, the idea being to distribute school houses as equitably as possible among a scattered population. A typical ruling provided that "the inhabitants from John Ransom's to Abraham Raymond's can build their own school . . . not extending further east than the mountain." [7]

The problems of obtaining teachers were also aired frequently in town meetings.

The School Committee is empowered to employ a schoolmaster for six months and a school dam or dams the rest part of the year for school to be kept in the several parts of the town according to the number of scholars for each part according to former votes.[8]

A typical "covenant" with a teacher covered a year's teaching, and salaries were in the neighborhood of £40 (lawful money).[9]

Whereas it appears probable that all the youth of Kent went to primary school, such education was not "free," as part of the expense was born by the pupils' parents. In general government financial support was quite generous in Connecticut. The colony treasury paid 40 shillings outright for each £1000 on the common list of any town. Kent's common list averaged about £10,000 in the eighteenth century, so this support was enough to pay one schoolmaster for six months.[10] More important, one fifty-third of all Kent land, (the School Right), was sold and the proceeds loaned at interest for support of the schools. A town meeting resolution provided:

The School Committee chosen from year to year shall have power to call on the original committee that sold the School Right and draw out the interest money to pay for schooling.[11]

A third source of public financial support would be town funds voted for a new schoolhouse. In 1750, for example, the town voted £120 for a school in East Greenwich Society.[12] Connecticut law provided that if public funds were not enough, the deficiency should be made up, 50 percent by the town and 50 percent by the parents of students.[13] Such assessments on parents were occasionally necessary at Kent. For example:

The School Committee should measure and find a center between James Stuart's and Reuben Swift's and erect a school to be supported one half by scholars attending and the other half by the town so long as the money shall last.[14]

Just as the records show that Kent possessed enough schools, teachers, and funds to provide a rudimentary education, they also show that the population was indeed literate. Practically all inhabitants affixed their signatures to land deeds at some time or other. No member of a Kent family who was raised in the town had to employ the "mark" device of an illiterate person. Kent education, then, was democratic in the sense that all acquired it. A groundwork was laid for democratic ideas if the pamphlets or books spreading such doctrine should ever reach the town.

Until after the Revolution, democratic aspects of the school system at Kent were probably overshadowed by the conservative nature of the curriculum. The acts passed by the General Assembly indicate a concern for orthodoxy. There was to be nothing frivolous or radical taught in the colony schools. Pupils were to master the "Three Rs," the catechism, and the laws relating to capital punishment.[15] Although Greek and Latin were to be taught in grammar schools (one for each county), these institutions were scarce, and Litchfield County had none until after the Revolution.[16] Private academies might have supplied this educational gap between primary grades and Yale College, but the government was fearful that "these might train up the youth in ill principles," and so they were outlawed in Connecticut until 1790.[17]

A close scrutiny of schools was maintained in the towns by selectmen, grand jurors, and the School Committee. The Code of 1750 ordered these officials to "visit and inspect" and "keep a vigilant eye." Where improper teaching was permitted to continue, the negligent selectmen were liable to a fine of 20 shillings.[18] Not only were Kent selectmen conservative and painstaking in their duties, but they were supported by the School Committee which was always composed of the town's top leaders. Timothy Hatch, Joseph Fuller, Nathaniel Berry, and Jabez Swift comprised the School Committee during the 1740s and 1750s.

The idea that education in Kent taught respect for magistrates and town leaders derives support from the close relationship between education and the Church. One of the pastoral duties of a Cyrus Marsh or a Joel Bordwell was to make the rounds of the schools and put the pupils through their catechism. One gathers that at Kent this was a solemn proceeding well calculated to "awe" the anxious pupil.[19] These pastors also acted as tutors for the sons of John Mills and for the few others who planned to enter the ministry and needed extra instruction to enter Yale.[20]

In conclusion we may note that the youth of Kent had learned to read and write, and had memorized the catechism and the laws on capital punishment; all this under the "vigilant eye" of a Timothy Hatch (selectmen, justice, and head of the School Committee) and a Cyrus March (pastor and later justice of the peace). When the time came to seek advice on how to vote in town or colony affairs, it seems probable that their education had made it easy and natural for them to "think as their leaders thought."

The Church at Kent

The "Church of Christ" at Kent, which was formally incorporated on April 29, 1741, helped to preserve steady habits and respect for authority. To the extent that Puritan orthodoxy still prevailed in western Connecticut in the mid-eighteenth century, the Kent church was indeed a bulwark of conservatism. On the other hand, where older ideas were breaking down, the "bulwark" was correspondingly weakened. The vicissitudes of Puritan theology form a vast backdrop to the history of Connecticut and New England during the seventeenth and eighteenth centuries. Only an outline of religious developments can be attempted here, enough perhaps to provide a setting for ideas and events in Kent.

"A PURITAN STRONGHOLD" [21]

The Puritan theory of government was grounded on the idea of original sin. If Adam had not fallen, no governments would have been necessary; but the sinful nature of man, confirmed by the Bible and experience, meant that man must live under the close scrutiny of magistrates.[22] Men should not stray from the fold. They should seek salvation together as a covenanted group, bound by covenant to each other and to God. Social solidarity then re-

quired "uniformity of thought and action." [23] Above all, it required the magistrates to lead toward the fulfillment of God's will
and the people to humbly and respectfully follow.[24]

After 1657 numerous forces tended to break down this ideol-
ogy. The development of the scientific method, of rationalism, and
of capitalistic and democratic ideas all played a part. As newcomers less pious than the "Saints" poured in, as the frontier conditions broke up the older communal forms of living, and as toleration of dissenting sects became necessary to prevent abrogation of
charters by the British government, the conservative influence of
the Church declined.[25]

In the "Puritan Stronghold" of Connecticut the greatest
changes wrought by the new forces occurred in the status of
Church membership. The Halfway Covenant, the Saybrook Platform, and various toleration acts of the General Assembly altered
the old concept of "one covenant, one body."

The Halfway Covenant of 1657 was the all-important first step
in broadening church membership and diluting the purity of the
original covenanted group. A synod of Massachusetts and Connecticut clergymen agreed that baptized inhabitants "who under-
stood religion" and were not "scandalous in their behavior" could
become church members (and thus make their children eligible
for baptism). The General Assembly of Connecticut recommended adoption in 1657. Most clergymen were gratified at enlarged church membership and many parishioners were doubtless
pleased at such a face-saving arrangement. They might outwardly
conform, enjoy the prestige of church membership, yet evade the
spiritual demands of orthodox Puritanism.[26]

From the Halfway Covenant it was but a short step to the
Saybrook Platform of 1708. Although this second statement of
policy was mainly concerned with the form of church government (it established a Presbyterian form of organization with
"consociations" serving as administrative units in each county),
it also indorsed (indirectly) the concept that mere belief or faith
was sufficient to entitle a communicant to full Church membership.[27] After acceptance of the Saybrook Platform in Connecticut,

there were conservative protests against the ease with which non-believers secured admittance to church membership, but the government failed to respond.[28]

Liberalization of church laws in Connecticut operated in two directions. While it was becoming far simpler to join the Church (after 1708 the desire to join and the formalities of admission were all that was necessary), the conditions of those outside the fold were also made easier. By an act of 1727 the General Assembly provided that although Anglicans must continue to pay equal Church rates along with all townsmen, these funds could be used to support their own church and minister. Quakers and Baptists were exempted from such taxes by an act of 1729 "provided they could produce a certificate showing membership in their own society."[29] The question then arose as to whether such dissenters could participate in town meetings, which were also parish meetings. After much agitation of this question the Connecticut General Assembly passed a compromise measure in 1746. Under this law, dissenters could vote in town meetings but not on Church affairs.[30]

The Great Awakening in Connecticut was both a revival of religious fervor and a twisting of original doctrines into new versions of protestantism.[31] Whereas the "Old Light" opponent of the Awakening stood for the principle of a learned clergy which alone might possess the intellectual capacity to solve the riddles of their complex doctrine, the "New Lights" believed in a simplified and "humanized" theology.[32] The Great Awakening was carried by "New Light," evangelical preachers, who sought a hearing in the various towns. Conservatives secured legislation to check such practices. In 1742 an act referred to the evil done by wandering ministers and provided that no preacher could visit a town unless approved by a majority of the town voters.[33] On the surface the "Old Lights" prevailed, particularly in western Connecticut; and through the middle years of the eighteenth century the colony remained in many respects a "Puritan Stronghold."

The American Revolution marked a major turning point. Although the Congregational clergy supported the patriot cause and gained prestige thereby,[34] the churches deteriorated during and after the war. Their postwar weakness has been attributed partly to dislocations of the war but mostly to the "spread of deism and French rationalism." [35] Thomas Paine was in vogue and the well known deism of Connecticut-born Ethan Allen "symbolized the rising revolt against the established order in New England." [36]

CONGREGATIONALISTS AND DISSENTERS IN KENT

In Kent, as in New England generally, much of the old Puritan doctrine remained while innovations were also present. If Connecticut Puritanism was the most conservative in New England, then perhaps Kent's "Old Light" orthodoxy made this town a conservative stronghold in Connecticut.

On April 29, 1741, eleven Kent men founded the Congregational Church in that town by publicly making a covenant with each other and God. They realized it was an "awful thing to transact with the living God." Nevertheless they counted on God's divine grace to uphold their faith. They "covenanted to walk together . . . to seek each other's spiritual good . . . to watch over each other . . . and to submit ourselves to such as are set over us in the Lord." [37] Most of the town's inhabitants soon joined the new Church by "taking the covenant." In May Daniel Comstock, Junior, Samuel Canfield, and ten wives of the original founders joined.[38] At least thirty-five more joined the first year, and a steady stream became members throughout the 1740s.[39]

Having covenanted among themselves to "submit to such as are set over us," the townsmen of Kent followed Pastor Cyrus Marsh and Justice Timothy Hatch in rebuffing any preachers of the Great Awakening who sought a hearing. Such "corrupt teachers" as James Clement, Richard Hallett, and Benjamin Ferris did appear in Kent, and the handful who listened to them "lost their Gospel Privileges for showing such unchristian disrespect."

The conservatives in Kent were impressed with the wisdom of the Act of 1742 requiring a majority vote to admit a visiting minister. However, with so scattered a settlement, Pastor Marsh did require assistance and it would be inconvenient to vote approval each week. The solution was to elect a permanent selection committee. Named to this committee were the town's three most conservative leaders, Timothy Hatch, Daniel Comstock, Junior,[40] and Joseph Fuller.

As the ferment of the Great Awakening continued to agitate other parts of Connecticut, Kent voters left no doubts as to where they stood. In colony elections they supported such "Old Lights" as John Bulkeley and withheld their votes from such a "New Light" as Hezekiah Huntington. On the allocation of funds from the "Church Right" acquired in the original division of the town they voted: "The money shall be used for support of a gospel minister according to the Ecclesiastical Establishment of this Government [the Saybrook Platform] *and no other*." (Italics mine).

Perhaps the most obvious mark of conservatism in Kent was the effort to enhance the prestige of town leaders by the seating arrangement in the meetinghouse. In 1744 it was voted in town meeting, "We shall seat each person according to age, dignity, and list [property in tax list]."[41] It was more important for a Barnum to sit where his "list and dignity" entitled him than to remain back with the rest of his family. The pews showed a hierarchy of dignity and property with Hatch, Hubbel, and Fuller awarded the front seats. We cannot tell how long this seating system lasted at Kent but presumably it endured as long as the original meetinghouse was used until 1774.

A number of liberal influences in the church establishment are also discernible in the records at Kent. It seems clear that church membership was open to all who wished to join and conform to the required standards. There were no references to "the elect" or even to a Half-Way Covenant. When the ministers from the different towns held "Consociation Meetings" at Litchfield and discussed membership, they referred to "baptized persons" only, thus implying that there were no other degrees or grades of "belonging."[42] The records also suggest a desire to hold on to the members they had. When occasionally a parishioner lost his gospel privileges for drinking excessively, creating a disturbance on the Sabbath, or attending a "disorderly meeting," he could obtain restoration of full privileges by "a humble confession." This requirement was difficult for the timid or the stubborn but some could take it in stride. Every year or so the records noted that

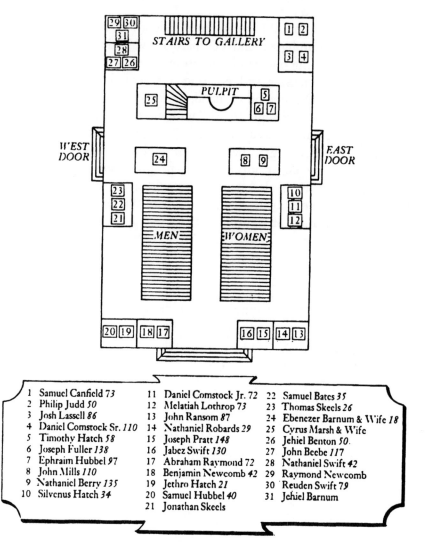

STAIRS TO GALLERY

PULPIT

WEST DOOR

EAST DOOR

MEN   WOMEN

1 Samuel Canfield *73*	11 Daniel Comstock Jr. *72*	22 Samuel Bates *35*
2 Philip Judd *50*	12 Melatiah Lothrop *73*	23 Thomas Skeels *26*
3 Josh Lassell *86*	13 John Ransom *87*	24 Ebenezer Barnum & Wife *18*
4 Daniel Comstock Sr. *110*	14 Nathaniel Robards *29*	25 Cyrus Marsh & Wife
5 Timothy Hatch *58*	15 Joseph Pratt *148*	26 Jehiel Benton *50.*
6 Joseph Fuller *138*	16 Jabez Swift *130*	27 John Beebe *117*
7 Ephraim Hubbel *97*	17 Abraham Raymond *72*	28 Nathaniel Swift *42*
8 John Mills *110*	18 Benjamin Newcomb *42*	29 Raymond Newcomb
9 Nathaniel Berry *135*	19 Jethro Hatch *21*	30 Reuden Swift *79*
10 Silvenus Hatch *34*	20 Samuel Hubbel *40*	31 Jehiel Barnum
	21 Jonathan Skeels	

Kent Meetinghouse, 1743–1774

"Each person shall be seated according to age, dignity, and list, in the year 1747." [a]

[a] Kent, Land, I, 21–43. The numbers following the names are the common list figures for 1747.

"Joseph Pack humbly confessed his drunkeness and was restrored to gospel privileges." [42]

It is almost impossible to judge the depth of religious feeling of the Kent churchgoer and compare it with that of his great grandfather. On the one hand, the promptness of the Kent settlers in obtaining a minister and erecting a meetinghouse suggests a pious outlook. On the other hand, strict colony laws required these actions. For example, to do without a minister for a year brought a large fine; [43] and an act of 1733 spelled out an elaborate procedure for building a meetinghouse. The town clerk was to keep the county court informed of progress and if there was negligence, the General Assembly "would assess on said society such sums of money necessary to complete the work." [44]

In the formation of Church societies one again detects a strong concern over money. The quarrels between societies over boundary lines and membership suggest that some were less concerned with the souls of their fellow covenanters than with what their neighbors could contribute to church finances. A 1752 petition to the General Assembly from the East Greenwich Society protested against their boundary with the New Preston Society, an arrangement which deprived them of six families. They could "ill afford to lose them for only thirty-five of us are rateable and our total list is but £1467." [45]

Whereas virtually all townsmen were members of the Congregational Church throughout the 1740s and 1750s, a fragmentation commenced around 1760. The Anglicans, strong in Fairfield County to the south, made inroads at about this time. Slosson's History, written in 1812, stated that a private quarrel arose between "a family connected with the minister" (possibly the Mills family as Pastor Bordwell's wife was Jane Mills) and the family of "an inhabitant" (the Swifts). "This last and his family became Episcopalians. He built a small church . . . and died in 1772." The "rebel" was Reuben Swift and, according to Slosson, after he died nothing further was done until 1810. [46] Records of the Society for the Propagation in Foreign Parts suggest more Anglican activity than did Slosson. The Reverend Solomon Palmer was appointed an "S. P. G." missionary for Litchfield County and took up residence in New Milford. In 1760 he reported, "There are subscriptions raising for the building of a Church in Kent . . . at a place convenient for about fifty families from different towns." [47]

There were no Baptist Societies in Kent but a few Kent men joined this sect in the town of New Fairfield to the southwest. The "certifications" are occasionally recorded in the Land Records. "This may certify that this day (March 3, 1770) John Hendricks has given himself up to the Baptists' Society." [48]

After the Revolution there were apparently large numbers of "certified" inhabitants. Writers referred to "infidel opinion coming in like a flood" and of "young men thinking of themselves as wiser than their fathers." [49] To become "certified" was frequently a device to avoid Church rates. One simply claimed membership in some distant or ephemeral church. In 1802 Daniel Parker was ordained pastor for the Ellsworth Society in northeast Kent and Sharon and has left a disturbing picture of conditions. "Preachers of every description had passed through and many of the inhabitants were certified in other denominations, mostly to avoid the expense." He referred to the "many who did not want any regular preacher" and to "their virulent hostility to church and society." [50]

THE ABEL WRIGHT CASE

It is difficult to form a final conclusion about the extent to which the church was a conservative force in Kent with so many factors in the equation and with most of these varying over the years. The story of Abel Wright's difficulties with the church and town authorities may afford a brief but clear look at the status of Kent leadership and church influence during the 1740s.

Abel Wright was a leading citizen of Kent. An original settler, he had purchased three proprietary shares at the Windham auction and had become Kent's largest property owner in 1740. (His list was £152 and his nearest rival was John Mills at £108). He was the town's most active land speculator. He was selectman, frequent moderator, town agent, petition writer, and captain of militia. Finally, he was an original charter member of the Kent, First Society (Congregational) Church. [51]

Wright apparently was caught up in the "New Light" ferment. He invited three "New Light" preachers, James Clement, Benjamin Ferris, and Richard Hallett, to discuss religion at his home in Kent on July 1, 1743. Also present were Abel's wife, Mary, neighbors Samuel and Sarah Latham, and Samuel Alger's wife, Rebeccah. For listening to these "notoriously corrupt teachers" Wright and the neighbors who had attended his "disorderly meeting" were summoned to appear before the Church Meeting of August 4, 1743. Wright made a spirited defense (oral, unfortunately) but was found guilty of "open contempt of the pastoral authority which Christ hath left to this Church and of unchristian disrespect to Him." The group was suspended from gospel privileges until they made satisfaction.[52]

Wright did not take kindly to the suspension of privileges nor to the pastor, Cyrus Marsh, who had apparently headed the persecution. Though his neighbors might crawl back, he had no intention of "confessing." Instead, he turned his attention to the teachings of the Moravian missionaries who were preaching to the nearby Indians.[53] Stirred up by the Moravian doctrine, Wright decided to spread the word to his friends, the Barnums. He argued with Ebenezer, his wife Abigail, and with Gideon Barnum. Gideon asked Wright how he dared speak as he did "being the Moravians were frowned on by the government." Wright replied that "they were the most instructive men he ever saw." They were good men. They had taught him "about the merits of Christ and practical, good relegion." However, Abel Wright made little headway with the Barnums and Gideon's final thrust was, "I believe they are Papists!" Even more imaginative, Abigail feared the Moravians would come and kill her in her bed.[54]

Wright visited from house to house. He argued with the Delanos, with Barnabas and Phoebe Hatch, with the Barnums again, and finally with Kent's first citizen, Timothy Hatch. But the Kent people were shocked at his actions and words. He had persuaded the Moravians to speak in English and marveled at their telling him that man was not always in a state of grace. "Sometimes you are in grace and sometimes you are so far out as to be half devil." It made good sense to Abel but was blasphemy to the rest. Timothy Hatch had the last word when he stated that the Moravians were under the frown of the government and therefore all men ought to frown on them.[55]

Abel Wright sounds a bit like one of Vernon Parrington's liberals casting out for new ideas and resenting the hidebound orthodoxy of his neighbors.[56] But the opposition was too much for him. A petition was despatched to the General Assembly urging that his captain's commission be revoked. The government collected the evidence on which this account is based but its decision is not known. Wright had had enough and moved back to Fairfield in 1744. He braved Kent again in 1760 and kept the town's general store until his death in 1770.

The episode has an ironic twist as far as Parrington's thesis is concerned. Instead of "village yeomen" raising the torch of liberalism against mercantile wealth, the opponents have reversed their roles. The liberal protagonist is a merchant, the biggest speculator and largest property owner in town. Signing the petition against Wright were thirty-eight "yeomen" of Kent.[57]

As indicated above, the Wright case is but a fragmentary account of a single episode. This brief glimpse does suggest, however, that the "frown of the government" may have been important. Wright had been popular enough to attain the town's highest electoral positions. When his thought deviated from that of the government and other town leaders his popularity and influence were ended.

The Kent inhabitant enjoyed economic democracy. As to political democracy, his right to participate in local affairs was virtually complete; and while only three out of four could participate in colony elections, even here democracy was only partially limited. Social democracy, however, was far from complete. The average citizen (we have used David Whittelsey as an example) found the top town offices preempted. The town leaders had reached their posts largely through ability; but once in them, they constituted a sort of permanent, elite, leader class. The schools and church demanded respect for authority. The leaders sat in the front pews, affixed such titles as captain or esquire to their names, and expected the town to "frown when they frowned." For most of the eighteenth century the Kent voter appears to have frowned on cue and generally kept his "steady habits."

Democracy at Kent

We have undertaken a study of democracy as it existed during the eighteenth century in the town of Kent on Connecticut's western frontier. This analysis of economic opportunity (the ability for all to participate in the material resources of the community), of political democracy (the extent of popular control of the machinery of government), and of social democracy (the absence of class barriers to the attainment of positions of prestige and authority) has involved a study of conditions within the community and of the town's external relationships with an "eastern, mercantile class."

Kent was settled in 1738 by forty families that came neither as a single, covenanted church congregation (seventeenth-century custom) nor as a conglomeration of individual land speculators (eighteenth-century practice). The Kent pioneers were indeed land speculators but they came in groups (nine families from Danbury, five from Colchester) along traditional migratory paths, about one-third via the east-west axis from the Connecticut River and two-thirds north from Long Island Sound. Although all Kent land was sold at auction and distributed by the notorious eighteenth-century proprietor system, the Kent records show that this method could be equitable and efficient. The General Assembly proved farsighted and vigilant in eliminating problems of proprietor absenteeism or delinquency.

Arrived at Kent, the settler found fertile (but stony) farming land, one of New England's larger deposits of iron ore, and abundant water power for saw, grist, or fulling mills. Such economic opportunity induced in the settlers, not placid contentment, but an almost frenzied determination to try a hand at everything. Virtually every family settled on a farm which provided not only subsistence needs but usually produced a salable surplus. There was a remarkable tendency for farmers to seek additional profits in ironworks, sawmills, and other non-agricultural enterprises. Most enticing were possible profits from land speculation. The original Kent settlers engaged in such a ferment of land deals that many registered tenfold gains on their original investments. Accompanying the quest for profits was a peculiar moral attitude. Even church deacons were not above dissembling and conniving. To summarize, the Kent settlers sought profits and "the better things." The stately colonial houses that crown Kent hilltops today testify that many found them.

In mid-eighteenth century Kent threats to economic opportunity were largely unrealized and Turner's questions about "class struggles" and "populist tendencies" would be answered in the negative. Absentee land control was negligible. Indebtedness was heavy but payments were orderly, oppressive attachments were scarce, and there was no clear pattern of frontier debtors opposing eastern creditors. However, economic opportunity, which appeared exceptionally bright at Kent from 1740 to 1777, was darkened after the Revolution by the pressure of population (swollen by the high birthrate) against a limited supply of land. Discontent stemmed from this crowded condition, not from any earlier oppressive acts of a wealthy, absentee class.

An evaluation of political democracy at Kent required two studies: first, of the ability of a Kent man to raise his voice as a freeman in colony affairs and second, of his right to participate in local government. Only half the adult males of Kent were freemen at any given time, but from 60 to 75 percent could have met the property qualification for freemanship and thus been able to vote in colony elections. The nonfreemen were not a class apart but were mostly apathetic freeholders or else sons or brothers of freemen, young men who within a few years would secure enough property to vote. Just as the freemen of Kent were of the same class as their nonvoting townsmen, so they were closely connected by kinship and interest to the ruling magistrates of Connecticut. Kent supported the existing order partly because political procedures encouraged stability and partly because Connecticut's government served its interests. Political democracy appeared complete at the local level. Proprety qualifications did not bar an inhabitant from voting or holding office. Furthermore, popularly elected town officials and not appointed justices of the peace constituted the real civil authority in the town.

Although economic opportunity and political democracy proved more widespread at Kent than what is usually pictured in eighteenth-century New England, social democracy in this town was restricted. Positions of top prestige and leadership were preempted by a few men. The password to the inner circle was not "proprietor," "gentry," "squire," or even "property," though most of the leaders were the town's wealthiest men. Kent did have an "elite of ability." However, once an able man entrenched himself in an office, he could hold it against other able aspirants. The schools, the church, and long-standing custom enhanced the dignity of the incumbents. The town was conditioned to think, to frown, to vote, and to reelect as its leaders directed.

Throughout this study of democracy at Kent we have tended to hover directly over the town, and most of our pictures have been closeups. In concluding we should venture a final appraisal of the significance of these Kent pictures. We should move our camera back, broaden our perspective, and note Kent's relationship to the major events of the late eighteenth century when, in the space of thirteen crowded years, the town played its role in the American Revolution, the Shaysite "contagion," and the ratification of the Federal Constitution.

The American Revolution drew a mixed response from the town. A population raised on an economic tradition of land speculation and individualistic venturing would not be expected to make unselfish, economic sacrifices during the Revolution. It did not. Kent's main contribution was some propertyless "volunteers" to the Continental line.[1] The propertied farmers made their brief appearances with the militia at the Lexington Alarm and the Danbury Raid.[2] An occasional Swift, Ransom, or Slosson served as a regular officer, but most Kent men of property were at best "home-front" heroes. Kent lagged in meeting her quotas of both men [3] and supplies, and she dragged her feet more than any other western town in paying state and continental taxes.[4]

A town enjoying democratic, representative government would be expected to defend her "liberties" against British threats. In particular, a town which respected its central government and habitually "frowned as the General Assembly frowned" could be expected to follow where the government led. The Connecticut General Assembly led the way into the American Revolution and Kent followed without a recorded dissent. During the whole war only five Kent property owners were accused of Tory leanings and three of these were absentees. (The local men were Jacob Bull and Abel Wright's son, Jonathan.) [5]

After the war the Shaysite "contagion" reached Kent and her sister towns. Shaysite strength was most evident in Sharon, Norfolk, Salisbury, and Cornwall.[6] We would expect some radical feeling at Kent. Many third-generation inhabitants who had inherited only one-twentieth of their grandfathers' proprietary holdings had dropped to the "poor" economic category. Their heavier taxes in the 1780s were making a dim economic outlook even dimmer. Less land meant less opportunity to qualify as freemen; and some potential freemen seemed increasingly disillusioned with the paternalistic system of government. Finally, the Revolution had brought upheaval, emotional stirrings, disillusionment, and legal wreckage, all of which were capable of fanning radical flames.[7] But our survey of Kent would also tell us that Shaysite feeling could hardly be expected to erupt there. Foundations for a class war were undermined by the ties of kinship in Connecticut society. The General Assembly had been benevolent too long and had made too many friends for a revolt against its authority to hope for success. There were no Kent crowds swarming to close courts or to prevent imprisonments or property attachments, for no one at Kent had been imprisoned for debt and virtually no one had lost property. Despite the erosion of economic and political opportunity, Kent remained basically a prosperous and conservative town rather than a depressed and radical community.

Our knowledge of Kent would prepare us for her role in the ratification of the Federal Constitution. The decision to ratify or reject was left to representatives of the towns meeting in convention in January, 1788. These town delegates were chosen not by the freemen alone but by "all who are qualified to vote in town meeting." [8] Kent, with practically all adult males eligible to participate, chose a fitting representative. They named Jedediah Hubbel, a selectman, justice of the peace, moderator, town agent, and a "town leader" like his father, Ephraim, before him. Shaysite elements in the town may well have opposed Hubbel. (We have no record of the town vote.) But just as radicals had not possessed strength to precipitate an eruption earlier, similarly they lacked numbers and influence to block the election of an old style "town leader." We may assume that Jedediah Hubbel, esquire, favored order and was appalled at anarchy. Connecticut's founding fathers, Oliver Ellsworth, esquire, Roger Sherman, esquire, and William Samuel Johnson, esquire, urged adoption of the Constitution.[9] Hubbel and the majority of Kent adult males nodded in solemn agreement.

Kent is manifestly an exception to prevailing interpretations concerning eighteenth-century settlements. Although the town conforms somewhat to established versions of social democracy, it deviates notably in the areas of economic and political democracy. This history of an "exceptional town" on the New England frontier may provide some counterbalance to those radical communities which historians have found plagued with internal and external class rivalries. It may also suggest methods for utilizing such abundant (but generally neglected) local records as land volumes, tax lists, and freeman rolls so that more towns may be reexamined along the lines undertaken at Kent.

Chronological Summary of Kent History

1684	First recorded visit of white man to Kent area, Benjamin Wadsworth.
1710	Indian raid from Canada passes through Kent region.
1711	Scouts from Danbury and Woodbury patrol Kent region.
1716	Benjamin Fairweather buys tract including Kent from Chief Waramaug.
1719	General Assembly, seeking orderly settlement, orders "no trespassing" in Western Lands.
1724	Last Indian raid from Canada to penetrate Kent region.
1726–37	General Assembly orders surveys, drafts several plans for disposal of Western Lands.
1737	Final act "Ordering and Directing Sale and Settlement of all Townships in Western Lands."
1738	Windham auction. Kent sold in fifty shares to proprietors submitting highest bids.
1738	Stephen Pain erects first cabin in Kent.
1738	First reference to iron mine in Kent.
1739	Kent incorporated. Settlers obtain "town priviledges."
1739	First schools authorized and erected.
1739–40	Hardship winter. Extreme cold reported.
1740	First meeting of freemen.
1740	First meetinghouse authorized (on Goodhill). Raised 1742, occupied 1744.
1740	First trainband, or militia company. Timothy Hatch, captain.
1740	Population, forty-two adult males.
1741	Church of Christ (Congregational) incorporated. Cyrus Marsh pastor until 1758.
1742	Kent made part of Litchfield Probate District.
1743	Land west of Housatonic annexed to Kent.

1743   Kent visited by New Light preachers, James Clement, Richard Hallett, and Benjamin Ferris. Local New Lights condemned.

1744   Moravians preach at Kent.

1744   King George's War. Kent calls self "much-exposed frontier town."

1744   Barnum ironworks operating at Spectacle Pond.

1746   Common field used for pasture only.

1747   Patent confirms land to Kent proprietors.

1747   Merryall boundary dispute; town enlarged on southern border.

1747   First bridge over Housatonic.

1747   Last Indian alarm. Raid to border of Kent rumored but never takes place.

1748   During Great Awakening Kent reaffirms Old Light position.

1750   Eastern part of town becomes East Greenwich Society.

1751   Kent a part of newly formed Litchfield County.

1753   Southern part of town becomes New Preston Society.

1756   Jabez Swift serves as first Kent deputy to General Assembly.

1756   French and Indian War. Kent militia on Crown Point expedition.

1756   Bull's ironworks authorized.

1756   First official census at Kent: population of 1000 inhabitants.

1758   Mine at Ore Hill in operation.

1758   Joel Bordwell replaces Cyrus Marsh as pastor for First Society.

1760   First report of Anglican group at Kent.

1760   Kent's economy largely subsistence but some evidence of export of iron and farm surplus; imports of luxury clothes via general stores.

1770   Baptists in Kent.

1770   Anti-British feeling in Kent. Town supports colonial non-importation movement.

1774   Kent votes support of Continental Congress.

1774   Kent population reaches 1922 inhabitants.

1775–76 American Revolution. Kent militia in Boston and Long Island campaigns (sixty-six men serve).

1776   End of common field.

1777   Virtually all townsmen sign Oath of Fidelity.

1777–81 Only two Tory sympathizers recorded in Kent.

1778   Kent militia at Danbury Raid.

1779   Part of New Preston Society permanently separated from Kent becoming part of new town of Washington, incorporated 1779.

1780–82 Kent quota for Continental Line set at thirty-four men; town actually furnishes twenty-nine.

1786   East Greenwich Society permanently separated from Kent. Becomes town of Warren.

1787   Shays' Rebellion. No record of specific agitation in Kent. Conservatives win elective offices. Contemporary observers note "unrest" and "Shaysite contagion."

1787 Methodists in Kent.

1787–88 Ratification of Constitution. Kent town meeting (all adult males eligible to vote) elects conservative delegate to ratification convention at Hartford. He votes "Yes" on Constitution. Litchfield County votes twenty-two "Yes" and nine "No."

1796 Kent has seven taverns, six forges, five general stores; iron goes to slitting mills at Canaan and Washington.

Original Proprietary Shares

The purpose of the following table is to summarize data on purchase and resale of the original fifty proprietary shares sold at the Windham auction in March and April, 1738 to the proprietors of Kent.

Names preceded by a number are original purchasers (e.g., 11 Ebenezer Bishop). Names without a number are second purchasers (e.g., Nathaniel Slosson under Bishop indicates Slosson bought the share from Bishop).

Italicized names became Kent residents. Names in roman type remained absentee.

Numbers with parentheses indicate owners of shares who had settled in Kent by 1741 (date of the petition by resident proprietors against absentee proprietors). Numbers without parentheses indicate owners of shares who remained absentee into the 1740s and 1750s.

Purchasers of Original Shares	Original Home of Buyer	Purchase Date	Price Paid (in pounds)
(1) Humphrey Avery	Groton	3/7/38	185-16- 0
Benjamin Brownson	Farmington	5/4/38	200- 0- 0
2 Humphrey Avery	Groton	3/8/38	165- 0- 0
Philip Cavarly	Colchester	9/21/39	
(3) Abel Barnum	Danbury	4/27/38	189- 5-10
Joshua Barnum	Danbury	10/10/39	
(4) *Ebenezer Barnum*	Danbury	3/8/38	189- 5-10
(5) *Ebenezer Barnum*	Danbury	3/8/38	189- 5-10
(6) *Ebenezer Barnum*	Danbury	3/8/38	189- 5-10
(7) *Ebenezer Barnum*	Danbury	3/8/38	189- 5-10
Abel Wright	Mansfield	4/9/38	
(8) Nathaniel Barnum	Danbury	4/27/38	189- 5-10
Samuel Lewis	Colchester	5/28/39	220
(9) Josiah Barrs	N. Fairfield	?	
William Roberts	?	?	
10 Samuel Benedict	Danbury	4/27/38	189- 5-10
Josiah Starr	Danbury	5/8/39	189- 5-10

Purchasers of Original Shares	Original Home of Buyer	Purchase Date	Price Paid (in pounds)
(11) Ebenezer Bishop	Stamford	3/7/38	180-10- 0
Nathaniel Slosson	Norwalk	11/11/38	236-10- 0
(12) *Thomas Beeman*	Stonington	3/7/38	185- 7- 0
(13) *Nathaniel Berry*	Tolland	3/8/38	182- 0- 0
(14) *Nathaniel Berry*	Tolland	4/26/38	190- 0- 0
(15) *Samuel Canfield*	Danbury	4/26/38	181- 0- 0
16 Thomas Casson	Voluntown	3/8/38	202- 2- 0
John Smith	Voluntown	'40	
17 Philip Cavarly	Colchester	3/7/38	200-10- 0
Abigail Strong (dau.)	Colchester	'55	gift
Philip Strong	Colchester	'56	gift
(18) *Daniel Comstock, Sr.*	Fairfield	3/8/38	187- 0- 0
(19) *Daniel Comstock, Jr.*	Fairfield	3/8/38	200- 0- 0
(20) Jonathan Dunham	Colchester	3/8/38	189- 5-10
Azariah Pratt	Colchester	'39	
21 Jonathan Dunham	Colchester	3/8/38	189- 5-10
(22) Francis Fenton	Wellington	3/8/38	184- 0- 0
Thomas Beeman	Stonington	'39	200- 0- 0
(23) Joseph Hatch	Tolland	4/27/38	152- 0- 0
Barnabus Hatch	Tolland	'41	gift
(24) *Ephraim Hubbel*	Fairfield	3/8/38	181- 0- 0
25 Jonathan Hubbel	Newtown	3/8/38	196- 0- 0
26 Eleazer Hubbel	Newtown	3/8/38	190- 0- 0
Peter Hubbel	Newtown	5/8/39	190- 0- 0
27 Eleazer Hubbel	Newtown	3/8/38	190- 0- 0
Richard Hubbel	Newtown	5/8/39	190- 0- 0
(28) *Philip Judd*	Danbury	4/27/38	189- 5-10
(29) John Knapp and	Danbury	4/26/38	185- 2- 0
Noah Rockwell	Danbury		
Thomas Lewis	Colchester	'39	200- 0- 0
(30) *Samuel Lewis*	Colchester	3/8/38	187-15- 0
(31) *John Mills*	Stratford	4/26/38	166- 0- 0
(32) *John Mills*	Stratford	4/26/38	181-15- 0
(33) Samuel Minor	Woodbury	4/26/38	184- 0- 0
Nathaniel Sanford	Newtown	'40	235- 0- 0
34 John Mitchell	Woodbury	4/26/39	193-13- 0
35 Knel Mitchell	Woodbury	4/26/38	180- 0- 0
(36) *Jonathan Morgan, Sr.*	New London	3/8/38	189- 1- 0
(37) *Jonathan Morgan, Jr.*	New London	3/8/38	198- 0- 0
(38) Thomas Newcomb	New Haven	3/7/38	?
Benjamin Newcomb	New Haven	6/5/39	350- 0- 0

Purchasers of Original Shares	Original Home of Buyer	Purchase Date	Price Paid (in pounds)
(39) *John Porter*	Danbury	4/26/38	172- 5- 0
Benjamin Hamilton	?	'39	
(40) *Joseph Pratt*	Colchester	4/27/38	182- 0- 0
John Beebe	Colchester	4/30/38	
(41) John Seeley	New Milford	3/8/38	220- 0- 0
Stephen Noble	New Milford	'40	
(42) *Thomas Skeels*	Woodbury	4/26/38	169- 0- 0
43 John Smith	Voluntown	4/27/38	177- 0- 0
44 Zephaniah Swift	Lebanon	3/7/38	201- 2- 0
Jabez Swift	Sandwich, Mass	'39	175- 0- 0
(45) Thomas Tozer	Lyme	3/7/38	195- 6- 0
John Ransom	Colchester	8/27/39	
(46) Jacob Wanzer	New Fairfield	4/27/38	189- 5- 0
Nathaniel Roberts	?	'39	190- 0- 0
47 Elisha Williams	New Haven	3/8/38	193- 0- 0
Ebenezer Marsh	Litchfield	'40	250- 0- 0
(48) *Abel Wright*	Mansfield	4/27/38	200- 0- 0
(49) *Abel Wright*	Mansfield	4/27/38	171- 0- 0
(50) *Abel Wright*	Mansfield	4/27/38	193-13- 0

Kent's First Settlers, December 1, 1739

In a petition for town privileges dated September 19, 1739, Samuel Lewis indicated thirty-two proprietors had settled in Kent. On the list below numbers 1–32 are these original settler proprietors. Numbers 33–45 are nonproprietors present in late 1739.[1] Also indicated are amounts of property shown for each man on the common list of 1740 (these would include the £18 poll tax). Original offices held in 1739–40 are shown. Finally, ownership of nonagricultural enterprises is indicated.

	Proprietor Settlers	Property on 1740 List (in pounds)	Town Office	Nonagricultural Enterprise
1	Ebenezer Barnum	40	Selectman	iron
2	Ebenezer Barnum, Jr.	27	Lister	iron
3	Gideon Barnum	37	Grand Juror	iron
4	Jehiel Barnum	31	Collector	sawmill
5	Joshua Barnum	52	Highway Surveyor Sealer of Measures	iron
6	Samuel Bates	21	Lister	
7	John Beebe	39	Constable	sawmill
8	Thomas Beeman	67		
9	Nathaniel Berry	48	Highway Surveyor	potash works
10	Samuel Canfield	47	Tithingman	
11	Daniel Comstock	75		tannery
12	Daniel Comstock, Jr.	35	Fence Viewer	tavern
13	Joseph Fuller	55	Treasurer	iron
14	Benjamin Hamilton	39	Tithingman	
15	Timothy Hatch	70	Selectman	
16	Ephraim Hubbel	90	Selectman	

[1] These lists have been pieced together from Kent Land Records, I, pp. 1–566; tax list of 1740; and minutes of proprietors' meetings. Kent, Proprietors, pp. 1–28.

Proprietor Settlers	Property on 1740 List (in pounds)	Town Office	Nonagricultural Enterprise
17 Philip Judd	29		
18 Samuel Lewis	85	Town Clerk	
19 John Mills	108	Grand Juror	gristmill
20 Jonathan Morgan	50	Fence Viewer	sawmill
21 Jonathan Morgan, Jr.	—	Fence Viewer	iron
22 Benjamin Newcomb	42		
23 Joseph Pack	65		
24 John Porter	55	Selectman	
25 Azariah Pratt	37	Selectman, Leather Sealer	sawmill
26 John Ransom	31		saw, grist, fulling mills
27 Nathaniel Roberts	34	Highway Surveyor	sawmill
28 William Roberts	33		sawmill
29 Thomas Skeels	44	Collector	gristmill
30 Nathaniel Slosson	42	Brander	pound (horses)
31 James Stewart	36		sawmill
32 Abel Wright	152	Selectman	merchant
Non-Proprietor Settlers			
33 Alexander Carey	21		
34 Elisha Hamilton	18		
35 Silvenus Hatch	21		
36 Melatiah Lothrop	25		sawmill
37 Thomas Judd	25		
38 Samuel Latham	21		
39 Ebenezer Lyman	26		
40 Stephen Pain	20	Highway Surveyor	iron
41 Caleb Morgan	—	Lister	iron
42 William Porter	19	Hayward	
43 Abraham Raymond	—		tavern
44 Gideon Root	18		
45 Samuel Wright	18	Hayward	

Notes

Preface

1. Kent and the towns of Connecticut's Western Lands fully earn the designation "frontier." They were, to use Frederick Jackson Turner's definition, "the meeting point between savagery and civilization. Again, following Turner, they were "at the edge of settlement." In contemporary documents the term "frontier" was frequently applied to Kent and her sister towns, particularly during King George's War when the new settlements were vulnerable to French and Indian attack via a wilderness corridor stretching along their western boundaries. The present study, by covering Kent history down to 1800, may appear to move beyond the frontier epoch. However, it is proposed here to keep and use the word just as Turner and his followers did. Turner, James Truslow Adams, Lois Matthews, Curtis Nettles, and others dealt with dozens of New England towns, such as Westminster, Rutland, or Palmer, Massachusetts, whose frontier credentials were neither markedly superior nor inferior to those of Kent. As Turner put it, "The term [frontier] is an elastic one and for our purpose does not need sharp definitions."

2. The most striking parallel to Kent is an Honors Research Essay, King, "Proprietors of Middlebury." Inhabitants of the Kent of 1745 showed striking similarities to the inhabitants of the Middlebury of 1785.

Part I: The Settlement of Kent

1. Local historians do report a scattering of settlers in Sharon and Salisbury before 1738. Starr, Cornwall's historian, believes loggers were active in Cornwall and Kent and that New Milford cattle may have been pastured there before the auctions of 1738. See Reed, *Amenia*, p. 12; Starr, *Cornwall*, p. 26; Crofut, *Guide to Conn.*, I, 414–15; Sedgwick, *Sharon*, pp. 22–23.

1: Preliminaries to Settlement

1. Wadsworth, *Journal*, pp. 102–10. Wadsworth kept a journal of his trip from Boston to Albany to Hartford in August, 1694. He accompanied

the Massachusetts Commissioners who went to Albany to treat with the Five Nations. He returned with the Connecticut Commissioners down the Hudson via Greenbush, Kinderhook, and Fort Turconnick. From here he passed through the wilderness of Connecticut's Western Lands and emerged in civilization at Woodbury, Connecticut.

2. Kurath, *Linguistic Atlas*, pp. 93–100. See also Deming, "Litchfield Settlements" and "Conn. Settlements"; also *State of Conn. Register*.

3. Kurath, *Linguistic Atlas*, Map 28, fails to indicate this reversal. He shows a movement from Hartford county directly to the Western Lands. Following Kurath is Garvan, *Architecture in Conn.*, p. 13.

4. Deming, "Conn. Settlements," pp. 22, 23, 46.

5. *Ibid.*, pp. 22, 45.

6. *Ibid.*, pp. 44, 45.

7. *Ibid.*, pp. 25, 47. Most settlers along Long Island Sound had come directly from England. Norwalk was an exception, as it appears to have been settled for unknown reasons by a group from Hartford.

8. Kurath, *Linguistic Atlas*, pp. 91–101. Migrations from England were completely cut off in 1640–60 but were fairly constant at other times.

9. The following Kent families in the "B's" were fourth-generation descendants of a mid-seventeenth-century settler: (Bates), *Bates Bulletin;* (Beebe), Beebe, *Beebe Family;* (Benedict), Benedict, *Benedicts in America;* (Benton), Benton, *Samuel Slade Benton;* (Boardman), Goldthwaite, *Boardman Genealogy;* (Bostwick), Bostwick, *Bostwick Family;* (Bulkley), Jacobes, *Bulkley Genealogy.*

10. Beebe, *Beebe Family*, pp. 23–25. Genealogists assign numbers to each member of the family. The first male arrival in America is 1, his eldest child is 2, his second child is 3, and so on. Members of the second generation have numbers from 2 to 15; the third generation, from 15 to 70; the fourth generation, from 70 to 150. John Beebe at Kent was 96; John Beebe of Canaan was 73; Samuel Beebe of Salisbury was 83. These numbers suggest minimum totals of family members at the birth of the numbered individual. Genealogists miss some family members because of missing records.

11. Comstock, *Comstock Family*. Daniel was number 126 at birth. When he reached Kent the early Comstocks had died but infant Comstocks were reaching the 200s.

12. Fuller, *Descendants of Edward Fuller.*

13. Orcutt, *Indians*, p. 22.

14. Slosson, "Kent," p. 3. Barzillai Slosson was a grandson of an original Kent settler, Nathaniel Slosson. His manuscript history was written in 1812 and is the earliest known descriptive writing about Kent. The original manuscript is at the Yale Library; copies are at the Kent Town Clerk's Office.

15. Orcutt, *Indians*, p. 78.

16. *Ibid.*, p. 79.

17. The corridor remains something of a wilderness today, serving as the route for the Appalachian Trail (a footpath from Maine to Georgia). This trail and the main axis of the Taconics pass through the western part of Kent.

18. Orcutt, *Indians*, p. 81.

19. *Ibid.*, p. 84.

20. *Ibid.*, p. 90.

21. Conn. Archives, War, IV, 136.

22. Conn. Hist. Society, Misc. Papers, Box 605.

23. Roger Wolcott was deputy governor from 1744 to 1750. The Committee on War was established in October, 1743, and was empowered to build forts. The destruction of Saratoga referred to in the petition was probably the raid of 1746.

24. Conn. Hist. Society, Misc. Papers, Box 605.

25. *Ibid.*

26. Starr, *Cornwall*, p. 26.

27. See Deming, "Conn. Settlements," pp. 52–54. Captain James Fitch acquired most of Windham County from the Mohegan Indians and "the profits must have been enormous." John Mason and John Reed also enjoyed profitable land relations with Indians east of the Connecticut River.

28. *Public Conn. Col. Records*, VII, 44.

29. Deming, "Conn. Settlements," pp. 24, 25. In 1650 Nathaniel Ely and Richard Olmstead on behalf of themselves and other inhabitants of Hartford petitioned the government for permission to plant a settlement at Norwalk. The Court agreed provided the usual rules were followed: immediate improvement of the land, calling a minister, settling at least thirty families, etc.

30. *Public Conn. Col. Records*, VI, 127.

31. Deming, "Litchfield Settlements," p. 2. The dispute dated back to the Andros regime when the panicky Assembly, fearing loss of its Western Lands, deeded them to Hartford and Windsor. A question had remained as to whether this emergency action held good after the danger had passed. The 1726 compromise line was the answer.

32. *Ibid.*, p. 3. *Public Conn. Col. Records*, VII, 44. Hartford and Windsor quickly established the towns of New Hartford, Winchester, Hartland, Harwinton, Colebrook, Barkhamstead, and Torrington. Lands were given to residents of Hartford and Windsor in proportion to their "common list," that is, their taxable property.

33. For details of surveys and plans see *Public Conn. Col. Records*, VII, 44, 109, 343, 386, 412, 459; VIII, 38, 180. Also see Conn. Archives, Towns and Lands, 2d Series, II, 104 a, b, c. Surveying committees were dispatched in 1726, 1727, 1731, and 1732. Disposal plans were debated in 1731 and 1733.

34. *Public Conn. Col. Records*, VIII, 128–36.

35. Proceeds from the sale were allocated to all the towns of Connecti-

cut in proportion to each town's "tax-list" totals. Such funds were ear-marked for support of the schools. Actually the purchasers at the auctions (that is, the new proprietors) submitted not cash but promissory notes, or "bonds." These "bonds" were distributed to the various towns and it befell their selectmen to collect on such "bonds" when they became due. *Public Conn. Col. Records*, VIII, 128–36.

2: Settlement: The Speculative Settler Proprietors

1. The earliest technical study of the New England land system was Egleston, *Land System of the New England Colonies* (1886). Egleston documented the controversies between proprietors and nonproprietors. The next important monograph was Lois K. Mathews, *Expansion of New England* (1909). Influenced by the frontier thesis of Frederick Jackson Turner, she was impressed by land speculation and a tendency for the "less prosper-ous" to move to the new towns while the "conservative elements" remained behind. In 1914 Turner wrote specifically of New England: "First Official Frontier of the Massachusetts Bay." Turner suggested that the New England frontier was a "field for investment of eastern capital and for political con-trol by it." The most thorough and important study of the New England land system was Roy H. Akagi, *Town Proprietors of the New England Colonies* (1924). Akagi provided details and documentation for Turner's ideas about speculation, settler grievances, and class struggle. James Truslow Adams' studies of the New England land system have placed most emphasis on class-struggle aspects. His concern over the "struggle of the common man to realize the doctrine of the Revolution" is a main theme in his trilogy *The Founding of New England* (1921), *Revolutionary New England, 1690–1776* (1923), and *New England in the Republic, 1776–1850* (1926). Adams' indignation at the oppression of the settler was most forcefully expressed in *Provincial Society* (1948).

For Connecticut the most thorough study of the land system and its operation is Dorothy Deming, "Settlement of the Connecticut Towns." Miss Deming's conclusions are similar to those of Turner, Adams, and Akagi. Authors of textbooks used for college courses in colonial history draw on these monographs and reinforce the idea that the legacy of the land system was speculation and sharpened antagonism between frontier and seaboard. See Curtis P. Nettels, *Roots of American Civilization* (1940) and Oliver P. Chitwood, *A History of Colonial America* (1948). The most recent text, Oscar T. Barck, Jr. and Hugh T. Lefler, *Colonial America* (1958) underplays class struggle but does mention that in part "the eight-eenth century witnessed an increasing tendency toward social stratification which was in part the result of . . . extensive land speculation by the 'better sort,' " p. 308.

2. Akagi, *Proprietors*, pp. 44–48. Akagi devotes a section to contrasting the system's operation in the seventeenth century with that of the eighteenth. In the seventeenth century he praised compact settlements, covenanted groups moving under a common impulse, and an absence of nonproprietors, underprivileged settlers, or "eastern men of property."

3. Akagi, *Proprietors*, p. 3.

4. *Ibid.*, pp. 30–44. In 1640 at Dedham, Massachusetts nineteen petitioned for a five-mile tract "above the falls." These nineteen became the entire body of proprietors and the entire body of original settlers. The original settlers at Hadley in 1659 and Suffield in 1669 were nearly identical with the body of proprietors.

5. *Ibid.*, p. 33.

6. *Ibid.*, pp. 86–98.

7. *Ibid.*, p. 210. Akagi cites Narragansett Township Number Four. Out of 126 original proprietors "hardly any" remained after twenty years.

8. *Ibid.*, pp. 217–18. Of the original sixty proprietors in Dorchester, N.H. only one settled there. Cornwall and Winchester, Connecticut, contained considerable land owned by absentees.

9. Akagi, *Proprietors*, p. 197. Mathews, *Expansion*, p. 92. Turner, *Frontier*, p. 65.

10. Akagi, *Proprietors*, p. 211. Williams, a signer of the Declaration of Independence, also speculated in Kent lands.

11. Kent, Proprietors. Original and second purchasers along with their absentee or resident status are shown below in Appendix II.

12. Akagi, *Proprietors*, p. 15.

13. Kent, Proprietors, pp. 1–5.

14. Under the New England proprietor system, a right, or proprietary share, entitled its holder to no specific parcel of land but to a portion of all the land of the town. Kent was divided into fifty-three portions (the extra three were for minister, church, and school), and thus each shareholder, or proprietor, had a claim to one fifty-third of the town. Proprietors obtained title to specific plots of land by meeting together and ordering surveys and divisions. Tradition and surveying expediency dictated that the town land, or "common," be digested in small mouthfuls. At Kent the proprietors' surveying committee launched the "first division" by marking off a 4000 acre strip of land running along the east bank of the Housatonic for the entire length of the town. This tract was then surveyed into fifty-three "equivalent lots" for which the proprietors would draw in lottery fashion. At the drawing "Samuel Messenger shall be the man to enter the men's names in the plan as they are called, and Mr. Jonathan Morgan shall be the man to draw the lots." At the first division drawing, Thomas Beeman drew lot 46. Ebenezer Barnum, owning four proprietary shares, drew lots 30, 42, 49, and 53.

15. See Turner, *Frontier*, p. 54; Adams, *Provincial Society*, p. 45; Mathews, *Expansion*, p. 99; Akagi, *Proprietors*, p. 25; Deming, "Conn. Settlements," p. 53.

16. Appendix III.

17. Turner, *Frontier*, p. 65. "The transition was slow but steady. In the Connecticut auction townships [Kent, etc. . . . .] the transfer from the socio-religious to the economic conception was complete and the frontier was deeply influenced by the change to land mongering."

18. Deming, "Conn. Settlements," p. 53.

19. Whittelsey, *Ancestry of John Pratt*, pp. 11–17.

20. The writer does not propose to cite sources for each separate office held by each individual. He has tabulated all town offices held from 1740–60 and from 1774–77. This information was obtained from minutes of Kent town meetings in which all elected officers were listed. At Kent these minutes of town meetings are at the back (and upside down) of the Land Records, Volumes I–V. The writer has recorded officeholding data on individual cards for each Kent inhabitant.

21. Kent, Church, 1741–1869, I, 1–2.

22. *Public Conn. Col. Records*, VI, 394. This act prescribed how and when lands should be divided. It gave proprietors authority to sell their shares and outlined rights and duties.

23. The first meetng of March 8, 1738, at Windham took place the day after the auction and so lacked the legally required advance warning of six days. The General Assembly later approved. "Their proceedings being regularly done shall be held good." Conn. Archives, Towns and Lands, VIII, 55.

24. *Public Conn. Col. Records*, VIII, 128.

25. At least three studies on New England settlements employ these name-counting methods. Most well known is the recent work by Robert E. Brown, *Middle Class Democracy and the Revolution in Massachusetts, 1691–1780* (1955). The present writer knew nothing of Brown's work until the Kent research was nearly completed. It has been interesting to observe how the similar research methods have produced somewhat similar conclusions. An unpublishd Honors Thesis by a Middlebury College student, Julia King, "Town Proprietors of Middlebury" (1956), employed research methods similar to those used at Kent and produced similar conclusions. On a different subject, ability of inhabitants to meet Connecticut franchise requirements, Chilton Williamson, "Connecticut Property Test and the East Guilford Voter: 1800" (1954), also tabulated individual names and found a broader franchise than is usually indicated.

26. Akagi, *Proprietors*, p. 157. Akagi credited Connecticut with full participation in the evils of speculation and absenteeism. Of the auction townships including Kent he wrote: "In these auctions the spirit of speculation reaches its height." See also Nettels, *Roots of Am. Civilization*. He mentions

the auctions of 1738 where towns were granted to "speculative promoters instead of to bona fide settlers." p. 529. See also Adams, *Provincial Society*, pp. 247–49. "But in case after case a large number, often a majority, and occasionally the entire body of grantees remained behind in the comfortable towns."

27. Appendix II shows the original owner and the initial sale of each proprietary share.

28. Kent, Proprietors.

29. The act as printed in the *Public Conn. Col. Records* says three years, but the writer believes this is a misprint. Deeds recorded for proprietors all say two years. Most conclusive, the patent issued in 1747 to the Kent proprietors in return for their having fulfilled conditions says two years. Conn. Archives, towns and Lands, II, III a, b, c, d, e.

30. *Public Conn. Col. Records*, VIII, 135.

31. See below, Appendix II. Five absentees kept the following six shares: Cavarly, 2, 17; Hubbel, 25; John Mitchell, 34; Knel Mitchell, 35; Smith, 43. In selling out, the proprietors sold mostly to locals but occasionally to another absentee. The following shares, though sold by their original owners as the deadline approached, did remain absentee through the 1740s: 10, 16, 26, 27, 44, 47. Share 47 was sold by Zephaniah Swift to his kinsman Jabez who intended to move to Kent. Jabez did not reach Kent until 1743 or 1744 so the share was technically absentee during those years before Jabez arrived. Altogether there were twelve absentee shares between 1739 and 1743.

32. Conn. Archives, Towns and Lands, VIII, p. 59.

33. Turner, *Frontier*, p. 65. Adams, *Provincial Society*, p. 248. Nettels, *Roots of Am. Civilization*, p. 529.

34. Kent, Proprietors, p. 2.

35. *Ibid.*, pp. 8, 19, 20, 27, 31, 33, 35, 38.

36. A rod being 5½ yards, a twenty-rod highway was 110 yards wide. At Kent, the most important road was the twelve-rod highway from Cornwall south through Kent to New Milford. Wider roads were less important and received less use and maintenance. Highways tended to be mere rights of way. They were kept wide (especially poor ones), to give the traveller ample leeway to pick his way around stumps, boulders, and boggy spots.

37. *Ibid.*, p. 3.

38. *Ibid.*, pp. 5–8.

39. Kent, Land, I, 26. Minutes of town meetings appear upside down at the back of the Land Record volumes.

40. *Ibid.*, p. 30. "According to their list" meant according to the proportion of taxes they paid.

41. Turner, Akagi, and Adams take the opposite position. They suggest that it was in the proprietors' interests to be delinquent and to oppress the settlers. See Turner, *Frontier*, p. 56; Adams, *Provincial Society*, p. 249.

Adams wrote: "[The attitude] . . . of the poor, hard-working pioneers would be one of extreme resentment against those capitalists who were reaping unearned increment upon their land holdings, while at the same time refusing to bear their share of burdens and treating the settlers very much like a colony of slaves who were to toil for their masters rather than themselves."

42. *Public Conn. Col. Records*, VII, 137–38. An act of 1727 defined the relationship between proprietors and town.

43. Kent, Proprietors, pp. 11–48.

44. *State of Conn. Register*, pp. 290–91.

45. Turner, *Frontier*, p. 65. This idea probably originated with Turner. He wrote: "In summing up, we find many traits of later frontiers in this early prototype, the Massachusetts frontier. It lies at the edge of Indian country and tends to advance . . . . It is built and is settled by the combined and sometimes antagonistic forces of eastern men of property [the absentee proprietors] and the democratic pioneers. The East attempted to regulate and control it." What Turner called an "attempt" Adams and Nettels called an accomplishment. See Adams, *Provincial Society*, p. 248. "In case after case (the absentee proprietors) remained behind in the comfortable old towns and from there controlled absolutely all matters of Taxation and government." See also Nettels, *Roots of Am. Civilization*, p. 529. "Speculators . . . controlled town governments as absentee voters."

46. Historians of the New England land system may have unintentionally mislead readers by their failure to indicate the importance of incorporation. Turner, Adams, and others state that absentees gained political control, then cite examples such as Westminster (settled 1739, incorporated 1759), where the settlers were indeed powerless for twenty years. By failing to indicate the changes incorporation produced, these historians may have created an impression that there was a semipermanent proprietary overlordship.

47. *Public Conn. Col. Records*, VIII, 266.

48. *Public Conn. Col. Records*, VI, 394; VII, 137, 138.

49. Kent, Proprietors, p. 8.

50. *Ibid.*, p. 10.

51. Conn. Archives, Towns and Lands, VIII, 59.

52. *Ibid.*, VIII, 60.

53. See Sedgwick, *Sharon*, p. 29. Starr, *Cornwall*, p. 26. All towns received permission to tax at two to four pence per acre. *Public Conn. Col. Records*, VIII, 13, 19, 79, 136, 140.

54. Below, Appendix III.

55. Deming, following Akagi, Adams, and others, feels that Connecticut was no different from Massachusetts. "The Court lost control of the land, for the conditions of settlement were left in the hands of the purchaser." Deming, "Conn. Settlements," p. 53.

Part II: Economic Opportunity in Kent

1. There is no particularly appropriate terminal date for this study. Changes in Kent came gradually, almost imperceptibly. However, it was necessary to continue through the year 1796 because the most complete tax records and property breakdowns happen to be available for that one year.

3: The Drive for Profits

1. One of the more sentimental historians of eighteenth-century settlements is Dorothy Canfield Fisher, *Vermont Tradition*. Her ancestors from Kent and New Milford brought lilac shoots to Arlington, Vermont, and a clear spring was, according to Canfield tradition, an important factor in the selection of the new homesite.

2. Adams, *Provincial Society*, p. 249. Adams considered the slave-master analogy appropriate for settlers and absentee proprietors of Westminster.

3. See Hofstadter, "Myth of the Happy Yeoman," pp. 43–53. Hofstadter suggests that where the yeoman practiced only subsistence farming, he did so out of necessity (lack of transportation and markets) and not because he was enamored of this way of life. The yeoman farmer wanted profits.

4. Such an analysis can be made by the use of local records. The method, however, becomes technical and complicated. The researcher soon becomes involved in the ever-changing intricacies of the tax lists (the essential source), the values of currency, the complexities of crop rotation, and the uncertainties of dietary habit. Only the summary findings will be attempted here. For more complete details see the original Columbia doctoral dissertation on which the present work is based. Grant, "History of Kent," microfilm copy of complete manuscript available from University Microfilms, Ann Arbor, Michigan (Mic 57-4760), pp. 55–81. Also see Appendixes on taxation, currency, and crop rotation.

5. Kent, Misc. Papers.

6. "Total" includes property only. Polls are omitted. These "common list" totals fall far short of actual farm valuations as indicated by probate inventories. To obtain a true value of one of the 103 Kent farms, multiply the "common list" total by a factor ranging from 2 to 7. For detailed explanation see original dissertation, Grant, "History of Kent," Appendix V, pp. 348–49.

7. Unfortunately, insufficient data has been located even to begin to piece together the entire economic mechanism. Where did Kent's surplus go? Where did the money come from that financed the land boom? Important as these questions are, the writer does not feel warranted in spinning out some conjectural hypothesis. We do know that surpluses were produced and that money was circulating in Kent. In 1851 an address by William Church mentions the role of the general stores and county merchants

in 1790. "The county merchants were the great brokers and stood between farmers and markets. They received all his produce and supplied all he wanted to buy." Kilbourne, *Litchfield Bar*, p. 19. Kent had several general stores, and an inventory of Abel Wright's in 1770 tends to substantiate Church's comments. Wright had a variety of imported consumer goods and a stock of local farm produce: wool, flour, wheat, cider, butter, and cheese. Wright owed money to twenty-one creditors including three New York merchants. There are a few more fragments. Barzillai Slosson in his "History of Kent" mentions the sale of iron at Canaan and Washington around 1800. Timothy Dwight notes the cheese-producing fame of western Litchfield County. Old-timers at Kent refer vaguely to Poughkeepsie, N.Y., as a commercial point for Kent products in the 1800s.

8. Divide dollars by 3⅓ to obtain pounds. No correction for inflation or price level changes is necessary. "Common list" valuations were in "lawful money" and were unaffected by other fluctuations.

9. Conn. Archives, Revolutionary War, XIII, 301–4.

10. Two Geer brothers, Silas and Ezra, came to Kent in 1751 and, settling on present-day Geer Mountain, proceeded to populate the area. Ezra married Elizabeth Skiff and twelve children were born between 1751 and 1773. Ezra Geer probably had the same-sized farm when he was raising his family that he had in 1796, for the tax figures remain quite constant throughout the years.

11. See Grant, "History of Kent," pp. 62–80. The original dissertation supports the statement that Geer produced a surplus with an involved analysis of dietary habits and acreage requirements for subsistence.

12. *American Husbandry*, p. 57.

13. Douglass, *Summary*, II, 203.

14. Dwight, *Travels*, II, 374.

15. Chastellux, *Travels*, pp. 37–54. French observers generally expressed delight at what they found in Connecticut. Equally enthusiastic were Warville, *New Travels*, pp. 68, 69, and Deux-Ponts, *My Campaigns in America*, pp. 53, 54. On the other hand, Englishmen were apt to notice that "the men are not over-nice in point of honesty." See Bemans, ed., *A Journal by Thomas Hughes*, p. 27. Also Janson, *Stranger in America*, pp. 81–100, made disparaging comments on his "Excursion in Connecticut." However, these unfriendly accounts did not deny the energy or success of the Connecticut farmers.

16. Chastellux, *Travels*, p. 38.

17. *Ibid.*, p. 41.

18. *Ibid.*

19. Kent, Land, Index. The index indicates the nature of all transactions, sale of forge, ore mine, etc.

20. *Ibid.*, I. The following prominent Kent families had iron interests in the eighteenth century: Barnum, Bates, Beach, Beardsley, Berry, Buel, Bull,

Carter, Chase, Cogswell, Comstock, Eaton, Eliot, Fuller, Geer, Hatch, Hopson, Hubel, Judd, Lewis, Mills, Morgan, Pain, Peet, Pratt, Rowlee, Swift, Spooner, and Winegar.

21. Slosson, "Kent," p. 6. See also Pease and Niles, *A Gazeteer of Conn.*, p. 250. They indicate seven forges in 1819 plus iron ore to the value of "several thousand dollars."

22. Eliot, *Field Husbandry*, p. 184.

23. Slosson, "Kent," p. 5.

24. Kent Land Records indicate Ransom built both house and mill soon after his arrival at Kent. The house and adjoining mill on Sandpit Brook remained in the family until sold to Abraham Beecher in 1793. Kent Land, V, 238.

25. These totals, obtained from the Index of the Kent Land Records, include all owners but omit men who were hired hands and lacked any share in ownership. We do not know precisely what men operated the mills but assume many operators were owners or their close relatives.

26. Slosson, "Kent," p. 5.

27. Kent, Proprietors, p. 26.

28. Slosson, "Kent," p. 6: "At the settlement of the town there was very little wood of any kind."

29. Atwater, *History of Kent*, p. 49.

30. Abel Wright and Company, Ozias Buel and Company, John and Reuben Swift, Mills and St. John, and Berry and St. John appear on Kent tax lists, 1770–1800.

31. Kilbourne, *Litchfield Bar*, p. 19.

32. Abel Wright, Kent, Probate, 1771. See Jensen, *New Nation*, p. 239: "The merchant's day books that have come down to us show that even during the Revolution the average farmer did not live on the luxurious scale charged by town dwellers. Only now and then did the hundreds of rural customers of merchants in towns like Worcester buy a few yards of calico or other imported cloth." Jensen's generalizations would not hold good for Kent. One may assume that then as now, some merchants carried luxury goods while others did not. Thus some daybooks would show luxury transactions while others would be limited to deals for essentials. Only a handful of daybooks in Connecticut have been preserved, and to generalize from these seems unsound.

33. Tabulated from Kent, Land, index:

ironworks	102	potash works	2
sawmills	30	blacksmith	9
gristmills	29	tannery	7
fulling mills	5	stills	2
dyehouses	4	stores	7
charcoal houses	2	taverns	10

34. Mathews, *Expansion*, pp. 76–134. Turner, *Frontier*, pp. 52–66. Akagi, *Proprietors*, pp. 157–97. Adams, *Provincial Society*, pp. 245–49. Chitwood, *Colonial America*, p. 445. Nettels, *Roots of Am. Civilization*, pp. 527–30.

35. Grant, "Land Speculation, pp. 51–71. Parts of this chapter draw on material first presented by the writer in the above article.

36. Kent, Proprietors, p. 2.

37. Tabulated from Kent, Land.

38. The Comstocks, a rare exception, did concentrate somewhat around lot 27. Daniel, Jr. bought lot 25 from Abel Barnum and lot 26 from Joshua Barnum after he had drawn 27. Later he bought 29 and 23. The Comstocks made a total of 71 scattered purchases so consolidation of holdings provided only a small part of their incentive.

39. Price trends tabulated from Kent, Land.

40. Slosson, "Kent," p. 6.

41. Conn. Archives, Towns and Lands, IX, 141.

42. *Ibid.*, IX, 141–43.

43. For more complete treatment see Grant, "History of Kent," 106–16.

44. Fuller, *Descendants of Edward Fuller*, p. 26.

45. Kent, Vital Records.

46. Kent, Land, I, II.

47. *Public Conn. Col. Records*, VI, 122.

48. Conn. Archives, Towns and Lands, 2d Ser., VIII, 177. Lassell always referred to himself in the third person.

49. Conn. Archives, Towns and Lands, 2d Ser., VIII, 180b.

50. See Grant, "History of Kent," pp. 116–25.

51. Kent, Proprietors, p. 2.

52. Conn. Archives, Towns and Lands, 2d Ser., II, 111 a, b, c, d.

53. Kent, Proprietors, p. 21.

54. *Public Conn. Col. Records*, IX, 455.

55. The following suggest a compromise settlement: (1) When one looks at the Proprietors' Map of Kent, one can see the disputed tract on the right hand border. It is clearly part of Kent, but it is subdivided in a pattern different from that used by the proprietors. Whereas the Kent proprietors always divided into small lots and pitches, this disputed tract was divided into twelve large lots including such specifically named tracts as "Fairweather's Lot," "Johnson's Lot," and "Eliot's Farm." Clearly the proprietors never got their hands on this land and never included it in any of their divisions.

(2) The inhabitants of Merryall who had petitioned against Kent became citizens of Kent. Stephen Noble, Ebenezer Washburn, and Nathan Eliot (Jared's son) appeared at this time in the Kent records and remained as citizens of the New Preston Society of Kent throughout most of the eighteenth century.

(3) There was precedent for such a compromise close at hand. In 1743

the land west of the Housatonic was annexed to Kent. The proprietors also wanted this land but the General Assembly denied them title. The inhabitants became residents of Kent and paid Kent taxes, but the General Assembly disposed of the land.

4: Threats to Economic Opportunity: Land Speculation and Absenteeism

1. Adams, *Provincial Society*, p. 249.
2. Figures tabulated from Kent, Land, I–IV.
3. Noyes, *Noyes-Gilman Ancestry*, p. 33.
4. Tabulated from Kent, Land. About half the 109 are certainly family members because the deeds spell out the relationship. "In consideration of the love and affection I bear for my son." Also included are some less certain cases where names and towns of origin are the same. Such individuals would be at least cousins.
5. Dexter, *Itineraries of Stiles*, p. 151.
6. Pack, of Cornwall, lived so close to the Kent meetinghouse and his route to the Cornwall Meetinghouse was so difficult that he obtained permission from the General Assembly to attend church in Kent. *Public Conn. Col. Records*, IX, 529.
7. Slosson, "Kent," p. 5. Slosson says that this mine was discovered soon after the settlement of the town. Because of the shining appearance of its ore, it was supposed "to abound in silver." Slosson goes on to say that "Five acres of ground including the precious treasure, was divided into sixty-four shares which were rapidly sold." However, the metal was not silver, the dream came to naught, and the proprietors of the venture lost considerably.
8. Proprietors only have been compared because: (1) The greatest champions for both sides were the proprietors. The group of 126 most active traders and the group of proprietors were virtually one and the same. (2) A table including all Kent land owners would tend to bog down on the 200–300 small tail-enders who lived in Kent for a short while only and often appear in the records for one transaction only. (3) In the 1740s the majority of adult males in Kent were proprietors.
9. The scoring system is based on counting lots in the first four divisions four points each. Lots in later divisions count only two points as these tracts were less valuable. Individual purchases or sales count only one point as most of these were mere slices of lots.
10. In selling, the proprietors conferred not only the share but also whatever lots and pitches had accumulated through the various divisions.
11. *Public Conn. State Records*, II, 172. Even after 1779 the researcher must be fortunate enough to find a "tax work sheet." These are scarce, the earliest for Kent being for 1796.
12. Conn. Archives, Towns and Iands, 2d Ser., VII, 201.

13. *Ibid.,* VII, 202, 203a.

14. *Ibid.,* VII, 208–210.

15. *Public Conn. Col. Records,* IX–XIV.

16. Turner, *Frontier,* pp. 51–61, implied that the government favored "influential capitalists." However, Turner, alone among authors using petitions, was suspicious of them. He warned: "If we were to trust these petitions . . . we might impute to these early frontiersmen a degree of submission . . . not wholly warranted by the facts." Where Turner could admire the independence and strength of frontiersmen, later writers were more impressed with their vulnerability. Akagi, *Proprietors,* pp. 290–97, stressed "undemocratic" and "feudal" control by eastern capitalists. Adams, *Provincial Society,* pp. 248–50, accepted settlers' petitions as factual and expressed indignation over "deaf" legislatures and wealthy absentees "who had the needful influence with the legislatures."

17. See below, Appendix II. Five absentees kept the following six shares: Cavarly, 2, 17; Hubbel, 25; John Mitchell, 34; Knel Mitchell, 35; Smith, 43. In selling out, the proprietors sold mostly to locals but ocasionally to another absentee. The following shares though sold by their original owners as the settlement deadline approached, did remain absentee through the 1740s: 10, 16, 27, 44, 47. Share 47 was sold by Zephaniah Swift to his kinsman, Jabez, who intended to move to Kent. Jabez did not reach Kent until 1743 or 1744 so the share was technically absentee during those years before Jabez arrived. Altogether there were twelve absentee shares between 1739 and 1743.

18. Agents can be recognized when the proprietors voted that settlement conditions had been met. At the meeting of April 20, 1743 it was voted that "Stephen Pain has fulfilled the settlement of William Burnham's right in Kent according to the act of the Assembly." Kent, *Proprietors,* p. 15.

19. The "common list" tax figures as shown in Appendix III make John Beebe, at £39, median among the thirty-two settler proprietors. Actually, the comparison between agent and resident proprietor would produce about the same results no matter who was selected as "typical."

5: *Threats to Economic Opportunity: Debt at Kent and Her Neighboring Towns*

1. Nettels, *Roots of Am. Civilization,* p. 663, generalized about upper class conservatives who believed "all offices of government should be controlled by the aristocracy . . . . the courts should not be unduly sympathetic towards debtors . . . or anyone disposed to challenge the supremacy of the upper class." Also implying that Massachusetts conditions were generally true in New England were: Charles and Mary Beard, *Rise of Am.*

Civilization, I, 306; Parrington, *Main Currents,* I, 259, 273–79; Jensen, *New Nation,* pp. 234, 308, 310, 326; Greene, *Revolutionary Generation,* pp. 337–40; Falkner, *Political and Social History,* p. 122.

2. Most material in this chapter is based on tabulations prepared from Court Records, Land Records (showing mortgages and attachments), and miscellaneous writs found in boxes in the basement of the Kent town hall.

For mortgage debts, see Kent, Land, Index, I. It is extremely difficult to distinguish an ordinary warranty deed from a mortgage deed where the transfer is provisional. Past town clerks have tried to ferret out the mortgages and indicate them in the index. One suspects they have missed anywhere from 5 percent to 50 percent.

For book debts and promissory notes, see the Probate Records. These are in various towns for different periods as Kent fell in first one Probate District and then another. See Godard, *Probate Papers.* Original probate inventories are now in the State Library, Hartford. Account books are scarce. The only one for 18th-century Kent is that of blacksmith John Converse at the Connecticut Historical Society, Hartford.

Court records for Litchfield County are at the State Library, Hartford. They are in eleven manuscript volumes. Vol. I covers 1751 to 1758, IX covers 1784 to 1787, etc. Sheriff's attachments are scattered through these volumes, usually at the end.

3. It is difficult to locate money lenders like Mills in the Probate Records because few men imitated him and died in the prime of life at the height of their economic activity. Most probate inventories are of aged relics living with children to whom they have previously given a major part of their estate "in return for keeping me and my wife for the remainder of our natural lives."

4. This smallpox epidemic must have been appalling. The tax lists show a population for East Greenwich Society in 1773 of 129 adult males. If 27 of these died for a percentage of 20, we may perhaps apply a 20 percent death toll to the entire Kent population. Especially tragic was the tendency for whole families to be wiped out. Joseph Carter, Jr. died with six others of his immediate family. In the year 1773 the Finneys lost Cyrus, John, Jonathan, Josiah, Josiah, Jr., Silvester, Zenas, Levina, Lucinda, and Sarah. Three more died in the next two years. Especially pathetic were the efforts to obtain medical aid. Wherever a probate inventory appears, there are bills from four or five doctors. The estate of Joseph Carter, Jr. owed sums to Drs. Ebenezer Man and John Chamberlain of Amenia, Joseph Perry of Woodbury, Seth Byrd of Litchfield, and finally Dr. Oliver Fuller of Kent. Feeling appears to have run high against innoculation. On March 7, 1777, the town voted: "That we will assist to the utmost of our power all enquiring officers and the civil authority in the prosecution of offenders in this

town who shall give or receive the smallpox by way of innoculation from this time forward."

5. For the other sixteen men the inventories are fragmentary or missing altogether.

6. John Converse, Account Book, Conn. Historical Society, Hartford.

7. Most of the charges were for shoeing horses and mending plow shares or other farm equipment.

8. *Public Conn. Col. Records*, VIII, 239; IX, 466. A few individual petitions asked for time extensions. Jonathan Dunham in Sharon was given until 1747 to pay. Josiah Starr, an absentee Kent proprietor, was given four extra years. The records reveal no foreclosures or dispossessions.

9. Kent, Land, Index, I.

10. Jensen, *New Nation*, p. 463. "In Worcester County in 1784 there were over 2000 suits for recovery of debts." See also Newcomer, *Embattled Farmers*, pp. 134–35. "Court records for all three counties [in western Massachusetts] bulked large with creditor suits . . . executions . . . reached a new peak in 1784."

11. Kent's population in 1752 included 129 adult males who had contracted an average of twenty debts apiece.

12. Starkey, *Little Rebellion*, p. 14.

13. Douglass, *Summary*, II, 197.

14. Litchfield Court, I, 347.

15. Altogether the concept that there was a distinct commercial-creditor group to whom the farmers were in debt has general acceptance among recent historians. Brown, *Mass. Democracy*, p. 31, has dissented emphatically: "Anyone who talks about 'debtor farmers' or 'debtor back country' and 'creditor seaboard' is indulging in pure armchair speculation for no one has ever established who the debtors were and what areas were debtor or creditor. . . . Debtors and creditors included all groups ranging from the poor to the wealthy."

16. Arthur Ross owed Simeon £100 and the farm's income was estimated at £7 per year. Therefore the farm was transferred to Simeon, not in perpetuity, but for fourteen years, long enough to recover his debt via the farm's income. Kent, Misc. Papers.

17. In a few cases it was absentee v. absentee. In 1770 Robert Livingston, Jr. attached Sharon land of Jonathan Trumbull, the prominent Connecticut merchant.

18. For descriptions of hardship in Massachusetts see Starkey, *Little Rebellion*, pp. 14, 15. For specific attachments see Newcomer, *Embattled Farmers*, pp. 135–36. On the oppressive role of the courts, Robert Taylor, reviewing Brown, *Mass Democracy*, *Mississippi Valley Historical Review*, p. 113, suggested that "the control which the justices exercised from the quarter-sessions bench approached tyranny." Also see Adams, *New Eng-*

land, pp. 156, 157; Douglass, *Rebels and Democrats*, pp. 151–52; Jensen, *New Nation*, p. 234.

19. *Public. Col. Records*, IX, 39. In May, 1744, the General Assembly set the figure at 48 shillings New Tenor or £8 Old Tenor. On a debt between 24 and 48 shillings one could appeal the justice's decision. Below 24 shillings no appeal was permitted.

20. In his scholarly and painstaking study of debt in Massachusetts, Newcomer notes the severity and great number of attachments. "Quite typical was this report of the constable at Brookfield: 'Sir, in obedience to this Rit I went to Mr. Watsons House and gave him a Somans and attached one thousand of shingles and left him to make a plea before your Honor.'" Newcomer implied that Watson lost his shingles. Were such a document to appear at Kent, the writer would label it "Sheriff's response to original writ." At Kent, Mr. Watson would have gone to court but kept his shingles.

21. Litchfield Court, I–IX.

22. Conn. Archives, Insolvent Debtors, I, 49.

23. *1750 Acts*, p. 8.

24. Conn. Archives, Insolvent Debtors, p. 184.

25. Morris, *Labor*, pp. 354–58. Morris cites a number of instances of debtors put to service in New England during the seventeenth century but shows none for the eighteenth.

26. Conn. Archives, Indians, II, 202.

6: Threats to Economic Security: Poverty at Kent

1. Nettels, *Roots of Am. Civilization*, p. 529, noted "the propelling of the landless out to the frontiers" and the "growth of a class of propertyless farmers." Chitwood, *Colonial America*, p. 445; "It became increasingly difficult for farmers of small means to get land even on the frontier." Adams, *Provincial Society*, p. 247, referred to frontiersmen as "poor men with pinched bellies . . . with only back breaking toil and their cleared acres between their families and starvation." On the other hand, Brown, *Mass Democracy*, stressed the idea that frontier society was middle class with most members owning adequate farm freeholds.

2. Conn. Archives, Towns and Lands, 1st Ser., VIII, 203a.

3. Kent, Land, I.

4. Conn. Archives, Towns and Lands, 1st Ser., VIII, 208.

5. Kent, Proprietors, p. 15.

6. Kent, Land, I, 40.

7. Nettels, *Roots of Am. Civilization*, p. 529.

8. Conn. Archives, Towns and Lands, 1st Ser., VIII, 61.

9. *Ibid.*, VIII, 61.

10. *Ibid.*, VIII, 199.

11. *Ibid.*, VIII, 188.

12. *Ibid.*, VIII, 193.

13. This holdout was not a poverty-stricken squatter, but Kent's aggressive opportunist *par excellence,* Joshua Lassell!

14. Conn. Archives, Towns and Lands, 2d Ser., IX, 16a.

15. *Public Conn. Colonial Records,* IX, 600.

16. Conn. Archives, Towns and Lands, 2d Ser., IX, 141.

17. *Ibid.*, 2d Ser., IX, 141a.

18. *Ibid.*, IX, 142, 143.

19. *Ibid.*, IX, 147.

20. Kent, Misc. Papers.

21. *Ibid.*

22. The present writer estimates that 95 percent of the adult males were literate. The signatures of women are rare but when they do appear as witnesses at Kent, only about 50 percent could write. The form of an illiterate person's signature was: His (Her) X Mark.

23. Conn. Archives, Towns and Lands, 2d Ser., IX, 211.

24. There were "two or three to the south." "Several persons had a great deal of the most valuable land." Of the "several persons" all but one took leases which totaled only 412 acres. What would be a typical leasehold? Probably about 100 acres. The final count then would show four lessors, plus Lassell who refused to take a lease, plus the two or three to the south: a total, then, of seven or eight. Assume smaller leases or squatters whom the committee missed through oversight and one might work the total up to twelve.

25. The most pathetic public charges at Kent were the Scatacook Indians. Living on a 1000-acre reservation in the southwest corner of the town, they posed a continuing economic and moral problem. However, they were the responsibility of the colony rather than of the town. Theirs was an "offbeat" problem not tied in with the economic or social fabric of the town. For these reasons their history will not be covered here.

26. A detailed analysis of Connecticut Poor laws is Capen, *Poor Law.*

27. *1750 Acts,* p. 190.

28. These papers are now in a drawer of the vault of the Kent Town Clerk's Office.

29. Capen, *Poor Law,* pp. 17, 18.

30. In some towns the actions of selectmen were indeed harsh. Morris, *Labor,* p. 15, cites Wareham, Massachusetts, where indigent widows were bound out after their sale at auction.

31. Kent, Land, III, 20.

32. *Ibid.*, III, 20.

33. Kent, Misc. Papers.

34. *Ibid.*

35. *Ibid.*

36. David Cogswell, the New Milford inhabitant employed in Kent, was presumably exceptional. He did not secure a Kent residence and his poll appeared on the New Milford common list, not the Kent list. The present section deals with low-property men who *did* "secure a Kent residence" and thus appeared on the Kent common list.

37. The years were selected to offer a spread but in particular because pertinent data appeared in those years. 1740 was the first year that tax and freemen lists appeared. 1745 is the only year for which we have a freemen's ballot. For 1751 we have a complete list of freemen. 1777 furnishes a freemen's list and a list of signers of the "Oath of Fidelity." 1796 is the first year for which we have a tax "worksheet" with detailed breakdown of property holdings.

38. This is the earliest year for which the detailed tax "worksheets" exist in Kent.

39. These common list figures include the £18 poll tax.

40. For details of Connetcicut freemanship qualifications, see below, pp. 107–10.

41. One should not be misled by the population drop between 1777 and 1796. This decline was not due to a fall in the birthrate nor to increased emigration. It reflected the split-off of most of the New Preston Society, which became Washington in 1778, and of the entire East Greenwich Society, which became Warren in 1787.

42. *Public Conn. State Records*, VI, 36, 173, 297, 414. These rates were no higher than had prevailed throughout the eighteenth century. Definitely burdensome was a special rate of 15 pence in 1781 "granted for the use of the United States." *Ibid.*, VI, 414. However, this was the only Federal tax Connecticut tried to levy in the 1780s and its collection was spread over the entire decade. Adams, *New England*, p. 130, wrote of Connecticut: "Not only were the postwar taxes unbearably heavy, but their incidence ruined the poor man." This would be an overstatement for Kent where tax collection appeared ineffective. Kent was listed among delinquent towns in 1787, but nothing seems to have been done about it. *Public Conn. State Records*, VI, 373.

43. Jensen, *New Nation*, pp. 337–39.

44. We have exact ages for 16 of the original settlers. Samuel Bates, 27; John Beebe, 39; Daniel Comstock, 44; Daniel Comstock, Jr., 26; Joseph Fuller, 41; Timothy Hatch, 45; Barnabus Hatch, 37; Benjamin Newcomb, 27; Joseph Pratt, 42; Azariah Pratt, 41; John Ransom, 31; Gideon Root, 19; Nathaniel Slosson, 44. Fragmentary data for the remainder suggests similar ages. Beemans, Barnums, Morgans, and Wrights die or leave in the late 1750s or 1760s.

45. About 15 percent of Kent's emigrants left a record of where they went. One finds such evidence by checking those deeds which record the last sales of the departers. Occasionally such a "grantor" had already

reached his new abode and referred to himself as "Joshua Lassell of the town of Amenia." On the other hand, a much higher percentage of immigrants revealed where they came from, for most bought their Kent home lot before arriving, "I, John Mills, of the town of Stratford," etc. Fragmentary returns made Amenia, N.Y. (just across the border from Kent) the champion recipient of Kent migrants. Brownsons, Chases, Chamberlains, Lassells, Lothrops, Marshes, Reads, Rowlees, Swifts, and Hatches moved to Amenia. Abel Comstock and Thomas Eaton were among the emigrants who went to the Mohawk Valley. Prince Bryant moved to the Wyoming Valley. Thomas Beeman moved to Nova Scotia and numerous families had sons moving to Vermont (especially Fullers, Carters, and Averills). Contrary to the thesis of continuous westward movement, many returned to the towns whence they had come (Barnums and Porters back to Danbury, Canfields and Sanfords back to New Milford, and Abel Wright back to New Fairfield). Aaran Pain seemed to have been on a circuit between New Milford, New Fairfield, and Kent.

Part III: Political Democracy at Kent

1. Indicating a narrow franchise was James T. Adams, *Revolutionary New England*, pp. 161, 315–16. Also Charles M. Andrews felt the colonies were undemocratic. See *Colonial Background of the American Revolution*, p. 201.

The literature of the Confederation Period and the Constitution is full of references to limited franchise. Charles A. Beard wrote that property qualifications "operated to exclude a large portion of adult males." See *An Economic Interpretation of the Constitution*, p. 71. Vernon Parrington referred to the "disenfranchised majority." See *Main Currents in American Thought*, I, 283. Merrill Jensen, on the other hand, admitted a wide franchise: "The great majority were small farmers and for the most part they were voters." See *New Nation*, p. 20. Jensen believed there was still minority control because the west was underrepresented. Elisha Douglass, *Rebels and Democrats*, also accepted the idea of limited franchise.

Two recent specialists in Connecticut history are of the limited-franchise school. Lawrence Gipson admitted the difficulty of the question and estimated "not one-fourth of the adult males were qualified voters." See *The British Empire before the American Revolution*: Vol. III, *The Northern Plantations*, pp. 84, 86. Oscar Zeichner followed Gipson. He found few freemen and few "admitted inhabitants," and so concluded, "It is apparent that during the colonial period the limits placed by the provincial government excluded all but a small minority from the privilege of exercising any serious political power." See *Connecticut's Years of Controversy*, pp. 7, 8.

The major study of voting qualifications is Albert E. McKinley, *The Suffrage Franchise in the Thirteen English Colonies in America*. Robert

Brown placed much of the blame for subsequent misconceptions on this monograph. The present writer is somewhat less critical. In Connecticut, McKinley made an excellent analysis of the voting statutes. However, Brown's two main objectives were well taken. McKinley was "fuzzy" on the distinction between adult male population and total population. Also he was the first of many to venture conclusions based on the number who voted in various elections. "Figures of the two elections shortly before the Revolution suggest but one vote in fifty or sixty of population." As Brown points out, the question is how many could vote, not how many did.

On the high side are some who attacked Beard's *Economic Interpretation of the Constitution*. Corwin felt 80 percent of adult males could vote. See "An Answer to the Economic Interpretation," *History Teacher's Magazine*, p. 65. Robert Brown launched his attack against the class-struggle thesis and the idea of a limited franchise in both *Middle-class Democracy*, Chap. 3, and in *Charles Beard and the Constitution*, Chap. 4. His research tends to establish his broad franchise idea and his footnotes are highly critical of the opposition.

Of the middle-of-the-roaders, Clinton Rossiter (12 to 50 percent) conducted a footnote war with Brown. Rossiter would appear to rely too heavily on McKinley. See *Seedtime of the Republic*, p. 461. Finally, for Chilton Williamson's figure of 65 percent for East Guilford, Conn., see "The Connecticut Property Test and the East Guilford Voter: 1800," *Connecticut Historical Society Bulletin*, pp. 101–4.

7: The Freemen of Kent

1. McKinley, *Suffrage*, pp. 423–27.
2. *Ibid.*, Chap. 13, "Connecticut."
3. *Public Conn. Col. Records*, IV, 11.
4. *Acts and Laws of His Majesty's Colony of Connecticut in New England*, Acorn Club, 1901, p. 40.
5. *Public Conn. Col. Records*, V, 129.
6. *Acts and Laws of State of Connecticut* (Hartford, 1796), pp. 274–81. Also see *1750 Acts*, p. 137. Also see Williamson, "Guilford," p. 103.
7. Williamson, "Guilford," p. 103.
8. *1750 Acts*, p. 50.
9. No personal property other than livestock seems to have been taxed before Oct., 1771, when certain vehicles were first taxed. See *Public Conn. Col. Records*, XIII, 513. Clocks, watches, and silver plate first appeared in 1779. See *Public Conn. State Records*, II, 172.
10. When Robert Brown wrote of Connecticut, "Its voting qualifications were less than those for Massachusetts," he was perhaps unaware of this possible "catch" in the definition of Connecticut personal property.
11. *1729 Acts*, p. 370.

12. McKinley, *Suffrage*, p. 415.

13. To prove that a simplified procedure increased the number of free-men after 1729, one would have to study the ratios of freemen to qualifiers before and after that date. The chances of finding a Freemen's List before and after 1729 for the same town are extremely slim. Before 1729 the lists were kept by the General Assembly. Today only a few are at the State Library in Hartford. After 1729 "Rolls of Freemen" were supposedly kept by town clerks and one would expect to find them in town vaults. Appar-ently the early ones were not kept in books but on loose sheets of paper. Kent lists do not appear systematically in a book until 1798. The writer has found lists dated 1743, 1751, and 1777.

14. Kendall, *Travels*, I, 46.

15. *Ibid.*, I, 47.

16. Kendall, *Travels*, I, 48.

17. Williamson, "Guilford," p. 103. A description of the technique em-ployed and possible limitations is included in Grant, "Kent," pp. 212-14, 346-56.

18. Kent Freemen's Rolls: Miscellaneous Papers.

19. The five were: Jonah Camp, committee for providing for soldiers' families; John Hitchcock, highway surveyor; William Parks, tax collector; Nathan Tibbals, fence viewer; and John Pain (of Kent), highway surveyor.

8: The Role of Kent Freemen in Colony Government

1. Jensen, *New Nation*, p. 20. Jensen found this condition prevailing generally, but not necessarily in Connecticut.

2. Labaree, *Conservatism*, pp. 23-24. See also Zeichner, *Years of Contro-versy*, p. 9.

3. *Ibid.*, p. 6.

4. The writer has found no statutory basis for this policy of no taxation and no representation for new towns. It was traditional policy in Connecti-cut. Each year *Public Conn. Col. Records* show the town representatives and the common lists for each town being taxed. None of the western towns appeared on either list in the forties. Kent, Sharon, and Salisbury appeared together for the first time on the list of taxed towns in October, 1756. (Cornwall first appeared in 1759.) Thus each new town, because of its newness and relative poverty enjoyed between fifteen and twenty years of tax exemption. Town representatives appeared around the time taxation commenced though the correlation was not precise. Sharon "jumped the gun" and had two representatives, John Williams and John Pardee, at New Haven in October, 1755. Kent first sent Jabez Swift as a lone deputy in May, 1757, and did not send two representatives until October, 1759. Daniel Lee then joined Swift. Kent continued to send two representatives until 1787 when Warren split off after which Kent and Warren each sent one.

Salisbury was first represented in 1757 and Cornwall in 1761. For a contemporary reference to this policy see Douglass, *Summary*, II, 167. "Every township sends two representatives except those marked * which are new or poor townships, pay no colony rates, and consequently send no representatives to the General Assembly." Kent and her sister towns all had the *.

5. Kent, *Land*, II, 7.

6. Conn. Archives, Ecclesiastical Affairs, IX, 349.

7. Kent and her sister towns were not concerned over the problem of paying the salaries or travel expenses of their deputies. These men were paid 7 shillings *per diem* and received a travel allowance of 7 pence per mile. *Public Conn. Col. Records*, IX, 287. Most important "The Assistants and the Representatives are paid out of the Colony Treasury." Douglass, *Summary*, II, 167. If a representative were absent without excuse, he was fined 10 shillings a day. If he secured leave from the House to be absent, he lost only his 7 shillings *per diem*. *1750 Acts*, p. 29. These rules appear to have been enforced and absenteeism on the part of town representatives was virtually nonexistent in Connecticut.

8. *Public Conn. State Records*, III, 269. Conn. Archives, Revolution, 2d Ser., X, 124.

9. Zeichner, *Years of Controversy*, p. III.

10. Douglass, *Rebels and Democrats*, p. III.

11. *Ibid.*, pp. 71, 136.

12. Conn. Archives, Ecclesiastical Affairs, IX, 349.

13. Douglass, *Summary*, II, 164.

14. For example, Adams, *Provincial Society*, p. 243. "It was not an age of paternalism and the legislatures were all too often on the side of the capitalists." By "capitalists" Adams meant the important "eastern" land speculators. Also concerned with the "permanent tenure" of Connecticut officials are: Zeichner, *Years of Controversy*, pp. 1–16; Labaree, *Conservatism*, p. 22.

15. The Connecticut Militia contained about 10,000 men aged 16 to 50, divided into 13 regiments. Each company of 64 men had three officers while companies of 32 had two officers. *Public Conn. Col. Records*, IX, 596.

16. *Ibid.*, IX, 163, 164, 596.

17. The writer has counted names in the index of the *Public Conn. Col. Records*, volume IX, 1744–50, and arrived at a total of 900. Although turnover was low among the highest officials, there was more rapid replacement among deputies and militia officers.

18. *Public Conn. Col. Records*, IX, 598–600.

19. Genealogies of each family are available at the Connecticut Historical Society, Hartford.

20. Conn. Archives, Ecclesiastical Affairs, X, 15–19.

21. *Public Conn. Col. Records*, IX, 398.

22. *Ibid.*, IX, 397, 528.

23. Conn. Archives, Travel, I, 368; II, 60, 321. There was much debate

about the location of the Housatonic River road. The General Assembly finally settled the question.

24. *Public Conn. Col. Records*, IX, 313.

25. Labaree, *Conservatism*, pp. 22–23, wrote in similar vein. "The re-peated re-election of the same men to the magistracy was an indication that the freemen of the colony were satisfied with their political state . . ." However, Labaree regarded the freemen as an exclusive class "using its power very largely for the benefit of its own members, often at the expense of other less privileged parts of the community." P. 2.

26. Douglass, *Summary*, II, 167.

27. Kendall, *Travels*, I, 41.

28. Labaree, *Conservatism*, p. 22.

29. Kendall, *Travels*, I, 40.

30. The following explanation is based on Kendall's account in 1807 which in turn drew on an "Oration" by Theodore Dwight in Hartford, July 7, 1801 before the Society of the Cincinnati. Other sources are the *1750 Acts*, the *Public Conn. Col. Records*, IX, and a Kent ballot or "proxy" dated Sept. 17, 1745, located among "Misc. Papers" at the Conn. Hist. Society at Hartford.

31. *1750 Acts*, p. 280.

32. Zeichner, *Years of Controversy*, pp. 20–27. Chapter two discusses the impact of the Great Awakening on Connecticut. The radical New Lights, mostly in the eastern counties, were dissatisfied with the Saybrook Platform and the cold formalism of the established church. Old Lights defended the establishment.

33. Freemen voted early in April. The freemen "brought in their votes" to the General Assembly on the second Thursday in May, at which time they were counted; hence the references to a May election, *Public Conn. Col. Records*, IX, p. 186.

34. The governor and deputy governor need not be among the twenty but in practice were nearly always the top two on the list. Secretary and treasurer were never taken from the twenty.

35. This process is described by Dwight's Oration in 1801. Records of votes in Conn. Hist. Society, Misc. Papers, confirm it. For example, in the nomination vote totals for 1738, Samuel Eels ranked ninth but was placed third on the basis of seniority. Wadsworth had the most votes but was placed fifth. Wm. Pitkin had the third most votes but was ranked thirteenth.

9: Local Democracy: The Town-Meeting Voter and Town Government

1. This label derives from the expression "all who are qualified to vote in town meetings." *Public Conn. State Records*, VI, 355.

2. Zeichner, *Years of Controversy*, p. 7. See also McKinley, *Franchise*, p. 422; Gipson, *Northern Plantations*, p. 87.

3. These designations have been worked out by the present writer. Contemporary designations were not only unwieldy but were altered from statute to statute. For example, the Code of 1750 identified the Class II town-meeting voter as "Settled and Approved Inhabitants, Qualified and Having Necessary Estate." Class III men were called variously "legal," "admitted," "approved," or just "inhabitants."

4. *Public Conn. Col. Records*, I, 651. Cited by McKinley, *Franchise*, p. 421.

5. *Ibid.*, IV, 486. Cited by McKinley, *Suffrage*, p. 421.

6. *Public Conn. Col. Records*, IV, 22. Cited by McKinley, *Suffrage*, p. 422.

7. "Last" may be too final a word. McKinley mentions the 1727 case but none thereafter. The present writer has examined all petitions entered in the *Public Conn. Col. Records* between 1743 and 1750. These petitions involved every conceivable sort of a mixup where machinery of government was operating: tax problems, debt problems, boundary disputes, lost papers, and procedural errors. But there were no more questions about town-meeting voters.

8. *Public Conn. Col. Records*, VIII, 586. This decision, also cited by McKinley to make the same point as the present writer's, has a confusing epilogue. The General Assembly, having told the town in effect, "You decide," proceeded to intervene and overrule the Voluntown procedings.

9. Gipson and Zeichner oppose these views. Gipson wrote: "But not even all male inhabitants were qualified . . . one had to be in possession of a freehold estate rated at fifty shillings on the tax lists or of personal estate valued at forty pounds." See Gipson, *Northern Plantations*, p. 87. Zeichner cited the same requirements and noted: "The local authorities heeded these orders carefully. They maintained a careful watch in their communities to make certain that undesirable newcomers did not settle among them or acquire political rights . . . . Only a small minority were admitted members of the towns." See Zeichner, *Years of Controversy*, p. 7.

10. *1750 Acts*, p. 99.

11. *Ibid.*, 99, 240–41.

12. *Ibid.*, p. 99.

13. *Public Conn. Col. Records*, IV, 111.

14. See Appendix II.

15. The work of listers was second only to that of selectmen in difficulty and importance. These tax assessors issued warnings, informed citizens of tax procedures, checked on absentees, managed the fourfold (they pocketed half of these fines themselves), and granted relief to those over-taxed. In cases of doubt, the listers were "to use their own judgment." *1750 Acts*, p. 135. Highway surveyors also had executive and policing functions. They were to report mal-lingerers to a justice of the peace.

16. This argument applies in 1739 when five out of twenty-seven were

substandard. In 1751, out of forty officeholders, only three were substandard: Joseph Carey, a highway surveyor, Zebulon Palmer, a fence viewer, and Henry Dains, a fence viewer. In 1777, however, not a single officeholder was below £34 in the common list. In fact, of the eighty-six men elected to Kent offices, all but four were £50 or above.

17. Freemen met independently and generally kept no records except their "rolls," usually on loose sheets of paper. We have found some of these. On the other hand, town-meeting records were well kept. Lists of town-meeting voters should be right with these records. That none have been found suggests that none were ever recorded.

18. The question of smallpox inoculation was hotly contested as those favoring the practice won in 1775 and lost in 1776. Colonial Kent's greatest recorded quarrel was the bridge controversy of 1771. A flood carried away Bonnie's Bridge (at the site of the present Route 341 bridge). Should the town pay for a replacement, in which event tax payers in present-day Warren and Washington would pay for a bridge in which they had no interest? A town meeting of March 7 said "Yes." A second meeting of April 8 claimed the original March 7 meeting had been improperly warned and was therefore illegal. The April meeting cancelled the bridge even though work had commenced and money had been spent for materials. The matter was taken to the General Assembly which dispatched two investigating committees. Three more town meetings were held as the air was filled with petitions and counter petitions. The dispute is not important to us (the town had to finish and pay for the birdge); but it is significant that although arguments about the legality of the meetings were marshaled by both sides, nothing was said about voters. See Conn. Archives, Travel, III, 298–303.

19. Kendall, *Travels*, I, 44–83. See also Douglass, *Summary*, II, 165–69.

20. Town-meeting-voter qualification was officially a "50 shilling freehold" compared to "40 shilling freehold" for freemen. *1750 Acts*, p. 99. However, freemen could vote in town meetings.

21. Supporters of the thesis that ratification procedures were undemocratic (Beard, *Economic Interpretation of the Constitution*, Chapter IX, "The Popular Vote on the Constitution") might conceivably contend that designation of town-meeting voters was not intended to be democratic, but perhaps was the reverse. However, freemen were also town-meeting voters so such a move would not have curtailed the electorate. Furthermore, the government of "a land of steady habits" would hardly have altered the status quo merely for the sake of meddling. The General Assembly must have wanted an enlarged electorate, and this was attainable only if the 1750 Code was a dead letter.

22. Taylor, review of Brown, *Mass. Democracy, Mississippi Valley Historical Review*, p. 113.

23. Kendall, *Travels*, I, 23, "The General Assembly is the branch from which all other authority proceeds and by which it may at any moment be

reclaimed. . . . in a word the General Assembly is the single depository of power; of power at once governmental, legislative, and judicial."

24. *1750 Acts*, p. 129.

25. *Ibid.*, p. 242.

26. *Ibid.*, p. 21.

27. Conn. Archives, Revolution, III, 420.

28. *Ibid.*, XV, 8.

29. *Ibid.*, XX, 190c. For 1781 Kent's quota was thirty-four. She furnished twenty-nine volunteers and five were designated by selectmen.

30. Cited by Kendall, *Travels*, I, 18.

31. *Ibid.*, I, 19.

32. Cited by Kendall, *Travels*, I, 16.

33. Ransom, *Ransom Family*, p. 74.

34. Litchfield Court, I, 57.

35. *1750 Acts*, p. 83.

36. *Public Conn. Col. Records*, IX, Index, 597–621. Ransom was appointed before Kent was represented. The usual procedure was for the General Assembly to appoint justices from its own deputy ranks.

37. Particulars and quotations of the events described above are taken from sheriff's writs. These are among miscellaneous papers in a drawer of the Kent town vault.

Part IV: Social Democracy in Kent

1. Kent, Land, Vital Statistics, Tax Records. Whittelsey came to Kent from Danbury in 1774 and bought land in New Preston Society along Chastellux's route. He was twenty-three years old on arrival. He married Joannah Taylor in 1778 and had registered births of four children by 1785.

2. Akagi, *Proprietors*, p. 157.

3. Bridenbaugh, *New England Town*, p. 8. See also Labaree, *Conservatism*, p. 2. On the other hand Brown, *Mass-Democracy*, p. 98, wrote: "The town officers were not controlled by an upper class aristocracy but by men who represented an average cross section of the population."

10: The Town Leaders of Kent

1. Akagi, *Proprietors*, p. 157. Akagi used the new western Connecticut towns to support this generalization.

2. Kent, Church, I, 3, 6.

3. Connecticut's famous intestacy law granted a double portion to the eldest son. However, probate records suggest that few Kent men died intestate. John Mills and Jabez Swift, who were killed accidentally, were exceptions. Other wealthy men (Hatches, Swifts, Hubbels, Berrys) left elaborate wills.

4. The author has found no statute confirming this practice but it seems to have been an unvarying rule. The moment a man attained the required office, the title appeared—never before.

5. We cannot prove what colonial moderators were doing. We do know that in both modern and historical bodies chairmen or moderators have been able to wield considerable influence through their powers of timing and their recognition of speakers. Traditionally moderators are poised, effective speakers, and are influential men.

6. *1750 Acts*, pp. 155, 159, 284. *Public Conn. Col. Records*, VIII, 379–87.

7. Morris, *Encyclopedia of American History*, p. 547.

8. Winslow, *Meetinghouse*, p. 198. "In some towns the bell tolled in signal of respect as the pastor crossed the green."

9. Miller, *New England Mind*, pp. 367–85, stressed the growth of secularism. Winslow, *Meetinghouse*, pp. 197–227 noted a growing contest between "pulpit and pew." She viewed the relationship between minister and people as "a strange blend of aristocratic privilege and democratic control." She found the latter prevalent after 1740.

10. Winslow, *Meetinghouse*, p. 208.

11. Kent, Church, I, pp. 3–12. Accusations against Abel Wright, Mary Wright, Samuel Latham, Sarah Latham, and Rebeccah Alger were signed by "Cyrus Marsh, Pastor, with concurrence of the bretheren." Wright blamed the pastor for his persecution.

12. Kent, Land, I, 26, 27.

13. Kent voted to call the Reverend Robert Silliman at its second town meeting on January 2, 1740. Negotiations with Silliman dragged on through five meetings and eventually broke down on the salary question. Marsh was ordained pastor on May 6, 1741, and his salary problem was argued in eight town meetings from 1741 to 1750. Kent, Land, I, 23–46.

14. Source materials do not provide answers. Kent Town and Church records say nothing about influence of the ministers in secular affairs. Even where ministers kept diaries they avoided this topic. See Winslow, *Meetinghouse*, pp. 201–6. Stiles, *Itineraries*, comments frequently on "hire and fire" or salary problems but says nothing of leadership.

15. Brown, *Mass. Democracy*, p. 98. Brown compared 58 Northampton officers with the town tax lists showing 227 men. He concluded: "The bottom 57% of the population had 65% of the town officials." This statement could be made for Kent and undoubtedly for other western towns.

16. Deputies are omitted because Kent had none until 1757. Proprietors are omitted because all 25 leaders listed were proprietors. The scoring system is somewhat deficient in that it fails to reflect the number of years a man held a given position. Where ties occurred, the author ranked the men according to length of service in the offices.

17. Although offices are listed in the order of property holdings of the men who occupied them, the sample is too small to set up any hierarchy of

offices based on property. Constables, averaging £103, were not necessarily in a higher economic class than leather sealers at £55. The highest leather sealer was above the lowest constable.

18. Deacon Comstock's library (as revealed by probate inventory) contained: "Watt's *Sermons*, Hervey's *Meditations, Letters, Sermons*, Rollins' *History*, Pemberton's *Sermons*, Champion's *Sermons*, *Penetential Crisis*, Mr. Williams' *Captivity*, Bragg's *Church Discipline*, Solomon's *Grammar* and *Martyr Book*."

19. Second-generation Hatches, Swifts, Berrys, Ransoms, Comstocks, and Beebes were second rank in Kent politics. Only Pratts, Fullers, and Hubbels produced second-generation leaders.

11: "Steady Habits" at Kent

1. Kent, Proprietors, p. 14.

2. Slosson, "Kent," p. 2. There were over twenty schools in the territory which originally comprised Kent. By 1812 Warren and Washington had split off taking their schools with them.

3. Brown, *Mass. Democracy*, pp. 113–19, stresses the importance of ability to read so that books and pamphlets could spread democratic ideas. "Education was a democratic rather than an aristocratic institution in colonial America."

4. Most historians have contended that education was essentially conservative. See Curti, *Social Ideas of American Educators*, pp. 1–23; Labaree, *Conservatism*, p. 91; Good, *History of Western Education*, pp. 373–75.

5. *1750 Acts*, p. 212.

6. Kent, Land, I, 36.

7. *Ibid.*, I, 53. The schoolhouses were well built as evidenced by the contract between the School Committee and a carpenter, Sylvanus Bliss, dated 1775. "Clapboard the said house all around and plane the clapboars and bead them . . . . Put in three new window frames and set the glass in five windows all which is to be done according to art and good workmanship . . . . Make writing benches on three sides of the room with a bench behind said benches aft to the sides of the house and there is to be two gangways through said writing benches . . . . And case all the timbers, and shingle the roof."

8. *Ibid.*, I, 53.

9. Kent, Misc. Papers, covenant with Nathaniel Durkee, 1777.

10. *1750 Acts*, p. 212.

11. Kent, Land, I, 56. Kent was less fortunate than the older towns. Those paying taxes prior to 1733 received all the proceeds of the sale of the Western Lands for support of their schools.

12. Kent, Land, I, 83.

13. *1750 Acts*, p. 213.

14. Kent, Land, I, 70.

15. *1750 Acts*, p. 20.

16. Kilbourne, *Litchfield Bar*, p. 22.

17. *Public Conn. Col. Records*, VIII, 501.

18. *1750 Acts*, p. 20.

19. Neither Marsh nor Bordwell left firsthand descriptions of their activities. Bordwell's colleague in Ellsworth Society (northwest Kent and Sharon), Daniel Parker, was both minister and school teacher. He describes his "visitations" in *Proscription Delineated*, p. 9. Bordwell's successor in Kent, William Watson Andrews (father of Charles McLean Andrews of Yale), has left an account of how he "made the pupils jump" in the nineteenth century. Andrews, *William Watson Andrews*, p. 48.

20. Kilbourne, *Litchfield Bar*, p. 23.

21. Chapter title, Gipson, *Northern Plantations*, pp. 75–107. Gipson felt that Connecticut in 1750 was "the last Puritan commonwealth."

22. For development of this thesis see Miller and Johnson, *Puritans*, pp. 182–85.

23. Gipson, *Northern Plantations*, p. 79.

24. Miller and Johnson, *Puritans*, p. 183.

25. Miller and Johnson, *Puritans*, pp. 1–19. See also Miller, *New England Mind*, pp. 366–82; Sweet, *Frontier*, III, pp. 1–5; Winslow, *Meetinghouse*, pp. 6–17; Smith, *Yankees and God*, pp. 179–84.

26. Smith, *Yankees and God*, pp. 180–81.

27. Miller develops this thesis in *New England Mind*, pp. 233–37, 266–67. He emphasizes the influence of Solomon Stoddard of Northampton. Stoddard, an anti-rationalist, rejected the traditional arguments about recognition of the elect. He believed that only God could recognize them and that therefore one might as well open the doors to all believers. Miller believes the Saybrook Platform followed Stoddard's ideas very closely. He particularly notes the omission of "covenant" and sees in this a diminution of early exclusiveness.

28. Hartford protested against leniency in 1711 but to no avail. Smith, *Yankees and God*, p. 241.

29. *1750 Acts*, p. 169.

30. *Public Conn. Col. Records*, IX, pp. 218–19. See also Kilbourne, *Litchfield Bar*, p. 14; *1750 Acts*, p. 165. The town and the parish coincided until the new constitution of 1818 separated Church and State. Although Church affairs could be brought up in town meetings, there were separate "society meetings" which dealt only with local Church affairs. There were four separate societies in Kent. A resident of the East Greenwich society elected his deacons and voted on the minister's salary at his local society meeting. He came down "off the mountain" to attend Kent town meetings at which he would vote for town selectmen, etc. To vote in a society meeting he had to be "of full age and in full communion with the Church."

31. Miller and Johnson, *Puritans*, p. 3.

32. *Ibid.*, p. 4.

33. *Public Conn. Col. Records*, VIII, 454.

34. Miller analyzes their problem in his chapter "A Secular State." *New England Mind*, pp. 367–85. The fundamental assumption of man's corruption and the need for government to impose God's will according to God's wishes was undermined by tolerance of dissenters. The clergy then came to identify their theological system, not with a restraining God, but with the doctrine of natural rights. God had ordained subordination among men but also granted inviolable rights and the right of Revolution. The clergy adopted this "patriot cause" with misgivings as they feared loss of the old "code of submission, obedience and social classification." The century's watchword was "happiness." Governments were to promote happiness and welfare. The patriots possessed this watchword and the clergy felt compelled to side with them.

35. Sweet, *Frontier*, p. 5.

36. *Ibid.*, p. 6.

37. Kent, Church, I, 1. The eleven original covenanters were: Samuel Bates, Ebenezer and Gideon Barnum, Nathaniel Berry, Daniel Comstock, Joseph Fuller, Samuel Lewis, Ebenezer Lyman, Cyrus Marsh, Azariah Pratt, and Abel Wright.

38. *Ibid.*, I, 2.

39. It is not practical to make a systematic check of who did or did not join because much of the record has been torn away and lost.

40. One of Daniel Comstock's books was Pemberton's *Sermons*. Ebenezer Pemberton was a conservative Boston minister part of whose writings were quoted by Miller and Johnson, *Puritans*, p. 18, to illustrate respect for authority. Pemberton (and probably Comstock) believed: "The welfare of the nation is served by each and every person's keeping to his proper station."

41. Kent, Land, I, 68.

42. Kent, Church, I, 14.

42. Kent, Church, I, 12, 15, 17.

43. *1750 Acts*, p. 165.

44. *Ibid.*, p. 153.

45. Conn. Archives, Ecclesiastical Affairs, I, pp. 489–90.

46. Slosson, "Kent," p. 9.

47. Webb, "Building of Our Present Parish Church," p. 1.

48. Kent, Land, VI, 455.

49. Kilbourne, *Litchfield Bar*, p. 37.

50. Parker, *Proscription Delineated*, pp. 9, 10. Parker was determined to glorify his own accomplishments, and his account is far from reliable. However, the conditions he described probably existed to some degree.

51. Kent, Church, I, 1.

52. *Ibid.*, p. 3. Rebeccah Alger "confessed" and was taken back the next April. In July, 1744, the Lathams "humbly confessed" and promised not to deviate again.

53. These missionaries arrived around 1740 and remained until 1770. They were most active just over the border in New York. See Slosson, "Kent," p. 4.

54. King George's War had commenced and Kent was full of alarms.

55. Conn. Archives, Ecclesiastical Affairs, X, 19.

56. Parrington, *Main Currents*, p. 126. Parrington had "village New England becoming surprisingly independent in spirit" as early as 1705. He based his chapter, "Stirrings of Liberalism," largely on evidence relating to three men, John Wise and two carters who refused to move aside for Governor Dudley of Massachusetts.

57. Conn. Archives, Ecclesiastical Affairs, X, 15–19. The petition to remove Wright's militia commission was supported by affidavits from which the above account was produced. The thirty-eight protests against Wright included over half of Kent's adult male population. Those opposed to Wright included Swifts, Hatches, Berrys, Barnums, Fullers, Comstocks, Judds, Skeelses, and Beebes. Neutral (or possibly pro-Wright) were Pratts, Hubbels, John Ransom, and John Mills.

Conclusion: Democracy at Kent

1. Volunteers with substantial property included John Barlow, Stephen Dodge, John Ransom, Nathan Slosson, and Jira Swift. However, of the eight men enlisting whose names began with "B" only one, Barlow, had property. Conn. Archives, Rev. War, XXX, 4c, 5c, 6.

2. *Ibid.*, X, 306. Also see Atwater, *Kent*, p. 81.

3. *Ibid.*, XXII, 9, 10. Kent's 1781 quota was 34 men and the town was five short. It was six short in 1782.

4. *Ibid.*, XXVIII, 28c. In 1785 Kent owed £3415 lawful money in back taxes. Salisbury owed second most. Shaysite towns Sharon and Cornwall owed the least.

5. *Ibid.*, XX, 306; XIII, 301; XXI, 334; XXVI, 38; XXXIV, 165; also *Public Conn. State Records*, III, 454, 455.

6. Evidence of unrest appears in a letter from J. C. Smith to Tapping Reeve of Litchfield. (Conn. Hist. Society, misc. papers.) Dated May 23, 1787, it reads in part: "Will the circumstances of the time warrant our legislature in proceeding to discipline and even expell its members for mere political heresy? Ought it not to be considered that Fitch [Hezekiah Fitch, Salisbury deputy who, strangely, voted "Yes" on the Constitution] acquired his popularity in Salisbury solely for his partiality to the rebel cause? . . . Does he not have the confidence of the people in unlimited degree? And will not his punishment at this time excite their indignation and fan the

flame of sedition which has been ready to burst forth in that town . . . .
Should an insurrection happen then Sharon is fully ripe to join them. Norfolk would not be backward and in short, all this part of the country would
be instantly in arms."

7. Minot, *Insurrection in Massachusetts*, pp. 16, 17. Minot believed "they
were just about quitting a well-fought contest . . . . The applause of the
world was fresh on their minds and they felt a title to retirement and repose
. . . . They could not realize that they had shed their blood in battle only
to be worn out by burdensome taxes at home." Minot has been criticized
for his "federalist bias." However, his stressing of the "disillusionment
theme" is probably sound.

8. *Public Conn. State Records*, VI, 355.

9. Sharon, Cornwall, and Norfolk (where Shaysite strength was stronger)
voted no. Western town votes were:

Town	Yes	No	Town	Yes	No
Canaan	2		Norfolk		2
Cornwall		1	Salisbury	2	
Goshen	2		Sharon		2
Kent	2				

Bibliography

Manuscript Sources

Connecticut Archives,
  Civil Officers, 1669–1756. Vols. I–III.
  Crimes and Misdemeanors. Vols. I–VI.
  Ecclesiastical Affairs, 1658–1789. Vols. I–IV.
  Finance and Currency. Vol. IV.
  Indians. Vols. I–II.
  Industry. Vols. I–II.
  Insolvent Debtors, 1762–1787. Vol. I.
  Lotteries and Divorces, 1755–1789. Vol. I.
  Revolutionary War, 1763–1789. First Series, Vols. I–XXXVII; Second
    Series, Vols. I–X.
  Towns and Lands, 1629–1789. First Series, Vols. I–VII; Second Series,
    Vols. I–VII.
  Travel. Vols. I–III.
  War. Vol. IV.
Connecticut Historical Society, Miscellaneous Papers, Box 605.
Converse, John. Account Book. Connecticut Historical Society.
Grant, Charles S. A History of Kent, 1738–1796. Columbia University Doc-
  toral Dissertation, 1957.
Kent
  Congregational Church Records.
  Land Records, Proprietors.
  Land Records. Vols. I–IX.
  Land Records, Index of Grantors and Grantees.
  Miscellaneous Papers.
  Probate Records.
  Vital Records
King, Julia. The Town Proprietors of Middlebury. Honors Thesis, Middle-
  bury College, 1956.

Litchfield County Court Records. Vols. I–XI.

Slosson, Barzillai. History of Kent. Manuscript at Kent Town Clerk's Office.

Printed Sources

Acts and Laws of Connecticut. New London, 1750; New London, 1729; Hartford, 1796.

Adams, James T. *The Founding of New England.* Boston, 1921.

—— *New England in the Republic.* Boston, 1926.

—— *Provincial Society.* New York, 1948.

—— *Revolutionary New England.* Boston, 1923.

Akagi, Roy H. *The Town Proprietors of the New England Colonies.* Philadelphia, 1924.

American Husbandry. Harry J. Carman, ed. *Studies in the History of American Agriculture.* New York, 1939.

Andrews, Charles M. *Colonial Background of the American Revolution.* New Haven, 1924.

Andrews, Samuel J. *William Watson Andrews.* New York, 1900.

Atwater, Frances. *History of Kent.* Meriden, Conn., 1897.

Barck, Oscar T. and Hugh T. Lefler. *Colonial America.* New York, 1958.

Bates Bulletin, Series III, April, 1920. (At Conn. Historical Society.)

Beard, Charles A. *An Economic Interpretation of the Constitution of the United States.* New York, 1913.

Beard, Charles A. and Mary R. Beard. *The Rise of American Civilization.* New York, 1930.

Beebe, Clarence. *Descent of the Family of Beebe.* New York, 1904.

Bemans, E. A., ed. *A Journal by Thomas Hughes.* Cambridge, England, 1947.

Benedict, Henry M. *Benedicts in America.* Albany, 1870.

Benton, Josiah H., Jr. *Samuel Slade Benton, His Ancestors and Descendants.* Boston, 1901.

Bostwick, Henry A. *The Bostwick Family in America.* New York, 1901.

Bridenbaugh, Carl. *The New England Town: A Way of Life.* Worcester, 1947.

Brown, Robert. *Middle Class Democracy and the Revolution in Massachusetts.* Ithaca, 1955.

—— *Charles Beard and the Constitution.* Princeton, 1956.

Capen, E. W. *The Historical Development of the Poor Law in Connecticut.* New York, 1905.

Chastellux, Marquis de. *Travels in North America.* London, 1787.

Chitwood, Oliver P. *A History of Colonial America.* New York, 1948.

Comstock, John A. *Comstock Family in America.* Los Angeles, 1948.

Corwin, Edward S. "An Answer to the Economic Interpretation," *History Teachers' Magazine,* 5 (February, 1914).

Crofut, Florence S. *Guide to the History and Historic Sites of Connecticut.* New Haven, 1937.

Curti, Merle. *The Social Ideas of American Educators.* New York, 1935.

Deming, Dorothy. "Settlement of the Connecticut Towns," Connecticut Tercentenary Commission of History, *Publications* (New Haven, 1933).

—— "Settlement of Litchfield County," Connecticut Tercentenary Commission of History, *Publications* (New Haven, 1933).

Deux-Ponts, William de. *My Campaigns in America.* Boston, 1868.

Dexter, Franklin B., ed. *Extracts from the Itineraries of Ezra Styles.* New Haven, 1896.

Douglass, Elisha P. *Rebels and Democrats.* Chapel Hill, 1955.

Douglass, William. *Summary, Historical and Political of the First Planting, Progressive Improvement, and Present State of the British Settlements in North America.* Boston, 1750.

Dwight, Timothy. *Travels in New England and New York.* New York, 1821.

Egleston, Melville. *The Land System of the New England Colonies.* Baltimore, 1886.

Eliot, Jared. *Essays Upon Field Husbandry.* Harry J. Carman and Rex C. Tugwell, eds. *Studies in the History of American Agriculture.* New York, 1934.

Faulkner, Harold U. *American Political and Social History.* New York, 1952.

Fisher, Dorothy Canfield. *Vermont Tradition.* Boston, 1953.

Fuller, William H. *Descendants of Edward Fuller.* Palmer, Mass., 1908.

Garvan, Anthony N. *Architecture and Town Planning in Colonial Connecticut.* New Haven, 1951.

Gipson, Lawrence W. *The British Empire before the American Revolution: The Northern Plantations.* Caldwell, Idaho.

Godard, George S. *Godard's Index of Connecticut Probate Papers.* Hartford, 1925.

Goldthwaite, Charlotte. *Boardman Genealogy.* Hartford, 1895.

Good, Harry G. *A History of Western Education.* New York, 1949.

Grant, Charles S. "Land Speculation and the Settlement of Kent, 1738–1760," *The New England Quarterly,* XXVIII (March, 1955).

Greene, Evarts B. *The Revolutionary Generation.* New York, 1946.

Hofstadter, Richard. "The Myth of the Happy Yeoman," *American Heritage,* VII (April, 1956).

Jacobes, Donald L. *The Bulkley Genealogy.* New Haven, 1933.

Janson, Charles W. *The Stranger in America.* London, 1807.

Jensen, Merrill. *The New Nation.* New York, 1950.

Kendall, Edward A. *Travels Through the Northern Parts of the United States.* New York, 1908.

Kilbourne, Dwight C. *The Bench and Bar of Litchfield County, Connecticut, 1709–1909.* Litchfield, 1909.

Kurath, Hans. *Handbook of the Linguistic Geography of New England.* Providence, 1939.

Labaree, Leonard W. *Conservatism in Early American History.* New York, 1948.

McKinley, Albert E. *The Suffrage Franchise in the Thirteen English Colonies in America.* Philadelphia, 1905.

Mathews, Lois K. *The Expansion of New England.* Boston, 1909.

Miller, Perry. *The New England Mind: from Colony to Province.* Cambridge, 1953.

Miller, Perry and Thomas H. Johnson. *The Puritans.* New York, 1938.

Minot, George R. *The History of the Insurrection in Massachusetts in the Year 1786 and the Rebellion Consequent Thereon.* Worcester, 1788.

Morris, Richard B. *Government and Labor in Early America.* New York, 1946.

—— ed. *Encyclopedia of American History.* New York, 1953.

Nettels, Curtis P. *Roots of American Civilization.* New York, 1940.

Newcomer, Lee N. *The Embattled Farmers.* New York, 1953.

Noyes, Charles P. *The Noyes Gilman Ancestry.* St. Paul, 1907.

Orcutt, Samuel. *The Indians of the Housatonic and Naugatuck Valleys.* Hartford, 1882.

Parker, Daniel. *Proscription Delineated.* Hudson, New York, 1819.

Parrington, Vernon L. *Main Currents in American Thought.* New York, 1927.

Pease, John C. and John N. Niles. *A Gazeteer of Connecticut and Rhode Island.* Hartford, 1819.

Public Records of the Colony of Connecticut. Charles J. Hoardly, ed. Vols. I–XV. Hartford, 1876.

Public Records of the State of Connecticut. Leonard W. Labaree, ed. Vols. I–VI.

Ransom, Wyth C. *The Ransom Family of America.* Ann Arbor, 1903.

Reed, Newton. *The Early History of Amenia.* Amenia, New York, 1875.

Rossiter, Clinton. *Seedtime of the Republic.* New York, 1953.

Sedgwick, Charles F. *A History of the Town of Sharon.* Sharon, 1842.

Smith, Chard P. *Yankees and God.* New York, 1954.

Starkey, Marion L. *A Little Rebellion.* New York, 1955.

Starr, Edward C. *A History of Cornwall, Connecticut.* New Haven, 1926.

State of Connecticut Register and Manual, 1955. Hartford, 1955.

Sweet, William W. *Religion on the American Frontier: The Congregationalists.* Chicago, 1939.

Taylor, Robert. "Review of Robert Brown, *Middle Class Democracy in Massachusetts,*" *Mississippi Valley Historical Review,* XLIII, No. 1 (June, 1956).

Turner, Frederick J. *The Frontier in American History*. New York, 1920.

Wadsworth, Benjamin. *Journal*. Collections of the Massachusetts Historical Society, Vol. I, Fourth Series.

Warville, Brissot de. *New Travels in the United States of America*. New York, 1792.

Webb, Charles H. "The Building of Our Present Parish Church," pamphlet at Kent Library.

Williamson, Chilton. "The Connecticut Property Test and the East Guilford Voter: 1800," Connecticut Historical Society, *Bulletin*, XIX (October, 1954).

Winslow, Ola E. *Meetinghouse Hill*. New York, 1952.

Zeichner, Oscar. *Connecticut's Years of Controversy*. Richmond, 1949.

Index